"An eagerly awaited investigation of major debates and challenges concerning the purposes of mass higher education in the contemporary world by one of the leading scholars in the field. In elegant prose he explores complex social, cultural, economic and political interactions associated with the expansion of higher education in the UK and internationally. This important book should be read by anyone interested in finding ways in which higher education might better realise the potential of individuals and wider society."

Maria Slowey, Higher Education Research Centre, Dublin City University

"Peter Scott draws on international comparison to call for a 'radical escape-forward' to address longstanding, widely regarded traditions in higher education, such as access conditions and modes of governance."

Ulrich Teichler, International Centre for Higher Education Research Kassel

"Offers important historical reflections on key issues faced by mass higher education today and proposes an alternative path towards an inclusive and democratic model of universal higher education."

Vincent Carpentier, UCL Institute of Education

"Peter Scott provides the essential historical narrative for our times. An engine of social, cultural and economic progress – higher education has left too many people behind. Helpfully, Peter provides us with a road-map. A must read."

Ellen Hazelkorn, Technological University Dublin

RETREAT OR RESOLUTION?
Tackling the Crisis of Mass Higher Education

Peter Scott

First published in Great Britain in 2021 by

Policy Press, an imprint of
Bristol University Press
University of Bristol
1-9 Old Park Hill
Bristol
BS2 8BB
UK
t: +44 (0)117 954 5940
e: bup-info@bristol.ac.uk

Details of international sales and distribution partners are available at
policy.bristoluniversitypress.co.uk

© Bristol University Press 2021

British Library Cataloguing in Publication Data
A catalogue record for this book is available from the British Library

ISBN 978-1-4473-6328-6 hardcover
ISBN 978-1-4473-6329-3 paperback
ISBN 978-1-4473-6330-9 ePub
ISBN 978-1-4473-6331-6 ePdf

The right of Peter Scott to be identified as author of this work has been asserted by him in accordance with the Copyright, Designs and Patents Act 1988.

All rights reserved: no part of this publication may be reproduced, stored in a retrieval system, or transmitted in any form or by any means, electronic, mechanical, photocopying, recording, or otherwise without the prior permission of Bristol University Press.

Every reasonable effort has been made to obtain permission to reproduce copyrighted material. If, however, anyone knows of an oversight, please contact the publisher.

The statements and opinions contained within this publication are solely those of the author and not of the University of Bristol or Bristol University Press. The University of Bristol and Bristol University Press disclaim responsibility for any injury to persons or property resulting from any material published in this publication.

Bristol University Press and Policy Press work to counter discrimination on grounds of gender, race, disability, age and sexuality.

Cover design: Robin Hawes
Front cover image: Kingston University Town House © Ed Reeve

Contents

Glossary		vi
Preface		xi
1	A 'general crisis'?	1
2	'Post-war' to post-millennium	19
3	The development of mass higher education	37
4	Themes and transformations	59
5	Higher education today	80
6	A further gaze	109
7	The UK in the 21st century	127
8	COVID-19 emergency and market experiment	150
9	What is to be done?	168
Coda		190
References		192
Index		201

Glossary

Like other sectors of public life in the UK, higher education is overrun by a riot of acronyms and agencies. Although they are explained in the text, this glossary is designed as a simple and easy-to-access guide. Cross-references to terms that appear elsewhere in the glossary are in **bold type**.

Three factors in particular help to explain the rapid turnover of acronyms. The first factor is that there has been a succession of different UK departments with primary responsibility for higher education – DES (Department of Education and Science), DFE (Department for Education – twice), DFES (Department for Education and Skills), DIUS (Department for Innovation, Universities and Skills), BIS (Department for Business, Innovation and Skills) … The main reason for this instability of departmental titles has been the question of whether to bundle education with training and skills, or with research, or both.

The second factor is that departmental and agency titles, and responsibilities, have changed as a result of the devolution of the primary responsibility for the whole of higher education and some research to separate bodies in England, Scotland, Wales and Northern Ireland after 1992 and, in particular, after the re-establishment of the Scottish Parliament and establishment of the National Assembly of Wales following devolution in 1999.

Finally, the changing architecture of UK higher education – partly the result of the development of the binary division between universities and polytechnics and its later abandonment in favour of a unified system, and partly of Scottish and Welsh devolution – has produced a shifting array of agencies: UGC (University Grants Committee); NAB (National Advisory Body); UFC (Universities Funding Council); PCFC (Polytechnics and Colleges Funding Council); HEFCE (Higher Education Funding Council for England); SHEFC (Scottish Higher Education Funding Council), which later dropped the 'Higher Education' when it merged with its further education equivalent to form the SFC (Scottish Funding Council); OfS (Office for Students); UKRI (UK Research and Innovation) …

ABRC	Advisory Board for the Research Councils, designed to coordinate the work of the research councils, succeeded by **RCUK**
Advance HE	A staff development and training organisation created by the merger of the **HEA** and the **LFHE**
BIS	(Department for) Business, Innovation and Skills [2009–16]

CATs	Colleges of advanced technology [1956–65], later technological universities
CDBU	Council for the Defence of British Universities
CIs	Central institutions funded by the **SED**, broadly equivalent to polytechnics in England and Wales
CNAA	Council for National Academic Awards, the agency that awarded degrees in polytechnics and colleges [1971–90]
CUC	Committee of University Chairs [of governing bodies]
CVCP	Committee of Vice-Chancellors and Principals, replaced by **UUK**
DES	Department of Education and Science [1963–93]
DFE	Department for Education [1993–99], [2016–]
DFES	Department for Education and Skills [1999–2007]
DIUS	Department for Innovation, Universities and Skills [2007–09]
EHEA	European Higher Education Area covering 49 countries, still including the UK, and principally designed to oversee the development of the Bologna Process
ERA	European Research Area, an initiative of the European Commission and the main vehicle for structuring European research programmes such as Horizon Europe.
ESRC	Economic and Social Research Council.
EUA	European University Association, bringing together more than 800 university rectors and rectors' conferences, such as **UUK**, in 48 countries, including the UK
Fachhochschulen	German higher professional schools, often translated into English as 'universities of applied sciences'
Grandes écoles	Highly selective professional schools in France, distinct from universities and at the apex of the higher education system
HEA	Higher Education Academy [2003–18], replaced the **ILT** and merged with the **LFHE** into **Advance HE**
HEC	Higher education corporation, the legal status of most **'post-1992 universities'**, as opposed to **'pre-1992 universities'**, most of which have Royal Charters
HEFCE	Higher Education Funding Council for England [1992–2017], replaced (in part) the **UGC** and was replaced by the **OfS**

HEFCW	Higher Education Funding Council for Wales [1992–], replaced (in part) the **UGC**
HEPI	Higher Education Policy Institute, an independent think-tank
HEQC	Higher Education Quality Council [1992–97], replaced the Academic Audit Unit of the **CVCP** and the **CNAA**
HESA	Higher Education Statistics Agency, a recognised national statistics body
HNCs/HNDs	Higher National Certificates (part-time) and Diplomas (full-time), two-year vocationally oriented higher education qualifications
ILEA	Inner London Education Authority, replaced the London County Council in 1961, responsible for schools, further and higher education, and abolished in 1987
ILT	Institute of Learning and Teaching [2000–03], initially a member-controlled body to promote higher standards of teaching, replaced by the **HEA**
LFHE	Leadership Foundation for Higher Education, established in 1998 and merged into **Advance HE**
MOOCs	Massive Open Online Courses, available to all to access online but not offering any kind of formal accreditation
NAB	National Advisory Body (initially 'for local authority higher education', and later 'for public sector higher education') [1982–88]
NSS	National Student Survey, an annual survey of students' views about the quality of their teaching, established in 2005, currently under review
OECD	Organisation for Economic Co-operation and Development, based in Paris, with 37 members, including the UK, most of which are developed countries
OfS	Office for Students [2018–], the regulator of English universities and other providers of higher education, which replaced the **HEFCE**
ONS	Office for National Statistics
PCFC	Polytechnics and Colleges Funding Council [1987–92], replaced the **NAB** and was replaced by the **HEFCE**

Polytechnics	Established between 1969 and 1971 by merging colleges of technology, business and art (and later education) in England and Wales, and designated as universities in 1992
'Post-1992' universities	Universities established since 1992, comprising the former polytechnics and some smaller colleges of higher education
'Pre-1992' universities	Universities that had already been established by 1992, sometimes described (misleadingly) as the 'traditional universities'
QAA	Quality Assurance Agency [1997–], replaced the **HEQC**, and incorporated the quality assurance divisions of the Higher Education Funding Councils
QR funding	Quality-related research funding: baseline research funding provided by Research England and, in Scotland and Wales, by their respective funding councils, based on the results of the **REF**
RAE	Research Assessment Exercise, first developed in the 1980s and replaced by the **REF** in 2008
RCUK	Research Councils UK [2002–18], succeeded the **ABRC**, and was replaced (in part) by **UKRI**
REF	Research Excellence Framework, a four- or five-yearly assessment of the quality and impact of research in UK universities which is used as the basis for distributing **QR funding**
Research England	A subsidiary of **UKRI**, which acts as a special-purpose vehicle to distribute **QR funding** to English universities
SED	Scottish Education Department, established in the 19th century and now subsumed within the Scottish Executive [now Government], its direct funding responsibilities transferred to the new Higher and Further Education Funding Councils in Scotland in 1992
SFC	Scottish Funding Council [2005–], responsible for distributing funding (for both teaching and research) to Scottish higher education institutions and further education colleges
SHEFC	Scottish Higher Education Funding Council [1992–2005], replaced the **UFC** and the funding responsibilities of the **SED**
STEM	Science, technology, engineering and medicine (or mathematics, in its original definition)

TEF	Teaching Excellence and Student Outcomes Framework, a part-peer and part-metrics based annual exercise that allocates 'gold', 'silver' or 'bronze' stars to institutions, currently under review
TNE	Transnational education
UCAS	University and College Admissions Service, the centralised admissions service that processes (most) applications from students
UFC	Universities Funding Council [1988–92], briefly replaced the **UGC** and was replaced by the **HEFCE** and equivalent councils in Scotland and Wales
UGC	University Grants Committee [1919–88], the celebrated 'buffer' between universities and the state, which distributed public funding to universities throughout the UK
UKRI	UK Research and Innovation [2018–], responsible for overseeing the research councils, and incorporating **Research England**
UNESCO	United Nations Educational, Scientific and Cultural Organisation, a UN agency based in Paris
UUK	Universities UK, representing the vice-chancellors and principals of universities in the UK, and successor to the **CVCP**

Preface

This book was written in the late spring and summer of 2020 and revised in the winter and spring of 2021 when the COVID-19 pandemic had not only fundamentally changed personal lives, creating the time and space for reflection that enabled the book to be written, but also disturbed the course of nations, societies, economies and cultures, and additionally had shaped in ways still unknowable the future trajectories of higher education systems and institutions.

It is a habit of historians to write of 'long' or 'short' centuries not aligned with the counting of the years. For many the 20th century was a 'short century', beginning in 1914 with the outbreak of the First World War and ending in 1989 with the Fall of Communism (in Europe, at any rate, reflecting a still powerful Eurocentric view of the world; a vigorous variant of communism is still dominant in China, the world's most populous country). For some, on the shorter-cycle pattern of France's post-war *trentes années glorieuses*, the years since 1990 can be framed as a short post-Cold War period, beginning in Western triumph (the conceit of 'the end of history') and degenerating through 9/11, the Afghanistan and Iraq invasions, the banking crisis and economic recession, the abortive Arab Spring and the civil war in Syria and the intractable 'war of terror' and culminating with the election of Donald Trump as US president and the self-harm of Brexit. Looking back from the troubled summer of 2020 it feels like another historical punctuation point, the humbling of the 'anthropocene' age so soon after it was announced, with global pandemic and global warming. History, still imperfectly tamed by human agency, is far from over.

In the tighter focus of political economy, shorter 'periods' are identified. Of particular relevance to this book are, first, the age of the welfare state between 1945 and its fatal erosion during the troubled 1970s, and of political consensus and the dominance of broadly progressive ideas during the same years; and, next, the age of … the market, the individual, neoliberalism (here there is a wide choice of labels) … which became established in the course of the 1980s, survived the 2008 banking crisis and subsequent economic recession only to confront new and tougher challenges in the next decade including so-called populism, increasing political (and ideological) polarisation that has strained the conventions of democratic life, and finally pandemic.

In the still tighter focus of higher education – the subject of this book – longer periodisations present themselves. The age of 'mass higher education', with its roots in the 1940s but emerging most strongly in the 1960s and still continuing today, seems to have transcended the supposedly epochal transition between welfare states and markets. Much of the detailed focus of debates about higher education, of course, has been on change

– the (comparative) decline of state funding; or the erosion of the so-called 'donnish dominion', that Arcadia of academic self-government; or the increasing contestation and declining autonomy but explosive growth of science, all of which had been originally gained in the pity (but glory) of world war and its immediate aftermath; and their gradual replacement, in some countries, by tuition fees paid by students and, in nearly every jurisdiction, by new conceptualisations – for some, demonisations – such as 'managerialism' or the 'entrepreneurial university', and by new regimes of knowledge production governed by notions of 'impact'. The detailed picture appears to be one of multiple disjunctures. But seen from afar and above, from the perspective of this pandemic year, these – important – differences are absorbed into a larger continuity. The impacts of expanding higher education systems on broader social and cultural change, and on economic and technological transformations, remain broadly similar. We are still in the 'long age' of mass higher education, now more than half-a-century old, just possibly drawing to a chaotic close but more likely enduring into the future.

This book is neither a memoir nor a piece of journalism nor an academic study of higher education. But it has elements of all three.

It is a memoir because I have witnessed, not only in a professional sense as a detached observer but sometimes in a more direct and personal sense, many of the events in the evolution of higher education in the United Kingdom, and also more widely in the world, which I describe in the next chapters. This historical account is not based on a close study of the archives but instead on multiple memories of 'being there' – as a journalist (mainly as Editor of *The Times Higher Education Supplement*), as a professor at the University of Leeds in the 1990s and, after a 13-year interlude as Vice-Chancellor of Kingston University, again at the UCL Institute of Education, as a board member at the Higher Education Funding Council for England (HEFCE) and later as Commissioner for Fair Access at the Scottish Government and in many other ancillary roles. Who is to say which is better 'history' – the vividly remembered conversation, uncheckable of course, or the documentary record in the form of the tailored minute? For example, I still have on a memory stick the minutes of all the board meetings of HEFCE I attended. But I have 'remembered' so much more than is apparent in the formal record.

I have not been a dispassionate observer. Disapproving, I watched up close the slow motion of exclusion of local government from any meaningful role in higher education and, approving, I observed the so-called 'repatriation' of Scottish universities long before devolution. I was a witness to the hollowing-out of university autonomy in the cause of accountability, regulation and – let's be honest – straightforward politicisation.

This book is journalism, in some of its writing style and in its polemical intentions. Although I have tried to be fair, I cannot claim to have wanted to be balanced. I have an agenda – in the past and still today. My values as a somewhat old-fashioned social democrat in the European tradition, as a Europhile and internationalist, and as a passionate believer in social justice, and necessarily in greater equality – and, in the particular case of higher education, 'fair access' – too, have never been hidden. Nor can I deny that, like a journalist, I often rely on sweeping phrases much more than, and at the expense of, close and rigorous analysis. This is a book that attempts, of course, to inform but also to persuade.

But it is also an academic study, in the sense that it is also based on more conventional academic writing. Some of this has been in the shape of synoptic books, for example on the central theme of mass higher education. Others have been more detailed research studies of national (UK) policy, governance and management, access and participation, and the internationalisation of higher education. The first type, synoptic books, have much in common perhaps with journalism, although it is to be hoped in a more disciplined way, and concepts are generally substituted for events and people. On balance this kind of academic writing is an aid to writing a book such as this. The second type, detailed research studies, are more difficult. The more you know, the less you can be sure. This second mode of working can raise disturbing doubts – what if the evidence does not support the grand generalisation you are poised to make? Sometimes these doubts must be listened to; at other times guiltily ignored. Evidence-based research and compelling, certainly polemical, argument have always had to coexist uneasily.

This book has nine chapters.

The first is an introduction, which discusses the successes of mass higher education but also its doubts, regrets and disappointments. To be brief – what happened to the utopia imagined two generations ago? How has the balance between the emancipation of the individual, and the public mind, the extension of the higher education franchise but also the consolidation (and legitimation) of social privilege worked out? Or the balance between the critical and progressive university and the managed and the entrepreneurial university? Do these contradictions between the achievements of mass higher education and lingering, or even increasing, doubts about whether it has lost its way deserve to be described as a 'general crisis'?

The second chapter looks at contemporary Britain and the wider world – the context in which these (hi)stories of higher education are situated. Britain two decades into the 21st century is very different from the Britain of 60 years ago when memories of wartime victory, austerity and solidarity were still vivid, if fading. So much has changed – in politics, as has been said, the shift from consensus to ideological strife, and from a welfare state to the 'market' (or, better, regulation) state; in the economy, the decline of manufacturing industry and the rise of (financial and consumer) services, the fetishising of 'tech' and the transformation of occupational structures; in culture, the rise of 'pop' and the intensifying presence of media, mass and social. In the wider world, new geopolitical patterns are emerging within a context of globalisation and cosmopolitanism (and the resistances they have provoked). Mass higher education, of course, has been a part of, and party to, these great changes.

The third and fourth chapters offer a historical account of UK higher education. Chapter 3 offers a chronology: the early promise of the Robbins era with its 'new' universities as cities on the (academic) hill; the rise and fall of the binary system with polytechnics as rival 'people's universities'; universities under post-1981 Thatcherite siege; the creation of a unified system in which an intensifying hierarchy invidiously substituted for formal segmentation; the public largesse (and state-imposed 'modernisation') of the New Labour years, the fragmentation of higher education in the UK with an especially vigorous (or deviant?) Scottish variant; the years since the 2010 Browne Report with high tuition fees (and high resistance to them), abandoned controls on student numbers but more intrusive regulation; and now – in England – the (temporary?) return of state-mandated *dirigisme* with an unhealthy dose of ideological prejudice.

The fourth chapter discusses the same 60-year period between 1960 and 2020, but from the perspective of four overarching themes or transformations: changes in 'steering' and regulation at the system level; the evolving architecture of coordination and funding agencies; shifts in governance and management at the institutional level and, more broadly, organisational culture; and, finally, new agendas and practices in teaching and research.

Chapter 5 examines higher education, principally in the UK, today. It starts with its vast enlargement – in the size of the system, in institutional scale, in student and staff profiles and in systemic architecture. The chapter then considers a series of transitions – at the system level in terms of governance, control, regulation, autonomy (or lack of it), funding and fees; at the institutional level in terms of organisational culture and the emergence of the managed and/or entrepreneurial university; at the ideological level in terms of reinvented concepts of 'excellence' that legitimate hierarchy and are reflected in the explosion of 'brands' and rankings; at the level of the curriculum and teaching in terms of the rash of new subjects, a shift towards the management of 'learning', and the both disruptive and exhilarating impact of technology; and at the level of research and, more widely, knowledge production in terms of new conceptualisations of knowledge and new regimes of assessment and control. As with the nation itself, these – UK – changes in higher education are set in the wider context of multiple globalisations and a dynamic but fragile internationalisation.

The sixth chapter offers a comparative gaze. After a brief sketch of global higher education in impressive aggregate and the various forms of internationalisation (pre-COVID-19, of course), it focuses on three key world regions: inevitably the US, the archetype and exemplar of mass higher education; Europe, which has played catch-up mainly through the mechanism of the Bologna Process, which has also served as higher education's contribution to the wider European project; and East Asia, where sophisticated higher education systems, glossed as 'Confucian' or 'post-Confucian', have developed. Their emergence clearly has the potential to shift global higher education's centre of gravity from its 20th-century North Atlantic fulcrum to East and South Asia in the course of the 21st century.

Chapter 7 reflects on how these transformed higher education systems and institutions shape and are shaped by wider changes in society and the economy. The emergence of a new 'graduate class', and even the making of a 'graduate society', is set against deep and chronic inequalities (of access and of life-chances). But do these trends replace or simply modify, and redescribe, more traditional categories based on social class? In the new – 'knowledge' and post-industrial – economy, universities act as hubs of innovation and creativity, but they also play a more down-to-earth role sorting and segmenting (and expanding and redefining) 'graduate' jobs. But are they decisive or ancillary forces in shaping the 21st-century economy? The 'clever cities', often with universities at their hearts, are also bases of cosmopolitan culture and home to new social movements, both opposed to more traditional values and institutions. Culture wars simmer and occasionally erupt. Are universities caught up – on the 'wrong side' – in emerging polarities between citizens of 'nowhere' and citizens of 'somewhere', or have they contributed to the consolidation or convergence of social and cultural attitudes?

Chapter 8 addresses the immediate challenges facing higher education, the impact of the COVID-19 pandemic and the faltering of England's experiment in applying market principles to the organisation of higher education.

The final chapter, inevitably, suggests a programme for reform. The regrets and disappointments of mass higher education some would propose to address by tactical retreat and elite consolidation. I believe they must be remedied instead by a radical leap forward, a renewal of growth towards a universal system of higher (or, better perhaps, tertiary) education that places more equitable access at the centre of democratic entitlements and obligations. This would be achieved by re-emphasising the role of universities as 'public' institutions with revived, and if need be re-imagined, civic responsibilities rather than as 'private' organisations trading in marketised (and monetised) 'knowledge' and selling socio-economic advantage to their graduates; and by reasserting their critical function at the heart of civic – and open – society in a more harmonious balance with their inevitable 'service' functions. That, at any rate, is the programme of this book.

1

A 'general crisis'?

First – two apologies. 'Crisis', which appears in the title of this chapter and subtitle of the book, is an overused word. Like 'paradigm', invariably linked to 'shift', it is rolled out far too often. So perhaps some kind of explanation is necessary.

As a long-standing admirer of the French historian Fernand Braudel, my instinct has always been to emphasise the *longue durée*, what endures or what changes slowly and deep inside history, at the expense of *histoire evènèmentielle*, the rush and bustle of politics and ideology that flares so brightly but is often quickly forgotten. But, carried to extremes, the Braudelian perspective perhaps leaves no room for crises, except perhaps fundamental crises, for example of sustenance – or, more topically, climate change. My use of 'crisis' in this book is in an intermediate sense, somewhere between restricting the word to describe these few and fundamental crises on the one hand, and on the other indulging the promiscuous overuse of the word to describe every fleeting shift of policy or ideology. In this book it is used to denote an accumulation of tensions, even contradictions, within systems and society rather than the ebb and flow of higher education policy on funding, markets, regulation, 'steering' and the like. The latter are discussed, often in some detail. But the primary focus is elsewhere on a modest, and modified, version of Braudel's *longue durée*.

The second apology is that this book is largely focused on the United Kingdom. This UK focus is only mitigated a little by the brief codas on other higher education systems that conclude some chapters, and also a separate chapter that looks at higher education in other countries. Even that is limited, because only the United States, the rest of Europe and East Asia are covered. The British have a reputation for insularity that is well deserved. My excuse is twofold – first, a frank admission that I know the UK best (for reasons I described in the Preface) and I have no pretensions to be a scholar of comparative higher education; but, second, the UK – both in terms of its higher education system and of its wider politics, economy, society and culture – offers a good case study because in most respects the UK, for all its claims to be exceptional, is in fact a fairly typical mid-to-large size European country that faces the same challenges that nearly all developed countries do in the 21st century. If I were to offer a more robust excuse, it would that I believe comparative studies of the development of higher education often, and inevitably, forego the fine-grain detail sometimes needed properly to understand both the growth of mass higher education and the wider evolution of society. Understanding is best expressed in terms of the dynamic between the particular – the detailed evolution of higher education within a national context, and the general – the trends and forces that impact on all higher education systems in developed countries. So, for those disturbed by too strong a focus on the UK, I urge them to treat this book as a case study.

A golden age

The development of mass higher education has produced what is arguably the university's golden age. The achievements of the medieval university, so unlike its modern form but nevertheless its nominal ancestor, were insignificant in comparison. The only rival perhaps was the period that began with the revival of the university in the 19th century, customarily said to have been triggered by the establishment of the University of Berlin in 1810. The ideals of free academic enquiry associated with Wilhelm von Humboldt, although derived from the values of the Enlightenment, were strongly tinged with ideas of duty to the state and later with nationalist ideologies or, at any rate, ideologies of state-building. However, the archetypal universities of the 19th century were perhaps to be found not in Europe but in the United States in the shape of post-Civil War land-grant universities, dedicated to popular education and technical science. It was during this period that the university became a global, rather than essentially a European, institution (with a few colonial outliers).

In the UK between 1800 and 1900 the number of universities grew from six (Oxford and Cambridge and four in Scotland) to 24. Only with two world wars, and the Great Depression of the 1930s sandwiched in between, did this momentum of university foundations falter. By 1960 the UK still had fewer than 40 universities. But in the past 60 years, the age of mass higher education, that number has exploded to more than 160. A favourite, rather flip, phrase is the claim that of all the scientists who have ever lived more than half are still alive today. In the case of UK universities such a claim is literally true, except that the share would be three-quarters, not half, of the universities which have been established in a single lifespan. Nothing on this scale has ever been seen before in the long history of the university.

If the number of students (or graduates) is measured rather than that of universities, the exponential character of the impact of mass higher education is even more striking. The number of students in the UK has increased 15 times over since the publication of the Robbins Report in the early 1960s, a key date when 'higher education' was first used to describe a system of institutions rather than simply a level of education, and when rapid expansion was authoritatively endorsed (Robbins Report, 1963). So much has happened, and so recently, that the contemporary university, for all its deep historical roots and superficial love of antique rituals, is an institution remade. An essay by the poet Philip Larkin on his early days as a librarian at Leicester just after the Second World War describes an institution not unlike a small grammar school (Larkin, 1983). The mass universities of the 21st century, with their tens of thousands of students and thousands of staff, and campuses spreading over whole city precincts clustered with 'statement' buildings more reminiscent of the world of corporate finance, dwarfing Victorian red brick and 1930s granite, belong in a different world.

Mass higher education

A number of labels have been used to describe the greatly expanded higher education systems that developed in the second half of the 20th century – 'the multi-versity', 'high-participation systems', 'mass higher education'. The first of these focuses on the transformation in the scale, and nature, of institutions (Kerr, 1963). The second, as the label suggests, focuses on participation levels (Marginson, 2016; Cantwell, Marginson and Smolentseva, 2018). The third focuses on the transition from earlier, more restricted (and elite?), university systems. Mass higher education, associated most closely with the work of the US sociologist Martin Trow, is perhaps the label that has stuck fast (Trow, 1973, 2010). Its appeal perhaps is the sense of development, evolution, even movement that it suggests. It is also more easily related to wider descriptions of social and economic (and cultural) change, of which an example contemporary with Trow was the writing of another US sociologist, Daniel Bell (Bell, 1973, 1976). Trow's three-stage transition, from elite to mass and then to universal higher education, even seemed to mimic, although on a quite different register, Bell's grander *schema* of pre-industrial, industrial and post-industrial society. Half a century ago, linear models of development, inexorably advancing and without the possibility of significant regression, were still popular. In our present less certain and more troubled age, these linear models have lost some of their appeal.

In the UK the label 'mass higher education' never acquired the easy familiarity, and acceptance, it enjoyed in the US, the land of its birth, or even in other parts of Europe. It remained an unsettling, and even uncongenial, idea. Perhaps it was at odds with the ethos of universities which placed, and still places, to the best of their capacity, great emphasis on small-group teaching (ideally tutorials), on a particular intimacy between students and teachers ideally in a residential setting, on low dropout rates, on organic links between research and scholarship and a university education – all attributes more traditionally associated with an elite university system. Perhaps the idea of mass higher education also obscurely jarred with the fundamental quality of English society, at once reformist and democratic but also class-bound and hierarchical. Perhaps it was just seen as coming from the United States, and therefore to be resisted whatever 'special relationship' there might be in other spheres, or perhaps it uncomfortably recalled (misleading, of course) perceptions of the chaotic universities of continental Europe. In any case, England (Scotland is subtly different here) never took to mass higher education as an idea, although without question a mass system has developed in the UK since 1960, and especially rapidly during the past three decades.

A general crisis?

The promise was that mass higher education would be the culmination of an educational revolution with roots far back in the 19th century. The Forster Act established universal elementary education in 1870; the Butler Act extended this principle to secondary education in 1944; and then a generation later in the 1960s it was extended again to higher education. The scale of social transformation produced in these earlier phases was to be repeated with equally benevolent results. Hundreds of thousands of young people – and adults, thanks to the newly established Open University – who had previously been excluded by their social origins, their gender, their ethnic backgrounds, or the schools they had attended would now be granted access. The character of a university education itself would be refashioned, no longer rooted solely in elite academic (and social?) culture but grounded instead in the daily experiences of diverse communities. So higher education would be embraced within the wider advance towards democracy.

However, it does not always feel like that – so far, at any rate. Mass higher education stands accused of overwhelmingly favouring the middle classes; entrenching and extending institutional hierarchies; enabling the emergence of corporate universities dominated by a new managerial class; sacrificing critical enquiry and radical thought to cults of 'employability' and 'impact' policed by 'metrics'; or even of 'woke' and 'cancel' culture. As a result, anxieties have accumulated – some well grounded in evidence, others groundless prejudice, but all contributing to a gathering sense of crisis. At the heart of this crisis is a confusion of regrets – Arcadia abandoned, or Utopia denied? The result is a weakening of belief in mass higher education, not just as established reality, the ways things are, but also as a reform project rooted in values and beliefs, the way things can be. Unlike Martin Luther five centuries ago, we seem not to be quite sure about the ground upon which to stand.

This introductory chapter makes a claim many will find startling, that mass higher education is experiencing a 'general crisis'. This general crisis arises because its undoubted achievements in reshaping the individual, society, the economy and culture do not seem to have been properly recognised. Doubts have gathered that mass access has either produced perverse outcomes or failed to deliver its original promise, which have allowed older prejudices that it was all a mistake in the first place to re-emerge from the shadows. This chapter looks first at those achievements, then attempts to identify some of the reasons for the apparent failure adequately to acknowledge them, and ends with a discussion of whether mass higher education is better described as an incomplete revolution or a revolution betrayed or denied.

Achievements and transformations

The development of mass higher education in the UK since 1960, without fear of exaggeration, has produced a social revolution. The expansion of universities and colleges has more radically changed the tone, perhaps, than the deep structure of British society (indeed, of world society). It has been deeply bound up in the advance of supposed 'classlessness', the belief that the old shackles of hierarchy, subordination and deference have been unlocked, producing new and more open social categorisations. Even fixed identities derived from class, race, gender and, indeed, nation are in the process of being complemented, if not superseded, by new identities based on educational level, and in particular participation in higher education. 'Going to uni' is now a familiar feature of social life and individual experience.

Mass higher education has clearly played an especially powerful part in the revolution in gender roles, which has been perhaps the most decisive social change of the past half-century. It is difficult to imagine feminism flourishing in the absence of greatly increased participation in higher education (or, indeed, the other way round). Expansion has also offered similar routes for advancement for people from minority ethnic groups, although less wide open and more muted ideologically. The clearest example is the changing face, quite literally, of the medical profession in the UK. Once White and male, medical students are now predominantly of Asian origin and increasingly female (although this shift is still reflected in access to the most prestigious medical specialties).

The impact of mass higher education on the economy, and occupational patterns, is also difficult to exaggerate. An ever-increasing influx of graduates has reshaped the labour market. Whether this reshaping has been reflected mainly in the inflation of status (and salaries) or in the real enhancement of skill levels, and in what proportions, although a matter of lively debate, is a secondary consideration set against its magnitude. The expanding higher education system has staffed the welfare state and public sector, which remain important destinations for graduates and key employment and economic sectors despite decades of the supposed hollowing-out of the state in the cause of the 'free market'. At the same time, expansion has staffed the expanding corporate bureaucracies and technical workforces within the private sector.

Mass higher education has allowed occupations such as (primary school) teaching and nursing to upgrade their academic and practical skill levels and also to acquire new professional status – unimaginable without the expansion of, in particular, the so-called 'post-1992' universities (former polytechnics which became universities after 1992). The links between universities and the development of so-called 'professional society', of course, were apparent even in the 19th century (Perkin, 1989). But the links between mass higher education systems and new modes of professionalism are even more intense.

Mass higher education's influence in science and intellectual life is equally profound. At first sight, top-level scientific advances may be particularly associated with, and largely confined to, the elite universities, and so not directly attributable to the development of a mass system. But these universities have flourished as the apex institutions in this much more extensive system. The expansion of higher education since 1960 has also created the social conditions for the sustenance of a wider 'scientific culture' – as well, of course, as contributing to the mass production of the PhD and postdoc researcher cadres on which the modern scientific research enterprise depends. The advance of what might be termed the 'technical sciences', far beyond the scope of traditional engineering, has depended crucially on the growth of a mass university (and college) system. Management sciences, foundational disciplines in mass higher education, have transformed business life. In wider intellectual life, although grand public intellectuals in the full-on French mould have continued to be treated with suspicion north of the Channel, the diversity and vibrancy of the mass student base has created the room for manoeuvre, and motivation, for new academic departures and has also served as the main seed bed for nurturing the multiple '-isms' of our age.

At first sight the impact of mass higher education on culture has been more muted. Hospitals, not universities, remain the favourite location for TV 'soaps'. The university novel, despite the successive best efforts of Kingsley Amis, Malcolm Bradbury or Tom Sharpe, has stubbornly remained a niche genre. Only the Open University seems to have penetrated more deeply into the wider popular imagination. Of course, art and drama schools, and even music conservatoires, have produced some of the iconic celebrities of (popular) music, theatre and fashion. In more structured ways, our mass universities have contributed to a cultural renaissance, often unwisely reduced to the flourishing of the so-called 'cultural and creative industries'. First, they have provided key elements of infrastructure – theatres, dance studios, concert halls, student union gigs. Second, they have provided key parts of the audience, especially for high culture. Our cultural sensibility has been shaped, maybe decisively, by the social and intellectual experiences offered by extended university systems.

Yet, despite this grand transformation, recognition of the achievements of mass higher education, and of its many social, economic, cultural and scientific impacts, is strangely muted. It is the National Health Service that has been regarded as Britain's 'national religion', even more so in the dark days of the COVID-19 pandemic. Other sectors, and institutions, also crowd out universities. The success of higher education seems to be a well-kept secret. Why? Four explanations are immediately available.

The novelty of mass higher education

The first, most prosaic and least disturbing, explanation is that truly mass access is a recent phenomenon. Although its beginnings date back to the late 1950s and early 1960s, it gathered force through the 1970s, despite the economic turbulence of that decade, and the 1980s, regardless of their ideological regression, both of which inhibited public investment in universities although for very different reasons. Only with the 1990s did access really take off, too recently perhaps to have penetrated deeply into the national psyche.

'Enemies within'

A second, and more substantial, explanation is the continuing influence of an 'enemy within', the opponents of mass higher education – or, to express the same idea in more moderate terms, those who have remained highly sceptical about its benefits. Their evident lack of commitment to mass access has acted as a drag on wider public acknowledgement of its achievements and may have sapped morale inside the university. Three main strands of oppositional opinion can be identified:

- The first strand of opinion comprises those who never believed in the expansion of universities in the first place, despite its magisterial endorsement by Lord Robbins and the impressive political consensus supporting it. Driven underground for the next half-century, they never abandoned their conviction that 'more means worse'. In recent years, resurfacing, their tactic has been to argue that too many school leavers go to university, and a proportion should instead be channelled into further education or work-based apprenticeships. Of course, there are entirely legitimate arguments for a rebalancing between higher and further education, which do not deserve to be labelled reactionary. But this reactionary strand of opinion has always lurked just beneath the surface of political life, even if it has remained a largely fringe position within higher education itself. In 2020 it acquired a strong ideological flavour, as prominent (Conservative Party) politicians explicitly rejected the university expansion of the past two decades, asserting that supposedly 'low-quality' and 'low-value' (in terms of earnings) courses should be

culled and students with 'inferior' qualifications diverted into lower-level technical education.
- The second strand comprises those who have accepted the necessity, and even the desirability, of mass expansion, but nevertheless continue to insist on the need for a strict hierarchy of institutions (and, of course, funding) to protect the elite universities. The more enlightened in this second group even welcomed the growth of newer institutions, fearing that in their absence elite universities might have come under more intense pressure to adopt socially inclusive (and academically radical?) policies. But many in this group perceived the ending of the binary system, and establishment of a unified system in which the distinction between universities and polytechnics was dissolved, as a threat. This helps to explain the stubborn persistence of the distinction between 'pre-1992' and 'post-1992' universities, which is largely incomprehensible to students themselves and the wider public. Once, the object of this second group was simply to emphasise the need for 'differentiation' between universities, still within a mass system. Today, the emphasis on 'world-class' universities serves a similar purpose – but may also reflect a retreat from the rather *noblesse oblige* indulgence towards mass higher education.
- To these two strands of opinion held among the opponents of mass expansion, or those highly sceptical about its benefits, can perhaps be added a third, whose scepticism is not about mass higher education in principle, rather the reverse. Instead, it is about the particular forms that mass access has taken. They object not only to the divisive language of 'differentiation' and 'world-class' universities but also to what they typically label 'managerialism', 'corporatisation', 'neo-liberalism' and 'marketisation'. With the exception of the last, these labels are not always helpful because they fail to distinguish between the structural characteristics of institutions within a mass system and more contingent ideological excrescences. This third group includes utopian idealists who value critical enquiry that challenges traditional academic orthodoxies ('hegemonies' is often their preferred description) and imagine equal collectives of free scholars in opposition to the corporate university. But it also includes more determined social engineers who see higher education as a wedge to bring about radical social and political change. To label this third group as 'enemies' of mass higher education, because their critiques may undermine the mass system as it currently exists, of course creates great resentment – perhaps fairly.

The cumulative effect of these strands of opinion among straightforward opponents of wider access, and among sceptics about mass higher education as it has developed in the UK, has been to undermine trust in mass access.

They have dented what would otherwise have been a sense of pride in its achievements.

The 'wrong side of history'

A third explanation for disenchantment with the idea of mass higher education is that it was first articulated, and had begun to be put into effect, at a very particular time and in very particular places. The very particular time was the 1950s and 1960s, which in retrospect can be seen to have been the time of 'peak' social equality. Wealth and capital had been destroyed in two world wars and the Great Depression in between, and the levelling effects of this destructive process had been reinforced by the socially progressive and egalitarian policies pursued by most post-war governments. Few imagined then that this trend towards greater equality would not continue unchallenged into the future. Even fewer could have imagined that it would be sharply reversed in the 1980s and beyond, leading to inequalities of income and wealth not seen since the 19th century.

The particular places where mass higher education was born were North America and, a little later, Western Europe. It is probably not an accident that the idea of mass higher education originally came out of California, a state that in its constitution guaranteed its citizens not just the 'pursuit' of happiness but happiness itself. In the US the social reformism of Franklin Roosevelt's New Deal, and the apparent consolidation of American prestige and power in the Second World War, were still fresh memories in the 1950s and 1960s. These memories were being renewed and refreshed by Lyndon Johnson's Great Society and, more controversially, by the radical and even revolutionary movements for civil rights for Black Americans and women's rights.

In Europe the rhetorical dial was never set so high. But there, too, social reformism was in the ascendant, whether the UK's welfare state or Germany's 'social market'. The past, dole queues and total war, had been decisively rejected. It was in this spirit that what is now the European Union (EU) was born, as well as the expansion of universities. For higher education this context was decisive. The development of mass systems was not an isolated current, but part of a much deeper river of social reform. The role of the state in its development, and its patronage of universities, seemed unthreatening, even inevitable – very unlike the adversarial surveillance that characterises relations between the post-welfare state and 21st-century higher education.

Mass higher education was born with a fair wind at its back. Its tragedy has been that it has come to maturity at a time when social reform has fallen out of fashion. Inequality is greater than at any time since 1914, for which it has even been unjustly blamed. Part of the rather awkward response of system-level and institutional leaders to this changed context has been to develop, sometimes with enthusiasm and sometimes with regret, corporate narratives which, they hope, are better attuned to the current *zeitgeist*. They recognise, better perhaps than their critics, that the old social reformist game is up – temporarily, we must hope. But repurposing mass higher education, with its utopian Enlightenment goals, in these new corporate narratives has nevertheless been a thankless and dispiriting task. There is also a fear that this repurposing lacks substance, or the suspicion that it lacks conviction, which feeds into the sense of general crisis.

In the UK during the past four turbulent and toxic years since the referendum on continuing membership of EU, there has been a further cruel twist. On the face of it, the sense that universities have ended up on the 'wrong side of history' has hardened (Hillman, 2020a). The fact that three-quarters of those without post-school qualifications voted for Brexit, while two-thirds of graduates voted to remain in the EU, has been taken by some to prove that universities threw in their lot with the old – and failed – order. Their liberalism, progressivism, internationalism (call it what you will) are exposed as the self-interested world view of an entrenched elite. It is certainly true that experience of higher education inclines people to be more 'liberal' in their social and cultural views, which makes universities even more suspect in the eyes of the conservative and nationalist opinion that is currently in the ascendant in the simmering culture wars that mark (and mar) contemporary UK society. Such a critique of higher education, of course, is deeply unfair and even absurd. Yet it has strengthened the conviction of the opponents of mass access that higher education has 'lost its way' (if it ever had any justification), and the fear that universities are now finding themselves on the defensive, and undeserving of public support.

Elites and insiders

The fourth explanation is that universities are ill adapted to operating in the more open arenas in which public opinion is now formed and political decisions taken. Quiet conversations in the Athenaeum or Whitehall have been succeeded by the clamour of soundbites and tweets. Although universities have been quick to embrace this febrile culture of 'branding' in terms of their own promotion, they have been curiously reluctant to devise a grander narrative, or 'story', about mass higher education as a whole (maybe because some do not believe in it?). Higher education has become a truly mass system over the past three decades, but it has remained, in key respects, a private world – by choice. In the past there was a hint of arrogance about the universities' assertion of autonomy (even privacy) that won them few friends. As mass higher education developed, such assertions were modified to distinguish between the 'public life' of universities, where public scrutiny and accountability were appropriate, and their 'private life', where autonomy needed to be robustly safeguarded. Yet universities continued, unwittingly, to communicate an off-putting *hauteur*.

Even today there remains a sense that the determination of policy for universities remains a quasi-confidential matter to be discussed out of the public gaze by political and academic elites or, at any rate, informed policy insiders. Admittedly these knowing insider exchanges now operate less through club chat and personal exchanges within a traditional elite and more through the activity of 'sector groups', such as the Russell Group of self-designated 'top' universities, and think tanks, like the Higher Education Policy Institute (HEPI) or WonkHE. But there remains a particularly 'private' quality about university affairs that goes beyond the habitual reticence of the UK's policy class and the instinctive defensiveness of most senior policy and administrative cadres. As in the days of the elite university systems of the past, there seems to be no pressing need for higher education to 'make its case', in broader social and cultural terms and to a wider public.

The result is a – comparative – failure of higher education to fire the public imagination about mass access. Universities in the UK are at a particular disadvantage. They have remained semi-detached public institutions, half-inside and half-outside the public domain. In the rest of Europe, until very recently, universities were firmly incorporated within state structures. This may have produced bureaucratic rigidity, but it also located exchanges between political and academic elites securely within formal arrangements. This is in contrast to the informality that characterised, and perhaps still characterises, the same exchanges in the UK. In the US, too, there was a clarity about governance arrangements in both state and private universities.

Paradoxically, of course, given the multitude of places where mass higher education now touches society that case has never been more compelling. But the publication of detailed lobbying documents on value-added, rates-of-return and multiplier effects is not able fully to compensate for this instinctive reticence. The price of autonomy, and resistance to popular scrutiny if not formal accountability, is a lack of wider visibility, which at times has been translated into a deficit of wider support. The problem may be that even when that autonomy has been frayed, as has plainly happened in the case of UK higher education, the comparative invisibility remains.

In a time of crisis this is a major deficiency. The COVID-19 pandemic has heightened fears that higher education in its present form will find it harder to return to 'normal' than other sectors and institutions because that 'normal' was already wobbling. Some – the NHS certainly, local government possibly – will emerge with renewed purpose and legitimacy, despite the organisational devastation they will have experienced. Universities, on the other hand, may find it easier to repair their balance sheets than their self-belief.

An incomplete – or failed – revolution?

However, these explanations for the puzzling failure to acknowledge the achievements of mass higher education – the comparative novelty of mass access, the influence of its unsubdued enemies, the awkwardness of switching from social reformist strategies and narratives to more corporate and entrepreneurial ones, and the continued reliance on private (and elite) networks in a more populist age – are clearly not the whole story. There are more fundamental reasons for the doubts about mass higher education, despite its many achievements, and these can be grouped under three main headings: sociological; institutional and organisational; and educational and cultural.

Sociological themes

The key question is whether mass expansion has tended to consolidate rather than erode social differences, both between different types of graduates and between graduates and non-graduates, or whether mass higher education retains the potential to promote more democratic access that can challenge these hierarchies?

The deepest fear of many of the supporters of mass higher education is that, as it has evolved, it is incapable of delivering socially progressive results and may instead have produced regressive outcomes which will be very difficult to correct. Of course, there are grounds for hope – or, at any rate, only moderate concern. Fifty per cent of the population now 'go to uni' in some form, although – crucially – 50 per cent do not (Department for Education/National Statistics, 2018). This divide creates not only social and cultural tensions but economic inefficiencies. To be fair, in Scotland participation is already higher with 60 per cent of young people going on to higher education and only 40 per cent still excluded (Scottish Government, 2019). So, in principle, there is no problem advancing the access frontier, and moving from mass to some form of universal participation in higher education. It will only take time, money, political will, public support and (perhaps) some degree of reorganisation of institutional patterns. Nothing fundamental to be concerned about. Revolutions take time to complete. We must be patient – and persevere.

But there are also grounds for anxiety. Arguably, mass access has not so much diminished differences between social groups but mainly recast them in new, and less obvious, ways. A familiar complaint is that the young White men from working-class backgrounds have been left behind. Even among graduates, social and cultural capital, and economic possibilities, are very unevenly distributed in ways that worryingly reproduce social origins and institutional types. This was, and is, most marked in the case of elite universities which continue to recruit disproportionately from the most socially advantaged groups, and this is where the correlation between class and access, and success, is at its strongest. Nor has mass access diminished differences between ethnic groups. Some minority ethnic and cultural groups have very high participation rates (higher than for White students) but others have among the very lowest participation rates. As a result, mass access may have had a similar effect among minority ethnic as it has among social groups. Also, although 'over-represented' in aggregate, minority ethnic groups are concentrated in lower-prestige institutions, in particular the big-city 'post-1992' universities.

The more optimistic argue that educational level has become a more open and fluid indicator of future social (and economic) status. But it is driven by, as well as driving, existing class demarcations. Educational level remains strongly correlated with social class. It would be too optimistic to suppose that, in aggregate rather than in terms of the experience of selected individuals (fortunate and often privileged), new indicators, such as a university education, have replaced existing demarcations derived from social class or ethnicity, or even gender. In some important respects, they may even have revalidated these social differences. Certainly, these new indicators and older demarcations have been woven together in deeply complicit ways. In the absence of significant social levelling, a 'graduate class' is still very much a middle class.

The – highly variable and stratified – status derived from participation in higher education may have given these persistent socio-economic inequalities new life by cloaking them in the disguise of meritocracy. And it should always be remembered that 'meritocracy', now almost universally but misleadingly linked to social mobility (and, therefore, a 'good thing'), was first used by Michael Young to describe the way in which it also conferred a legitimacy on inequalities that the older idea of 'aristocracy' no longer could (Young, 1958/1994). New people might now be in charge, but they still comprised an elite. In practice the social differences between old and new elites are more limited than is generally supposed. The old elites got better educated (and still sought to dominate entry to the 'best' universities). New elites adopted their habits. Co-option rather than replacement remained the dominant mechanism of social change. At the very least, these potentially more socially regressive outcomes of mass access need to be set alongside optimistic assumptions about the emergence of a classless 'graduate culture'. Increasingly, the dark side of meritocracy was revealed, encapsulated in the titles of two recent influential books by the American philosopher Michael Sandel and the British historian Peter Mandler – *The Tyranny of Merit* and *The Crisis of Meritocracy*, respectively (Sandel, 2020; Mandler, 2020).

The impact of mass access on the (graduate) labour market has been similarly ambivalent. On the positive side, in aggregate, it has allowed a much wider cross-section of the population to access professional jobs, provoking an endless debate about whether this has been driven predominantly by the need for a more skilled labour force or simply by a greatly increased supply of graduates (a fascinating debate, certainly, but one that is not relevant in this context, and will be discussed in a later chapter). On the negative side, the effect of mass access has been to systematise and stratify the professional jobs market. It has also allowed universities to establish a near-monopoly of routes into this market, by choking off older apprenticeship-based routes. Another inevitable outcome of mass access has been to restrict job opportunities for non-graduates, comparatively and absolutely.

The cultural effects of mass access too can appear ambivalent. The creation of new communities – physically centred on universities as national, regional and urban hubs, and generically defined by 'graduate' lifestyles, more advanced technical and entrepreneurial expertise and enhanced professional standing (and cross- and multi-cultural and cosmopolitan values?) – has sometimes been at the expense of gutting older communities based on local identities, more traditional values and class solidarities. The new demarcation between so-called 'clever cities' and their prosperous suburban and rural hinterlands, on the one hand, and, on the other hand, decaying industrial and market towns and impoverished rural communities outside the commuter and second-home belt may have sharpened rather than softened the traditional differences between metropolitan and provincial cultures.

Institutional and organisational themes

The key question here is whether the corporate university is the inevitable form that institutions must take in a greatly expanded system comprising more heterogeneous universities, or whether more democratic and collegial forms of organisation are still possible?

Contemporary universities, even those with academically selective intakes and glittering research profiles, are now mass institutions. As has already been said, they enrol tens of thousands of students and employ thousands of staff. They have budgets of hundreds of millions, even billions, of pounds. Their assets – property, buildings, equipment and intellectual property (and 'brand' values?) – are even more valuable. Their economic impact on their cities and regions, through direct and indirect expenditure, employment and their role in providing high-skilled graduate labour and cutting-edge research, makes them major players. Sometimes, almost literally, they are the 'only show in town'. The proliferation of their courses and scale of their research have produced centrifugal forces that have eroded any normative coherence possessed by earlier, and smaller, universities. Once the glib phrase was that mass or mega-universities are organisations held together by a common grievance over car parking. Today, there are many more grievances, but the thought is the same.

Their governance and management reflect this new scale, complexity and heterogeneity. An increasing management class, made up of academics in permanent or semi-permanent managerial roles and professional specialists in finance, human resources, information systems and so on, has emerged in response to these challenges of scale and complexity, to the role that universities now play as strategic agents rather than simply as 'holding companies' for academic departments, and also to the new demands of national policy and accountability regimes and the demands of operating on a global scale. Universities have been transformed into large-scale bureaucratic organisations – necessarily so in most respects, although the cult of 'managerialism' (with its corporate-style reward packages for vice-chancellors repurposed as 'chief executives' and the overblown growth of senior managerial and administrative cadres) may have been a gratuitous and unnecessary excrescence. As a result, universities can no longer realistically be imagined to be communities of learning or academic cooperatives embracing junior researchers and teachers as well as senior professors (whose own leading role is also under threat even in research universities).

These developments have attracted a range of labels, of which the 'managed university' or 'corporate university' are perhaps the most common. They raise important questions that bear on the reputation of mass higher education. Are these changes in organisational style and culture in universities largely a structural response to growing scale and complexity (and 'mission spread' as institutions take on more and more roles, dissolving any distinction between core and peripheral activities) – in other words, the arrival of mass higher education, or largely a response to changes in their external environment such as politicisation (often ideological imposition masquerading as public accountability) and marketisation (the bitter fruits of neoliberal political economy)? Are they inevitable or potentially reversible? There is no clear answer.

But one thing is clear; the 'managed' or 'corporate' university is not much loved. Distaste for the corporate university is widespread across UK higher education. It is shared by the conservatively inclined who look back to a, perhaps imagined, 'donnish dominion' and progressives who had hoped to see the establishment of a radical university. The DNA of the Council for the Defence of British Universities (CDBU), established following an article by the historian Keith Thomas criticising the current state of higher education in the *London Review of Books* (Thomas, 2011), has both conservative and progressive strands, both Oxbridge dons, determined to defend a quasi-aristocratic version of academic freedom against managerial encroachment, and radicals, opposed not only to managerial ambition and excess but also to the marketisation of English higher education and the perpetuation of traditional institutional hierarchies. Another UK organisation, the Campaign for the Public University, which is avowedly progressive in tone, has also at times expressed support, even nostalgia, for forms of institutional autonomy and academic freedom beyond the domain of politics where radical critiques of society can be developed. The suspicion that mass higher education has made the 'managed university' inevitable is clearly another reason why it remains unloved, and its achievements inadequately acknowledged. It is a powerful contribution to the sense of gathering crisis.

Educational and cultural themes

The key question here is whether the suppression of radical forms of critical enquiry, or at any rate their subordination to a jobs-targeted instrumentalism, is also an inevitable characteristic of a mass system, or whether it was – and is – possible still to conceive of more progressive forms of curriculum, learning and research that challenge intellectual hierarchies and orthodoxies.

Also potentially undermining the legitimacy of mass higher education is a third bundle of concerns that relate more directly to the curriculum and how it is delivered, student learning and emerging patterns of research. In its early years, the expansion of UK higher education appeared to offer opportunities for radical ideas to take root. The new universities of the 1960s devised 'new maps of learning' that emphasised interdisciplinary courses and new approaches to delivering the curriculum to students. Some of the newly established polytechnics moved away from subject-focused degrees and developed new modular structures designed to maximise student choice. A few even created Schools for 'Independent Study' that challenged the standard taxonomies – and, by implication, authority – of traditional academic disciplines.

But in more recent years these radical initiatives have been domesticated (de-fanged?) by emphasising their structural rather than intellectual features or have been abandoned entirely. A very different pattern, and especially language, developed: some elements were shaped by technology, such as 'learning management systems' or, most recently, 'massive open online courses' (MOOCs); some reflected a new desire to systematise the design of courses and manage how they are taught, which required the definition of approved 'learning outcomes' and appraisal of the 'performance' of teachers; some emerged in response to the imposition of external metric-based assessment regimes such as the Teaching Excellence and Student Outcomes Framework (TEF). The increasing emphasis placed on measuring 'student satisfaction' and 'value-for-money' (reductively in terms of graduate earnings) has compounded a sense that liberal, and scientific, education has been subordinated to an oppressive instrumentalism. A typical, and resigned, comment: 'In effect, the only functions that are now recognised for universities – whether by policy makers or senior university leaders – are the development of human capital and the enhancement of economic growth' (Holmwood, 2011).

Similar changes have taken place in research. The impact on the behaviour of both institutional managers and individual academics of the Research

Assessment Exercise (RAE) and its successor the Research Excellence Framework (REF) cannot be exaggerated. It transformed the culture of academic research. Other changes included the emphasis on increasing income by securing external funding and on measuring the 'impact' of research. Of course, the increased volume of research, as a direct result of the expansion of higher education, also changed its nature, what had been a semi-artisanal activity in many disciplines, especially the humanities, took on many of the characteristics of a quasi-industrial process.

Of course, there was some continuity with earlier examples of radicalism. In the curriculum, new subjects continued to emerge and traditional academic disciplines are sharply challenged. A good current example is the attempts to 'de-colonise' the curriculum by introducing hitherto marginal ideas and voices into subjects like literature and history, but also the social sciences and creative arts. However, while the 'new maps of learning' drawn up in the 1960s and even more radical experiments in some polytechnics during the 1970s and 1980s were not opposed in principle and mostly treated with indulgence even by sceptical conservatives, these more recent initiatives often provoked a strong ideological backlash.

As a result, the emerging tensions between radical ideas and recent shifts in learning and teaching may have added to the sense of unease about the impact of mass higher education. Similarly, the movement towards more open, socially distributed and contextualised research systems have become confused with highly reductive interpretations of 'impact' and narrow definitions of 'applied research', once again contributing to this sense of growing unease. As with the 'managed university', the key question now is whether these changes in education and research were inevitable within a mass system or whether they simply reflected the shift in the organisational culture, in other words the 'managed university' and external political and ideological choices that could be distinguished from the core process of mass expansion – and so, potentially, be reversible.

Finally, on a wider canvass than these specific developments in curriculum, student learning and research, there has perhaps been an intellectual, and cultural, void. No compelling narrative, or simple 'story', has been generated about the role universities have played in English national life, and the benefits of mass higher education. In contrast, in the US, 'college' – like the NHS in England – has some of the qualities of a 'national religion'. Even in Scotland there is a 'story', however mythic, that links universities, the Scottish Enlightenment, the so-called 'democratic intellect' and the pseudo-populist 'lad o'pairts' into a broader narrative about national identity (Davie, 1961/2013, 1986). In England potential alternatives to the high elitism of Oxbridge have failed to become established despite the development of mass access. In their place, the cynical pastiches of Kingsley Amis's *Lucky Jim* or Malcolm Bradbury's *The History Man* – and, of course, a thousand spreadsheets about graduate salary premiums, economic multiplier effects and the contribution of universities to gross domestic product (GDP). But nothing to excite the popular imagination, no 'story'. Weak foundations on which to build a justification, and celebration, of mass higher education.

Final words

UK higher education faces immediate, and urgent, challenges. Some are directly linked to the COVID-19 pandemic: uncertainty about future student recruitment when universities are unable to offer the full campus experience (and must fall back to a greater or lesser degree on online delivery of their courses); a dark fear that 'the party's over' for international student recruitment, and maybe internationalisation in a broader sense, which has been a key driver of institutional reputation (and a crucial additional income stream for many institutions); the near inevitability of financial retrenchment, austerity and worse. Other challenges are more deep-rooted – the slow-motion divorce from the European mainstream triggered by Brexit, which threatens the UK system's research base (the loss of European research funding and faltering recruitment of early-career researchers and more senior scientists); the imposition of an over-mighty regulator in England, the Office for Students (OfS), with a highly politicised agenda, and the enthusiasm of a Scottish Government more attracted to more traditional forms of bureaucratic centralisation for top-down 'restructuring'; an indifferent, or even hostile, public opinion unimpressed by overpaid managers, rumours of grade inflation, bragging (and name-calling) competition incompatible with keeping faith with 'public service', and hyperactive gaming of league tables that corrodes trust.

However, the argument in this book is that we must dig deeper for the real reasons for this disenchantment with mass access, the source of UK higher education's general crisis. To call them existential is going too far – but not perhaps by much. The innocent promise that the expansion of higher education was, and is, a key component of a wider social project, the advance of equality and democracy, has not been kept – or so it seems. Its contribution to economic efficiency is increasingly contested and, in any case, faith in the inevitability, and desirability, of growth is weakening. The utopian university of so many people's hopes and dreams, a space where free-thinking and critical ideas could flourish and the existing social order could be reimagined along more progressive lines, has morphed into a clunkish corporate institution. The very purposes of a university education in gloomy moments seem to have been diminished and undermined. Above all, there is a fear that these developments, although uninvited, have been inevitable – and that the possibility of turning back, or into, a new course is now uncertain. Although this book ends up in a more optimistic place, this is where it must start.

2

'Post-war' to post-millennium

The development of mass higher education in the UK since 1960 did not take place in a vacuum. Many of the changes that have taken place, whether in terms of national policy, institutional missions, organisational culture or teaching and research, cannot properly be explained without some consideration of the wider political, social, economic and cultural context. Mass higher education, above all, is contextualised higher education, to a degree that did not perhaps apply in the days of much smaller elite university systems. Put simply, UK higher education is different because the UK is different. The 1960s, where this story began, are now 'another country'.

The same contextualisation is needed to make sense of the wider evolution of higher education systems across the globe in the rest of Europe, North America, Latin America, Africa, Asia (in particular, East Asia) and Australasia. The bipolar Cold War world – one half (broadly) 'market', liberal democratic, social reformist and the other half (nominally) Communist – has been replaced by new geopolitical alignments, shifting (and often volatile) configurations, war and terrorism, all overshadowed by the spectre of climate change and environmental degradation (and now pandemic). New economies, and economic structures, have emerged. The stable landscapes of 20th-century industrial society have crumbled to be replaced by volatile 21st-century corporate visions. Global cultures have both cohered – through the action of the mass media, the advance of world brands, and the (dubious) rise of 'Globlish' among other phenomena – and also fragmented – through growing hybridity and increasing resistance.

These wider contexts are the subject of this chapter. The main focus, inevitably but regrettably, is on the UK. The wider UK context is discussed under four headings:

- 'The Sixties to Brexit': the political changes from 1960s to Brexit five decades later;
- 'Themes and trends': major themes such as over-centralisation of political power and decision making, and the replacement of consensus by new adversarial politics;
- 'Economic change': changing economic contexts, including the death of industrial England and the rise of neoliberal finance';
- 'A social and cultural revolution?': wider social change, such as the erosion of old solidarities and the rise of new 'identities' against a background of increasing inequalities, and a cultural revolution, rooted in the advance of

social liberalism and the unbundling of traditional forms and structures of creative expression in the context of instantaneity, brands and celebrity.

The Sixties to Brexit

The 'post-war' still lingered in 1960s Britain. At the start of the decade, the Second World War had ended only 15 years before. Most of the population, apart from those still at school, had active and personal memories of the war years and the years before. A flavour of Victorian Britain lingered too. Once inside the new suburbs and new arterial roads, cityscapes retained much of their Victorian look and feel – grand civic buildings, imposing schools and colleges, massed terraces. Comprehensive urban development – high-rise flats and motorways – lay largely in the future. Britons in 1960 had also recently experienced post-war reconstruction under Clement Attlee's Labour Government and benefited from the building of a comprehensive welfare state and had lived through the 1950s with their curious mixture of 'ups' (the new Elizabethan age), 'downs (Suez), and 'ups' again (Harold Macmillan's 'never had it so good' Conservative Government). Two generations later this is the stuff of history books like the two magisterial series written by Peter Hennessy and David Kynaston (Hennessy, 2006, 2017, 2019; Kynaston, 2008, 2010, 2013). But then it was recent and lived experience.

There are two ways of looking at the 1960s. Either they can be seen as the culmination of 'post-war', the – sometimes shaky – completion of the welfare state by Harold Wilson's Government that came to power in 1964, but also as a continuation of the 'never had it so good' era and an irreversible post-Suez retreat from empire. Or they can be seen as decade of rupture, like the Thatcher years 20 years later, with the rapid advance of social liberalism – the end of capital punishment, and the legalisation of abortion and homosexuality – and the embrace, almost fetishising, of 'technology' that has gripped every government since – Wilson's 'white heat of the technological revolution' speech and Concorde. Whatever view is taken, the 1964–70 Labour Government was a landmark administration, not perhaps in the same league as the Attlee Government, but probably equal to Thatcher and New Labour, the other two landmark administrations of the later 20th century.

In contrast, the 1970s are remembered as a decade of drift and crises – miners' strikes, the International Monetary Fund (IMF) bail-out, the 'winter of discontent'. They are often treated as an uneasy interlude between the 1960s and the 1980s, in both of which – for better or worse – there was a clear sense of direction. That judgement may be a little harsh. The post-war welfare state reached its fullest development during this decade. Public spending grew to its post-war peak as a proportion of gross national product (GNP). The UK, belatedly, became a member of the European

Economic Community (now the European Union), which represented an epochal redirection of its destiny and, until the car crash of Brexit in 2016, seemed irreversible. Closer to home, the 1970s saw the completion of the comprehensive reorganisation of secondary education (ironically by Margaret Thatcher in her first Cabinet post as Education Secretary) and the consolidation of the first stage of the development of mass higher education with the growth of the 'new' universities and the establishment of the polytechnics.

The conventional view has become established that the 1980s, dominated by Margaret Thatcher, represent the true rupture in British post-war political life. Before Thatcher, the welfare state, high taxes, strong trade unions and the consensus politics of 'Butskellism' (Rab Butler for the Conservatives and Hugh Gaitskell for Labour) were dominant. After Thatcher, the key characteristics were a shrunken state, deregulation and privatisation, a new confidence in the virtues of the 'free' market and, above all, some variety of political revolution, more apparent perhaps in the scale and intensity of opposition to it than in its concrete realisation. The 1980s were also regarded, at the time and in retrospect, as a similar rupture in many other countries – for example, parallel trends in the US during the Presidency of Ronald Reagan, and the failure of Francois Mitterrand in France to master the forces of economic liberalisation in the name of democratic socialism. In the UK, the underlying data on annual rates of growth in the economy, trends in public expenditure and even the shares of GNP devoted to public expenditure tend to cast some doubt on this belief in stark before-and-after rupture. Economic growth across the decade in the despised 1970s was pretty healthy too. But this belief is perhaps too well established, and contains too much truth, to be cast aside.

The Thatcher years certainly saw a change in national mood. A primary although neglected cause of this shift was the final departure from the national scene of those with direct adult experience of the Great Depression, the Second World War and post-war reconstruction and the building of the welfare state. This demographic diminuendo was perhaps more significant than the specific policies pursued by the Thatcher Government. The 'post-war' was finally over. That shift in mood had two elements. First, there was the sense that the public good as the guiding star of policy and politics was eroded, if not abandoned. As Margaret Thatcher famously asserted: 'there is no such thing as society only individuals'. This, and other pronouncements by Conservative politicians, gave the impression that this first element in the shift in mood was predominantly due to a change in ideology – the much-heralded Thatcherism. But a more prosaic, and structural, explanation is just as plausible. The very success of post-war reconstruction in increasing national wealth, and of the welfare state in reducing the chronic insecurity and personal uncertainties which had been the experience of previous generations, had created the economic and socio-cultural space in which individualism could flourish. Core social attitudes in fact have been remarkably stable over half a century.

The second element, more directly attributable to the style and actions of the Thatcher Government, was the erosion of political consensus – no more 'Butskellism' (or even its successor, the apolitical and technocratic tone of the Labour Governments of the 1960s and 1970s). The result was a revival of adversarial politics, and a quasi-existential clash of ideologies, not seen since the turbulent years between the end of the First World War and the General Strike. The Conservatives rediscovered ideology, which they had gradually abandoned during the pre-war years and, in particular, during the Churchill and Macmillan era post war (even if there had been a tentative rediscovery of ideology – the much quoted 'Selsdon man' – during the initial phase of the government of Edward Heath as a form of proto-Thatcherism). At same time, in the 1980s, the Labour Opposition abandoned the technocratic middle ground it had occupied.

In retrospect, this revival of ideology may appear to have been less complete than it appeared at the time. But it is difficult to deny that, to a considerable extent, the 1980s changed the political weather in the UK. The revival of adversarial politics, which has persisted to this day after a limited regression to consensus under New Labour, was powerfully assisted, of course, by the continuation of an unreformed (and unfair) voting system – and, more recently, turbocharged by an increasingly partisan mass media and, even more recently, the explosion of social media. In other words, adversarialism was essentially a contingent phenomenon based on favourable structural characteristics. Proportional representation in elections, a more measured mass media or even a circular debating chamber rather than an antique House of Commons might have curbed its ominous but apparently irresistible growth.

In structural terms there were three legacies of the Thatcher years. The first was the rapid growth of what might be called 'the para-state' – in other words, the expanding hinterland between the public and private sectors created by privatisation. This 'grey' hinterland was greatly expanded by the subsequent government of John Major, from 1990 to 1997, and even by the New Labour governments of Tony Blair and Gordon Brown. In the 21st century, this para-state has become one of the most dynamic, and profitable, sectors of the national economy, after financial services.

The second legacy was the destruction of a powerful trade union movement, in stark contrast to the rest of Europe. To some degree, the decline of trade union power reflected the erosion of the manufacturing and extraction industries where trade union organisation had been strong, and also the squeezing (and privatisation) of the public sector. But a powerful reason was the ideological determination of the Thatcher Government to strengthen the hand of managers – which had the incidental, but welcome, effect of weakening the rival Labour Party, which still depended on affiliated trade unions for much of its income.

The third legacy of the Thatcher years was the hollowing-out and subordination of local government, which of course tended to have the same beneficial effect in terms of partisan politics because many local authorities, particularly in cities, tended to be Labour strongholds. During the 1980s – and into the 1990s and 2000s – a far-reaching concentration of political power in Whitehall and Westminster took place. At the time it may have seemed the natural culmination of the long-term building of a national government under way since the 19th century. In retrospect, the UK has probably paid a high price in terms of responsiveness, resilience and agility for this over-concentration of power in London.

The government headed by John Major has sometimes been seen as merely an interlude between the fall of Thatcher and the victory of New Labour. As with the 1970s that may be a serious underestimation. The government lasted for seven years, with Major winning a decisive election victory, something which eluded the Conservatives for the next quarter of a century. It undertook a major reform of the structure of higher education, the ending of the binary system, arguably the most important change of direction between the original decision to establish the polytechnics 26 years earlier and the lurch towards creating a quasi-market system in English higher education following the Browne Report in 2010. The Major Government, in contrast to the Prime Minister's own mild manners, accelerated the pace of privatisation, including that most totemic privatisation of all, of the railways. Finally, it was during these years that the quiescent divisions within the Conservative Party on membership of the European Union (EU) burst into flame. The free-market and nationalist Conservative Party fringe, labelled 'bastards' by Major, lost the first skirmishes but ultimately won the war two decades later. These divisions have dominated national politics since, creating a toxic fracture matching, or even out-rivalling, those over the Corn Laws, Irish home rule and imperial preference in earlier times.

New Labour, which triumphed in 1997, and two subsequent elections, under its new Leader, Tony Blair, despite its claim to be 'new', was really a return to the enthusiasm for modernisation and technocracy that characterised the Labour Governments of the 1960s and 1970s. Another comparison is with the Attlee Government of 1945 to 1951, although only perhaps in terms of New Labour's ultimate failure to match that government's grit and determination to make irreversible reforms in society. Yet it established a political dominance exceeding that of the Conservatives during the Thatcher years or since 2010. So great was that dominance in its first term that, with the Opposition curbed and quietened, the UK came close to becoming a one-party state, to an extent never achieved by Margaret Thatcher in the 1980s. For a few years, adversarial politics abated. Two Conservative leaders came and went; it was only with the third, David Cameron, and his espousal of heavily New Labour-influenced 'compassionate Conservatism', that normal politics was resumed.

New Labour both completed and contradicted the Thatcher project – accelerating still further modernisation policies, many relying on market-like mechanisms (this was the high tide of New Public Management), but at the same time making unprecedented levels of investment in public services (from which higher education greatly benefited). Although it was not successful in reversing (or may even not have been interested in reversing) increasing income inequalities, it made impressive reductions in absolute poverty. New Labour also experimented with a new way of doing politics, focused on 'identity' and 'brand' and less on traditional political solidarities. It attempted to build support among wider but also more fluid swathes of the population – a successful strategy in the short run, although fraught with future danger. This new style of politics has now become pervasive.

However, New Labour's most decisive reform was to re-establish a Scottish parliament (almost three centuries after the establishment of a United Kingdom with a united parliament) and a Scottish Executive, later Scottish Government, to match; and to establish for the first time a National Assembly in Wales and a separate government. Like many reforms, this one was incomplete, even botched, with the respective powers of the UK Government and two new devolved administrations left unclear. Such was the dominance of New Labour at the end of the 20th century that it was casually and arrogantly assumed that any differences could be resolved by internal Labour Party discussions; little thought appears to have been given to the possibility that the three governments might be controlled by different political parties with different political agendas.

The consequences of this reform are still being played out 20 years later. Its ultimate trajectory remains unclear. But already it has produced substantial policy divergences, most notably in Scotland where the Scottish Government in effect opted out of the market-like reform of higher education introduced in England in 2010 and developed instead a distinctive Scottish, and increasingly separate, higher education system. One view of the long-term trajectory is that devolution has hastened the slow-motion break-up of the imperial UK state, what Tom Nairn once labelled 'Ukania', which began a century ago with the independence of Ireland. Another possible trajectory is that it will lead ultimately to the replacement of the highly centralised UK state centred on Whitehall and Westminster, and its broken politics, by a reformed federal state, including a revival of genuinely local government.

Two events derailed New Labour. The first was to follow the United States and support the invasion of Iraq and later the invasion of Afghanistan, a cemetery of old British imperial ambitions. Initially seen as a continuation of the liberal interventionism that had worked, just about, in the Balkans following the break-up of Yugoslavia, public opinion quickly turned against the Iraq adventure. Opposition was particularly intense within the Labour Party itself – although in an interesting historical footnote the number of Labour MPs who voted against their government on the Iraq war was exceeded by the number who voted against raising tuition fees in universities to £3,000 per year. The ultimate failure of the Iraq and Afghan adventures was to reactivate painful memories of imperial retreat and national decline, symbolised above all by the Suez invasion in 1956, which – fortuitously – had been temporarily put out of mind by the recovery of the Falklands Islands in 1983.

The second was the 2008 banking crisis, and subsequent economic recession, on which the new Prime Minister Gordon Brown exercised global leadership. But this did not yield any electoral advantage – rather the reverse – and Labour was denied a fourth straight election victory by their opportunist opponents. The banking crisis too stirred disturbing memories – on the traditional left, stoking resentment that bankers had been protected from their follies at the expense of ordinary people; and, among the government's opponents (and, encouraged by the right-leaning media, perhaps public opinion), reviving past associations between Labour and economic mismanagement.

The installation of a Conservative-dominated Coalition government, with the Liberal Democrats as (very) junior partners, followed New Labour's defeat in 2010. The new government under David Cameron imposed substantial cuts in public expenditure, according to the old 'austerity' playbook. The investment of New Labour in public services was reversed, with disastrous consequences for public health and social care that became apparent with the outbreak of the COVID-19 pandemic in 2020. Local government budgets were particularly savagely cut, further increasing their subordination to central government, a process thinly disguised by the creation of Potemkin Village-style mayors in major conurbations. The only exception was higher education which, in effect, was protected from the general austerity at the price of accepting much higher tuition fees, which later proved to be Mephistophelian bargain with the state. This get-out-jail-free card was duly noted, and resented, by other public services.

The new government also accelerated the market-like reforms initiated under the Thatcher and Major Governments but, ironically, espoused with relish and expanded by New Labour. One was a large-scale expansion of Academies, and an enforced reduction in the number of local authority schools, even if the probably inevitable development of large multi-school Academy chains was a long cry from the original intention of the policy to free individual schools from bureaucratic controls. A second was yet another reform of the National Health Service to establish clinical commissioning groups, with GPs ostensibly giving contracts to hospitals (a reform now in the process of being unbundled in the endless merry-go-round of NHS restructuring). However, the faith in technocratic solutions was undermined by the government's open endorsement of quasi-populist attacks on professional expertise. The Secretary of State for Education, Michael Gove, took to talking of the 'blob', to describe experts in education. This anti-intellectualism became established as a new strain in (or stain on?) political life.

But the dominant issue remained that of membership of the EU. Paradoxically, the result of the 2015 general election which gave the Conservatives a majority exacerbated the tensions on Europe, because they no longer had to rely on the Liberal Democrats, a strongly Europhile party, to remain in power. David Cameron, prime minister since 2010, had promised to hold a referendum on membership of the EU, confident that continuing UK membership would be endorsed by a similar margin witnessed in the rejection of Scottish independence the year before. A year later he resigned when his gamble failed and, by a very narrow margin, a majority voted to 'leave'. There then ensued one of the most turbulent, and toxic, periods in UK political history. For the next three years Cameron's successor, Theresa May, struggled to honour the promise to respect the result of the 2016 referendum by reaching a compromise on an orderly withdrawal with the EU which could also satisfy Conservative Members of Parliament, almost losing her majority in another election in 2017 in the process. Her successive failures paralysed political life. In 2019 she resigned and was succeeded by Boris Johnson, a leader of the 'Leave' campaign. In a third election, in December 2019, the Conservatives were returned with a comfortable majority. But the moment of triumph was short-lived, with the onset of the COVID-19 pandemic, which produced a new form of political paralysis.

It is hardly an exaggeration to compare the battle over membership of the EU with earlier crises, for example over Parliamentary reform in the 1830s or the Corn Laws a decade later. Just as they came to be seen as the inevitable growing pains towards progress and modernisation, so the crisis over Europe took on something of the character of a revolt against modernity. The struggle between 'Remain' and 'Leave' became the new fault line of political life. It also unleashed culture wars perhaps never experienced before in Britain – with monster public demonstrations by supporters of 'Remain' which far exceeded anything achieved (or even claimed) by the Chartists in the mid-19th century, and threats from the more extreme supporters of 'Leave' going far beyond the limits of respectable political debate. Resentment against austerity (and growing inequality), imperial nostalgia, a resurgence of a narrow English nationalism at the expense of British patriotism, anti-immigration sentiment (and outright racism) in response to the advance of multiculturalism and cosmopolitanism

– all contributed to a toxic mix that turbocharged the adversarial politics that had been evolving since the Thatcher years. Crisis and conflict became embedded in political life. At the same time, the instability of the archaic UK 'constitution' was painfully exposed with unprecedented clashes between the Executive, Parliament and the courts. The fragmentation of the UK also accelerated, with Scotland and Northern Ireland voting to 'Remain'. But it is too early, and too raw, to reach considered conclusions about the longer-term consequences of this most turbulent period in UK political life.

Themes and trends

But it is not too early to identify some long-term secular trends over the long half-century between 1960 and 2020. Four stand out:

The centralisation of political decision making at Westminster and in Whitehall

At the start of this period, local government retained substantial powers of political decision making which have been sharply eroded – tentatively in the 1960s and 1970s (one example is the imposition of a comprehensive pattern of secondary education by the Wilson Government); vigorously so in the 1980s by the Thatcher Government when party political and ideological conflicts came to the fore; and decisively during the New Labour years with its insistent programme of modernisation. In the past decade, the Conservative-dominated Coalition Government and then the subsequent Conservative Government completed this subordination of local authorities to the status of mere delivery organisations for Whitehall directives. The only countervailing force was the appointment of new-style mayors with executive powers in a few major cities, in particular London. The initial decision to establish the polytechnics in the 1960s, taken centrally, and their removal from local authority control in the 1980s were examples of the process of nationalisation. This process was not only confined to local government but extended to many other intermediate and supposedly autonomous public agencies and even civil society organisations receiving public funds. The abolition of the University Grants Committee (UGC) and the subordination of universities to more direct Departmental control is another example. The BBC, the Arts Council and the British Council were all exposed to more direct political pressure.

The decline of political consensus and the advance of adversarial politics

It would be wrong to exaggerate the degree of political consensus in the 1960s. But 'Butskellism' was not a media myth. As has already been pointed out, Margaret Thatcher, in her first incarnation as Secretary of State for Education between 1970 and 1973, in effect completed the comprehensive reorganisation of secondary education begun by her Labour predecessor Anthony Crosland. In a revealing exchange with her Labour shadow, Roy Hattersley, she even boasted that public expenditure on education had increased more rapidly on her watch than during the previous, Labour, Government. This particular episode, for obvious reasons, has been excised from the hagiographic accounts that focus on her subsequent time as prime minister. But, in the course of the 1970s, new fault lines appeared – on labour relations (provoked by the first, and successful, miners' strikes) and management of the economy (in the wake of the crisis in the middle of the decade). These fault lines fractured still further, and took on an explicitly ideological form, during the 1980s. The Conservatives abandoned their 'middle England' ground and shifted right, while Labour abandoned its faith in technocracy and shifted left. The temporary dominance of New Labour around the turn of the century briefly imposed a new consensus, only for it to fracture again after the Iraq invasion and the 2008 banking crisis and economic recession. Since 2010 polarisation has intensified, most toxically on Europe. By 2020 the UK had become among the most ideological of all European countries, its tradition of pragmatism shredded – forgotten or despised. This advance of adversarial politics also reflected and was assisted by new ways of 'doing politics', rooted in the aggressive use of social media and data analytics.

Experts – and their enemies

In the 1960s orderly habits of disinterested public administration still prevailed; the Robbins Report was a splendid example of the application of these habits. But over the next half century these habits were sharply eroded; choices once regarded as essentially 'administrative' came to be seen as 'political'. The technocracy of the 1960s, revived under New Labour, fell irredeemably out of fashion. Paradoxically, this shift towards the politicisation of public policy (with an increasingly ideological edge) led to a proliferation of the use of – rival – experts. More frequent use of phrases such as the need for 'evidence-based' policy in reality demonstrated its reverse, the advance of partisan policy making with its insatiable demand for supportive data. As a result, professional experts, once seen as standing apart from the immediate political struggle, became enmeshed in advocacy and controversy. Experts became targets of both radical-right and radical-left politicians, who resented any restraint their advice might place on the realisation of their ambitions, on disgraceful show during the COVID-19 pandemic. However, with the decline of political consensus and rise of adversarial politics between the 1970s and 1990s this may have been inevitable.

But, at the same time, the UK state became more and more dependent on expert systems, of all kinds, often based on new data technologies. Just as the websites and call centres became the ubiquitous interfaces in the market economy, sometimes dehumanising 'systems' replaced more traditional forms of contact between citizens and the state. This fed sullen resentments and sometimes provoked fierce reactions, exploited by populist politicians with other agendas for discrediting supposedly 'elite' (and liberal technocratic) experts tarred as the guardians of these 'systems'. By the end of the period, political life had come to be dominated by two contradictory impulses: resentment of experts who seemed to stand in the ways of political dreams, yet ever more frequent resort to expert and scientific support for policy. This love–hate relationship with professionalism, and expertise, represented a toxic and volatile mix.

Erosion of competence in public administration

As a result of the first three trends, there has been an alarming loss of competence in public administration. The over-centralisation of political decision making at Westminster and in Whitehall has produced the results that all such processes of centralisation produce: overload and a decline in pluralism and of local knowledge and sensitivity. The emasculation of local government has sharply reduced not only the ability of 'local' voices to be heard but also on-the-ground competence – compounded by increasing budgetary constraints. The advance of adversarial politics has elevated ideological partisanship and party-political 'loyalty' over skills and competence, as well of course as (deliberately) curbing pluralism. 'Success' is now defined in terms of short-term political advantage and ideological purity, often measured in terms of media reaction, rather than long-term reform. The UK has paid a high price in professionalism by focusing on who is 'one of us.' The use and misuse, and distrust, of 'experts' have also eroded the UK's tradition of disinterested public administration. All of this has been horribly on view as the UK government struggled during the COVID-19 pandemic. The initial marginalising of beleaguered public health services in favour of a highly centralised and essentially privatised 'test and track' system was the ultimate folly, as the reversal of this approach in the case of vaccinations confirmed.

Economic change

In 1960 the landscape, and geography, of the 19th-century industrial revolution were still visible. The UK economy was dominated, as it had been for almost a century, by manufacturing, extraction, trade, services and the state. In manufacturing, the focus was moving from capital to consumer goods and from heavy industry to light engineering. The extraction industries were still dominated by coal, although on the cusp of a dramatic shift to oil and gas. Services were spread across a range of sectors – administration, retail, hospitality … Although the City of London was already established as a global financial centre, its institutions – banks, high-street and merchant; insurance companies; brokerage firms – still operated in familiar and traditional ways. The so-called 'big bang', the liberalisation of financial markets, lay in the future. The state, expanding since the 19th century but much aggrandised since 1945, occupied a pivotal role in heavy industry, energy and transport, as well as in education, health and other public, or welfare state, services. The big industrial players were coal and steel, car (and to a lesser extent aerospace) manufacturing and chemicals.

However, things were changing. The next half century was dominated by competing narratives of economic decline and neoliberal reforms, for and against – but also by some underlying continuities, all dating originally from the 1960s:

- First, government became a far more active agent in the economy, even when, as under Margaret Thatcher, particular governments celebrated the efficacy of the free market and practised limited monetarist economic policies. The historical record was plain about the advancing agency of the state. The new Labour Government in 1964 established a Department for Economic Affairs (DEA) as a counterpoint to the Treasury. Although the DEA did not thrive, or indeed survive, and the Treasury quickly reclaimed its primacy within Whitehall, the core message of this reform, that it was the responsibility of government to develop a dynamic industrial strategy, was accepted by almost every successive government. The effectiveness of particular strategies has often been questioned. But no serious challenge to the need for such a strategy in the first place has been made.
- A closely related continuity was a commitment to investing in 'technology', begun in the 1960s in Harold Wilson's Labour conference speech with its ringing endorsement of 'the white heat of the technological revolution'. Again, no subsequent government has seriously resiled from that focus on technology-driven growth. The development of the supersonic airliner Concorde was an especially high-profile early expression of this fascination with 'technology', and it has resonated down subsequent decades, with HS2 as the latest example. From this fascination with 'technology' the later idea of 'knowledge society' emerged, with universities as key players.
- The same Labour Government tentatively began the process of attempting to modernise industrial relations when it published its White Paper *In Place of Strife* (HMSO, 1969), an especially delicate manoeuvre for a party

largely funded by trade unions. Not surprisingly this proved initially to be a false start. But curbing the supposedly excessive power of trade unions to block industrial change became the economic issue that was to dominate the next two decades.

The 1970s were dominated by the trade union 'problem'. The Heath Government's singular achievement in finally negotiating UK membership of the then European Economic Community was overshadowed by its failure to reform the trade unions. Confrontation ensued. The victory of the National Union of Mineworkers (NUM) in its first national strike since 1926, admittedly on the issue of pit closures rather than directly on the reform of industrial relations, elevated what had begun as a measured attempt to modernise industrial relations into a quasi-constitutional clash summed up in the question 'Who rules?'. While other European countries were able to focus on longer-term industrial development and investment, the UK was mired down in a dour struggle between trade unions and the state that dominated the political agenda and weakened the focus of industrial leaders on innovation and productivity. The eventual defeat of the NUM, and the trade unions more generally, by the Thatcher Government was achieved at great cost – not only the polarisation and bitterness produced by the defeat of the second miners' strike in 1984, one of the most cathartic events of the past half century, with its accusations of 'the enemies within' and images of long convoys of police vehicles heading north to the coalfields, but also the large-scale de-industrialisation of the UK. It was not just the mines that closed.

The way in which this issue had dominated political life and inhibited industrial progress, and the manner in which it was finally resolved, meant that any future growth of the UK economy had to be based on different principles and other sectors. The UK was not so able to build a dynamic economy on the industrial foundations of the past, as happened in Germany and, to a lesser extent, France where advanced manufacturing provided the basis for future growth. Instead, in the UK, greater reliance had to be placed on the development of service industries. The explosion of consumerism and credit was the inevitable result. This is also where the most important reform of the Thatcher decade, the liberalisation of financial services – the 'big bang' in the City of London – fits in. No doubt this emphasis on the financial sector as a driving force of the economy reflected the ideological preferences of the government. However, as a result of de-industrialisation, which earlier industrial strategies had failed to arrest and the Thatcher Government had witlessly promoted, there was little choice. Perhaps the enduring weaknesses of the UK economy – over-exposure to the volatility of global markets, stagnant productivity and the rest – can be attributed to this fundamental lack of choice.

The trade union 'problem' having been solved, the new Conservative Government headed by John Major in the 1990s focused on another favourite strand of the Thatcher Government's economic policy – privatisation. The main public services – gas, water and electricity – had been privatised in the 1980s, and the new government, more contentiously, added the railways (which, ironically, have now been effectively renationalised because of the collapse in demand during the COVID-19 pandemic). The Major Government also accelerated the subjection of the remaining public sector to 'market' disciplines. This theme was enthusiastically picked up by the incoming New Labour Government under Tony Blair, although the focus shifted from outsourcing to private companies to root-and-branch 'modernisation' still within the scope of the public sector. But as a counterpoint to 'modernisation', the recently elected New Labour Government was also determined to increase public investment and to create public services worthy of the new century. It exploited the new forms of innovative financial engineering developed in the private sector following the 'big bang', to create new ways of funding public expenditure, especially on capital projects. The so-called 'private finance initiative' enabled new hospitals and schools to be built, using private money secured by lease-back and similar arrangements. Other public–private partnerships, in which the private sector provided funding and the government took on the risk, also flourished.

As with the curbing of trade union power, privatisation (and modernisation) tended to crowd out other economic issues on which other countries were able to focus more of their efforts. Also, privatisation must be judged a failure – if its fundamental aim was to shrink the size of the public sector to prevent it crowding out more productive private sector investment. The core public sector, plus what can be reasonably be described as 'publicly planned expenditure' (student loans are a good example), plus the spreading 'para-state' of outsourced and thinly privatised services (of which a good example is the supposedly private rail operating companies), almost certainly consume a larger share of the GDP in the 2010s than the welfare state did in the 1960s. The case for privatisation, therefore, had to be made, not on the basis of economic theory, but on its practical benefits in terms of promoting greater efficiency. Here, the jury remains out.

After the emphasis on industrial strategy, the fascination with 'technology', the trade union 'problem' and privatisation, the fifth major theme of economic policy was the familiar struggle to manage the boom-and-bust of economic cycles, and in particular to maintain the confidence of global markets, especially after the economic liberalisation of the 1980s. Episode followed episode – the devaluation of the pound in the 1960s, when the upholding of its value against other currency was still treated as a matter of national prestige; the resort to an IMF loan in the wake of the inflation triggered by the increase in oil prices in the mid-1970s; the run on the pound on 'black Wednesday' in the early 1990s when it was forced out of the European Exchange Mechanism (a precursor of the common European currency, the Euro, which New Labour later declined to join); and the banking crisis of 2008, a global meltdown beginning in the US when the fragility – and falsity – of many of the novel forms of financial engineering developed in the wake of financial deregulation were exposed.

The final theme of economic policy was the progressive reduction of tax rates, on individuals and companies. Tax became toxic, exemplified by the reaction to the introduction of a new tax, the poll tax, ironically by the Thatcher Government, which provoked civil disorder. Keynesian remedies, increasing state expenditure to compensate for shortfalls in demand in the private sector, despite their theoretical attractions, were treated with suspicion. Controlling inflation, not boosting employment or growth, remained the primary focus of economic policy. The first resort, therefore, was to cut public spending. During this period there were two especially harsh episodes of 'cuts', which created a new political lexicon – the first, during the initial years of the Thatcher Government (burnt into the collective memory of the universities as the infamous '1981 cuts'); and, secondly, the decade-long 'austerity' imposed by the Conservative–Liberal Democrat Coalition Government that came to power in 2010. However, despite these episodes, which were balanced by two periods of rapid growth in public spending, during the 1960s and between 1998 and 2008, a decreasing proportion of current state spending was covered by taxation, with the increasing gap covered by more borrowing. The UK became, in multiple ways, a rentier state.

A social and cultural revolution?

There is an arresting contrast between the trajectories of the economy and wider society – the former marked by the advance of economic liberalism, albeit under tight state tutelage; the latter characterised by an equally remorseless advance of social liberalism. Of course, it has been argued that economic and social liberalism are two sides of the same coin, because both are rooted in the primacy of individual choice. That may work well enough at a conceptual level. But, in the lived experience in the UK since 1960, it is the dissonance between the two aspects of liberalism that is more evident. Advocates of the 'small state' have generally been equally strong advocates of traditional values, and social discipline. Advocates of LGBTI or transsexual rights have rarely been enthusiasts for deregulation of the economy.

Just as the 1980s have been conventionally seen as a pivotal decade in terms of the UK's political economy, so the 1960s have been regarded as a pivotal decade in terms of social and cultural change. Suggestively the first phase in the development of mass higher education – the expansion of student numbers following the Robbins Report, the establishment of the new universities on greenfields campuses and the creation of the polytechnics – took place during that decade, the first time perhaps that higher education decisively entered the wider narrative of change in UK society. Both characterisations of whole decades, of course, are caricatures verging on myths. But both are probably too entrenched ever to be shifted now. A book published in 2014 even had as its title '1965: The Year Modern Britain Was Born' (Bray, 2014).

At first sight the evidence to support this view is compelling. Kenneth Tynan saying 'fuck' on television (and Philip Larkin using the same word in a celebrated poem), the *Lady Chatterley's Lover* trial, the abandonment of the Lord Chancellor's centuries-old censorship of theatre plays, the abolition of the death penalty, the legalisation of homosexuality and abortion, the widespread use of the contraceptive pill, the Carnaby Street revolution in fashion, the full and final arrival of a TV culture (and the popularity of satirical programmes such as 'That Was The Week That Was' on the hitherto staid BBC), the emergence of popular music in the UK as a global phenomenon with the Beatles and later the Rolling Stones, even the establishment of the Open University … these were the iconic events and trends of the 1960s. Like 'Thatcherism' in the political sphere, the idea of 'the Swinging Sixties' has become too vivid to be denied. Certainly, the global image of the UK was radically transformed – out went Burberry and in came Mary Quant; gentlemen were elbowed aside by pop musicians, 'received' English by regional accents. Up to the start of the 1960s, popular music styles still recalled the Victorian and Edwardian music hall and its inter-war continuation. The Beatles and Rolling Stones came from somewhere completely different. A counterculture was born that has only grown stronger and more distinctive in the intervening years.

Yet, in many respects, social habits remained conservative, with the 1960s essentially seeing a continuation – and possibly an acceleration – of the slow distancing from the experience of world war, and pre-war depression and post-war austerity, that had already characterised the 1950s. It also took time to spread and entrench the social liberalism of the 1960s. It was still possible for the Thatcher Government two decades later to legislate to ban public libraries and schools stocking books that supposedly portrayed homosexuality as a valid alternative to heterosexuality, which is inconceivable today (and was ineffective at the time). At almost the same time, the Greater London Council's commitment under the insurgent leadership of Ken Livingstone to gay and lesbian rights was held up as conclusive proof of 'extremism', although now it is mainstream orthodoxy. But gradually social liberalism became dominant, and effectively unchallenged. It just took time.

It also took time for socio-economic structures, and the cultural values derived from them, to change. The key changes in the occupational structure arising from the shifts in the UK economy will be discussed in a later chapter. But one key change deserves to be emphasised – the increasing gap in incomes between rich and poor. The former benefited from the deregulation of financial services which vastly increased the rewards available to bankers and ancillary financial jobs, the advance of privatisation which offered windfall profits, and the declining burden of taxation. The latter found their bargaining power sharply reduced by the decline of trade unionism, the growth of new and often insecure jobs, and the declining value of social benefits.

The transformation of the UK into a multiracial and multicultural society, which had first emerged as a high-profile issue between the 1950s and the 1970s (from the original Notting Hill riots to the arrival of the Ugandan Asians), will also be discussed later. Changes in education, in particular the introduction of comprehensive secondary education and the first phase of university expansion, gradually but inexorably began to lift aspirations and horizons, although these changes could be seen as a continuation of earlier reforms, the Butler Education Act of 1944 or the impact of 'scholarship boys' on the tone of universities. But some of these fundamental shifts were already apparent in the way the 1961 census had been conducted. For the first time, additional questions were asked of a 10 per cent sample. Suggestively these extra questions asked for the first time about qualifications, indicating the future importance of educational level as a social signifier, and also about migration status, prefiguring the arrival of multiculturalism. It was also the first census analysed by computer, emphasising the impact of new technologies not simply on industrial processes but on individual lives. Education, ethnicity, technology – this is how society was changing.

Conclusion

During the decades after 1960 the UK was transformed. In political terms it became more toxically divided than it had been for almost two centuries. Since the 1980s its public affairs were conducted in an increasingly partisan and adversarial sprit. Decision-making power was over-centralised at Westminster and in Whitehall (located in a resurgent global London). But, at the same time, the UK was approaching the brink of its possible dissolution. Its capacity for competent, and disinterested, public administration was badly dented by austerity and privatisation.

In economic terms, old industrial England ebbed away to be replaced by a services economy powered by consumerism, a deregulated financial services sector market and new industries sometimes ideally based on high technology. In social and cultural terms, the UK came to be characterised by a social liberalism that went increasingly unchallenged as the decades passed. The UK also became a global brand in terms of popular culture. In this chapter the contribution that the development of mass higher education had made to the making of contemporary Britain (and of many other advanced countries too) has only been touched on in passing. However, it is within the wider context sketched out here that the development of UK higher education into a mass system, the subject of the next chapter, must now be situated.

3

The development of mass higher education

This chapter and the next offer a survey of the historical development of mass higher education in the UK since 1960, chronologically in this chapter and thematically in Chapter 4. They offer a sketch of the broader development of the system rather than a detailed account of policy making based on archives, such as Michael Shattock provided (Shattock, 2012a). The chronology sketched in this chapter is divided into five periods – higher education around 1960; reform and growth headlined by the Robbins Report and modified by the binary policy during the 1960s; advances but also setbacks between the mid-1970s and the early 1990s; the emergence of an unambiguously mass system in the 1990s and 2000s, accompanied by a contested process of 'modernisation'; and the period since 2010, with an attempted shift towards a higher education 'market' (at any rate in England). A final section in this chronology briefly sketches developments outside the UK. In the next chapter, four themes are explored in conclusion: (i) 'steering' and regulation at national and system levels; (ii) the political economy of higher education, in particular the reshaping of the system from binary to unified (and back again?), but also the fragmentation of the UK system into two, possibly three, national sub-systems; (iii) the transformation of institutional governance and management – from collegiality to managerialism; and (iv) new intellectual agendas, subjects, curricula and learning economies.

Higher education in 1960

In the early 1960s there were fewer than 200,000 students – studying at universities offering first and postgraduate degrees, at technical and art colleges offering advanced certificates and diplomas, and at colleges of education training mainly primary school teachers, the three sectors which, at the time, constituted 'higher education'. But it is an anachronism to talk about a 'system' of higher education before the Robbins Report (Robbins Report, 1963). Despite receiving an increasing proportion of their funding from the University Grants Committee (UGC), established in 1919, universities remained a collection of autonomous institutions. The Committee of Vice-Chancellors and Principals (CVCP), the ancestor of Universities UK, had yet to develop much beyond being a club that enabled vice-chancellors informally to exchange information and share views, and occasionally indulge in discreet lobbying. It is even an anachronism to talk about 'sectors'. Some further education colleges, especially in inner London, had links to the University of London (as 'institutions with recognised teachers'). But their place was in the wider world of local education authorities. Similarly, for the colleges of education, although under the loose tutelage of university institutes and departments of education (themselves occupying peripheral places in their parent universities), their primary reference points were again local education authorities or, if voluntary colleges, their presiding churches.

The universities comprised: Oxford and Cambridge, still very much seen as standing apart and also still with a high proportion of the total student population (both had more than 9,000 students); the University of London with its component Schools and wider hinterland, which also had a considerable share of the total number of students; the 'Civics' – civic universities founded in the second half of the 19th century and mainly located in the industrial north and midlands; the so-called 'red-brick' universities established after 1900 with a centre of gravity further south in England (Truscot, 1951). In addition, there were the four ancient Scottish universities, the University of Wales and Queen's University in Belfast. Altogether there were 113,000 students in universities in 1961–62. Most universities were small-scale, typically 2,000 to 5,000 students.

Advanced further education was led by the new colleges of advanced technology (CATs) established between 1956 and 1962 and no longer subject to local authority control. A second tier of regional colleges of technology, still under local authority control, offered a mixed portfolio of advanced and lower-level further education courses. Typically, students on advanced courses were still in a small minority in these colleges. The art colleges, as some have remained, were small and highly individualistic (not to say anarchic), and were only just beginning to offer standardised national qualifications. The colleges of education, 146 in England and Wales and a further seven in Scotland, often single sex, were not so much changed from the training institutions that had been established in Victorian Britain to train elementary school teachers, almost recognisable from a Thomas Hardy novel.

No national governance structure yet existed. Unlike the technical and art colleges and the colleges of education the universities were not even indirectly the responsibility of the Ministry of Education, standing apart from the rest of the education system. The UGC was directly responsible to the Treasury, reflecting the view that the relationship between the universities and the state was simply a matter of funding, not of policy. The favourite metaphor was that of the tree stump in the forest: politicians left the money on the stump and departed leaving the UGC to pick it up and distribute it to the universities. Like many metaphors, it came most sharply into view when it was ceasing to be true. But this remained the orthodoxy in 1960, even though the process already under way of identifying new universities clearly required the involvement of both national and local government. The first tentative steps had also been made to 'pool' funding for advanced further education between local authorities. But, apart from the CATs, technical colleges remained subject to local government. The major local authorities, such as the London County Council, the West Riding of Yorkshire, and Birmingham, had no intention of shirking or abandoning their responsibilities. Their colleges were the object of substantial civic pride.

The governance of individual institutions was also underdeveloped. With the important exception (then as now) of Oxford and Cambridge, universities were governed by lay councils typically made up of local professional and business leaders, although the influence of academic senates was increasing. But the business undertaken by both councils and senates was limited. It was only in the mid-1960s with the foundation of the new universities that something resembling dual governance shared equally between councils and senates became established, even if today that standard is regarded misleadingly as quasi-ancestral. In colleges, government remained hierarchical centred on the authority of the principal, who was subordinate to governing body which itself were subordinate to local politicians or church leaders. But, once again, the hand of governance was light. 'Management' was a still unfamiliar term. To the extent it was acknowledged at all, it was disapproved of. 'Administration' was sufficient (Moodie and Eustace, 1974).

However, it would be a mistake to imagine that, because of its organisational underdevelopment by later standards, higher education itself in 1960 was underdeveloped. On the contrary ... The prestige of the sciences, built on foundations laid by their contribution to the national effort during the Second World War, was exceptionally high. Let the discovery of DNA stand as proxy for a very large number of notable scientific advances. Scholarship in the humanities was equally impressive, acquiring new intellectual rigour, in method and thought. The social sciences continued their ascent begin in the 19th century. The curriculum was evolving rapidly. An example was the development of 'PPE' (philosophy, politics and economics) at Oxford as an alternative to 'Greats' (classics), as the proper preparation for a career in (elite) public service. PPE had first been offered in 1920 but only really came into its own after the Second World War. Technical education was moving forward just as fast: the technicians produced by further education were crucial to the modernisation of post-war Britain. Art schools were vibrant, already pregnant with the cultural explosion of 1960s that transformed national life (and decisively contributed to the birth of a popular global culture). Universities played a key role in this transformation of post-Victorian Britain. They were among the most important agents of modernity.

Robbins and Crosland

The Robbins Report of 1963 occupies an iconic place in the history of higher education in the UK. It is a deserved place, not only because in retrospect it has come to mark the catalyst for the subsequent growth of mass higher education but also because of its exceptional quality as an exercise in the making of public policy. The Committee on Higher Education chaired by Lord Robbins did not have the formal status of a Royal Commission, although its recommendations were more decisive than of those of many 20th-century Royal Commissions. Instead, it reported to the Prime Minister, Harold Macmillan. Such was its authority that its core message, if not all its detailed recommendations, almost immediately acquired general acceptance, even when there was a change of government less than a year later.

After its publication two big ideas became almost unchallengeable. The first was that there should be a 'system' of higher education, rather than a collection of separate institutions (universities and colleges of education) and scattered provision (advanced further education). The idea, let alone the desirability or inevitability, of a 'system' is so routine now that it is difficult to conceive of its novelty 60 years ago. Although the members of the Committee on Higher Education may not have anticipated all its long-term implications, the acceptance that there was a 'system' of higher education made it almost inevitable that some form of 'coordination' of that system would be necessary. Once the need for 'coordination' was recognised, it was a small step to accepting the need for some form of 'steering' and therefore limits on institutional autonomy.

The second was that the supply of places should be expanded to meet demand from suitably qualified applicants. Although the number of students in universities had increased in previous decades, Robbins put expansion at the heart of higher education, a place it has not (yet) lost. What made this more remarkable was that opinion in the early 1960s was far from unanimous about the need for growth. There was strong opposition, spearheaded by *The Times*, with significant support in, among other places, Oxbridge common rooms. This opposition to expansion was famously expressed by Kingsley Amis, no doubt soured by his experience as a lecturer at Swansea (which was also the basis of his novel *Lucky Jim*). He wrote: 'University graduates are like poems or bottles of hock and unlike cars or tins of salmon in that you cannot decide to have more good ones. More means worse' (Amis, 1960).

Today the case for university expansion is a commonplace (despite impotent grumbles that Tony Blair's 50 per cent target was a mistake), but at the time expansion did not go uncontested (Little, 1961).

The soon-to-be-famous Robbins principle stated that university places 'should be available to all who were qualified for them by ability and attainment'. The committee recommended that this would mean there should be 390,000 places by 1973–74, in other words a doubling within a decade, and 558,000 in 1981–82, the outer limit of Robbins' student number projections. This recommendation was derived from the careful and detailed projection of future demand undertaken by Mark Blaug and his team. This statistical exercise matched the highest standards of the Victorian 'blue books' and was far superior to the 'evidence-based' policy making of our own time. Like all projections, it did not turn out to be entirely accurate. The Robbins principle, of course, left room for detailed argument about how 'ability' and 'attainment' should be defined and measured. But the idea that student demand should determine the size of the higher education system has never been seriously contradicted.

In contrast to the dominant mode of policy making in the 21st century with its relentless Anglocentrism seasoned with limited and tendentious policy borrowing, the committee also based its recommendations on detailed consideration of the experience of other countries. In its own way, it was a model of comparative higher education. The main external reference point, inevitably, was the United States. It was through Robbins that the disturbing idea of mass higher education was imported into the UK and given an establishment imprimatur. Robbins himself in a later interview was frank about the influence of America on his thinking. He recounted how he had been influenced by a remark by R.H. Tawney that the benefits America had received from giving so many of its people at least 'the smell of a higher education' could not be underestimated (Scott, 1977).

The committee believed that the necessary scale of expansion could only be achieved by creating more universities. Its principal recommendation in this respect was that the CATs should be turned into technological universities, adding Bath, Surrey, Aston, Brunel, Bradford, Loughborough and Salford (and also Strathclyde in Scotland, although technically it was not a CAT) to the university roll. The establishment of the 'new' universities, beginning with Sussex, most revealingly in (or near) towns with suitably Shakespearean names, was already under way, an initiative shared between the UGC and central and local government (Daiches, 1964; Perkin, 1991) and often with bold ambitions for academic reform most notably outlined in the BBC's Reith Lectures given by the Vice-Chancellor of the University of Essex (Sloman, 1963). But endorsement of expansion by Robbins gave this initiative an additional and powerful impetus. The committee assumed that later some of the more developed regional colleges of technology would follow the CATs into the university fold …

And then came the binary policy announced in a speech by the new Labour Secretary of State, Anthony Crosland, in a speech at Woolwich Polytechnic in 1966 (HEPI, 2016), later developed in a White Paper (Department of Education and Science, 1966). Instead of increasing the number of universities beyond the former CATs, he proposed that 'polytechnics' should be established, created by mergers between colleges of technology and art colleges (sometimes fiercely resisted by the latter, in particular Hornsey and the West of England colleges of art, now components of Middlesex University and the University of the West of England, respectively). Crucially these new polytechnics would not be established as autonomous institutions funded through the UGC but would remain subject to local education authorities. Much has been made of the supposed 'rejection' of Robbins by Crosland. But careful examination of the binary policy makes it clear that in Crosland's eyes the key distinction was between the 'autonomous sector', that is, the universities, and the 'public sector', which he asserted should remain under 'democratic control', although he did play with ideas of a contrast between academic and vocational and professional education (Scott, 2014b). This was an attempt to justify concrete differences of political control by reference to more nebulous differences of educational mission.

Much was also made of the claim that the new polytechnics would develop into 'people's universities', distinct from the existing universities not only by remaining under 'democratic control' (in practice, by continuing to be maintained by local authorities) or even by their greater stake in vocational and professional education, but in a deeper sociological and even ideological sense (Robinson, 1966). The fact that their foundation coincided with the high tide of student radicalism appeared to confirm this hope. In practice, most polytechnics, although experimenting more freely than Oxbridge, London, the Civics and the red-bricks (but not new universities like Sussex) with multidisciplinary courses and new modular course structures that offered students greater choice, did not aspire to be radical alternatives (Pratt, 1992). But a few did, notably the North East London Polytechnic (now the University of East London), which was a bright radical star in the constellation of UK higher education for more than two decades (Rustin and Poynter, 2020).

Half a century later what is striking is not the differences between Robbins and Crosland, which faded as the distinction between 'autonomous' and 'public' sectors dissolved, but their essential agreement that the future of higher education lay with large, comprehensive, multi-subject institutions. UK higher education in 2020 continues to be dominated by such institutions, since 1992 all nominally universities. Robbins and Crosland were jointly responsible for this poverty of institutional forms, which is in marked contrast to some other countries. This lack of diversity is largely responsible for two enduring weaknesses. The first is that smaller specialist institutions continue to struggle in a one-size-fits-all system, unless they enjoy exceptional prestige (and funding), like the Royal College of Art. Regulatory, funding and governance structures have been developed with multi-faculty universities in mind. The new regulatory regime introduced in England by the Office for Students (OfS) has exacerbated the tensions created by 'one size fits all'. Secondly, there are continuing problems with delivering 'dispersed' higher education, whether through new (that is, private) providers or local colleges. This may have introduced into UK higher education a bias against wider access, an issue that will be explored later in this book.

Advances and setbacks

At first sight the two post-Robbins decades, the 1970s and the 1980s, have little in common. The view that the election of Margaret Thatcher in 1979 represented a decisive breakpoint in the history of post-war Britain is so entrenched that it is – almost – beyond contradiction. This may well be true across a wide range of aspects of political and economic (and even social) life, although in retrospect what is striking is some important underlying continuities. One of those continuities is in the development of higher education. Both decades presented universities, and now polytechnics, with formidable challenges.

The first of these challenges was increasing constraint on public expenditure, from the mid-1970s occasioned by 'oil shock' economic crisis and continuing economic difficulties, and from 1981 onwards as an act of deliberate state policy. For universities this was an unfamiliar and unwelcome development. It is often asserted, although the authority for this assertion has rarely been specified, that the UGC's advice to government on the 'needs of the universities' had always been accepted by successive governments without question or variation before the mid-1960s. The expansion of student numbers, and the greatly increasing cost of higher education, of course, changed the rules of that game for ever. Decisions taken even before Robbins effectively to abolish all tuition fees and to offer students generous maintenance grants led to the State becoming the near-monopoly funder of higher education just when the total cost of higher education was escalating, making intensified political scrutiny inevitable.

The second challenge, which shaped and was shaped by the availability of public funding, was a new debate about projections of future student demand, which now became the key variable in future planning. Again, acceptance of the Robbins principle made this inevitable. The result was a succession of divergent projections. Robbins had calculated that 596,000 places would be needed in 1981–82. The 1972 White Paper *Education: A Framework for Expansion* increased that to 741,000 (Department of Education and Science, 1972), only for the total to be progressively scaled back to 560,000 in successive government expenditure plans. As there was a widespread assumption that demand would fall back in the later 1980s and early 1990s because of demographic factors, the metaphor of 'tunnelling through the hump', that is, deliberately not meeting demand in full in the short term in order to avoid an over-supply of places later, became popular. The 1985 Green Paper even warned that institutions might have to close when student demand fell in the 1990s (Department of Education and Science, 1985), in retrospect a bizarre prediction in the light of the explosion of student demand during that decade. All these projections, of course, proved to be wrong. By 1992 there were to be just short of a million students in higher education and this total continued to grow faster than ever before. But alarms about public spending 'cuts', and to-ing and fro-ing about future student demand, occupied much of the policy space over these two decades.

The third challenge was learning to live with increasing state interference. This had already begun in the wake of Robbins. The UGC was made responsible to the new Department of Education and Science. The UGC also issued its first 'letter of guidance' to universities, a timid document by later standards. University books were opened to the scrutiny of the Comptroller and Auditor General and the House of Commons Public Accounts Committee (Public Accounts Committee, 1967). Then, in 1969, Shirley Williams, the minister responsible for higher education (later Secretary of State for Education), published her '13 points' (cited in Shattock, 2012a, p 143), a tentative list of possible reforms including experiments with two-year degrees, more intensive use of buildings, sharing of facilities and a reduction of funding per student (and, in particular, staff–student ratios) . This list was brushed aside without much ceremony by university vice-chancellors. Later home-grown attempts to promote greater efficiency also produced limited results, despite the retrospective, and almost demonic, reputation gained by the 1985 Jarratt Report (Jarratt Report, 1985).

Eleven years later things had got more serious (Scott, 1989; Ryan, 1998). Margaret Thatcher's government sharply reduced public funding for universities, leaving the UGC with the grim task of sorting out the details. The UGC could have opted for a policy of 'equal misery' but instead adopted a highly selective approach ranging from no reduction for some universities (for example, York) to cuts of more than 40 per cent for others (including Aston and Salford). Its reputation never recovered from the controversy that followed. The '1981 cuts' were engraved on the universities' collective psyche. Later in the 1980s the growing power of the state over higher education took on something of the character of an ideological confrontation. The University of Oxford declined to award the Prime Minister Margaret Thatcher an honorary degree and her Secretary of State for Education, Keith Joseph, insisted that the then Social Sciences Research Council (SSRC) should drop the 'sciences' in its title or face abolition. This nominal denial of the scientific status of the social sciences continues to this day in the title it was obliged to adopt, the Economic and Social Research Council (ESRC).

Throughout the 1970s and 1980s the 'steering' of higher education by the state took on a new and more intense character (Bird, 1994). In the 1970s, as part of the concentration of the non-university higher education into the newly formed polytechnics, teacher training effectively ceased to be a separate sector. Many colleges of education were closed; others were merged into polytechnics (with a handful of exceptions when they were merged into universities instead, for example at Warwick); some survived to diversify to become more comprehensive arts and social science-based institutions which eventually became universities in the late 1990s and 2000s.

The governance of higher education was also transformed by state action. From the start local authorities struggled to retain control over the polytechnics (Sharp, 1987). Relations between local politicians (and officers) and polytechnic directors became increasingly fractious. The first attempt by the Thatcher Government to 'nationalise' the polytechnics was successfully resisted. Instead, a curiously hybrid coordinating body was established, the National Advisory Body (NAB), initially 'for Local Authority Higher Education' and then 'for Public Sector Higher Education' when its remit was expanded to embrace the voluntary (that is, church) colleges. The NAB had a byzantine two-tier constitution with a jumble of national and local politicians, Whitehall officials, polytechnic directors and college principals. The juxtaposition of 'national' and 'local' in its original full title highlighted the essential incoherence of the compromise it represented.

The Conservative Government's second attempt to 'nationalise' the polytechnics and other colleges succeeded (Watson and Bowden, 1999). In the Education Reform Act 1987 local authorities were stripped of their historic role in higher education, and the institutions were established as independent corporations (with suitably 'corporate' governance arrangements). The NAB was replaced by a Polytechnics and Colleges Funding Council (PCFC). The UGC had staggered on for a few years after the '1981 cuts' only to be abolished by the same Act and replaced by a new Universities Funding Council (UFC) lacking the UGC's residual independence as a 'buffer body' between universities and the state. During these two decades the 'ancient constitution' of higher education was, in effect, torn up. Institutional autonomy and local responsibility were replaced by national state control.

Yet, during these two same decades, expansion continued unabated. The establishment of the polytechnics between 1969 and 1972 gave an unparalleled impetus to the expansion of higher education outside the universities. Half a century later these institutions, universities since 1992, had become the largest sector of English higher education. Their foundations were laid down, and their dynamic development began, in these two decades – in particular, after 1981 when growth in universities was constrained by the UGC's ultimately unsuccessful attempt to protect as far as possible the 'unit of resource' (funding per student). This unintended spill-over of displaced students was the making of the polytechnics even if the foundations of their success had been laid down during the 1970s. The contrast with the scattered provision characteristic of advanced further education before Crosland is marked. The policy of concentration, a bolder reprise of the creation of the colleges of advanced technology after 1956, changed the landscape of UK higher education.

For another set of institutions, the new universities established in the 1960s, the 1970s were also a formative decade. It was then that they really became established at the heart of the university system rather than being on the periphery of the Oxbridge-London-Civics core. Although their most ambitious growth plans, inspired by the development in California and other US states of new campuses, were not achieved, their presence and influence in the UK were irreversibly established. Alongside the growth of the polytechnics and the new universities, a third element of expansion was the increasing enrolment of international students. The impetus for this, paradoxically, came from another decision by Crosland to require universities to charge full-cost fees for international students by withdrawing any public subsidy, which was resisted longest by Oxford and Bradford (strange bedfellows). This financial incentive was – and is – a powerful inducement to international student recruitment. It was during this period that the presence of increasing numbers of international students changed the face of UK higher education. They provided not only additional income that helped to mitigate cuts in core funding but contributed to the growth of a more open and cosmopolitan culture across all major institutions. This process of internationalism rapidly eroded the provincialism that had once characterised many universities, apart from Oxbridge and London (and one or two of the major Civics).

Second wave

The 1990s and 2000s were the decades when a truly mass higher education finally reached maturity in the UK. Student numbers grew rapidly from fewer than a million in 1990 to 2.5 million in 2010. The constant preoccupation with the impact of demographic change on the demand for higher education, which had dominated policy and planning during the previous two decades, died away. Instead, the focus switched almost exclusively to increasing the supply of places in universities and colleges to match a growing demand that was now taken almost as a 'given'. The introduction in the late 1980s of General Certificates of Secondary Education (GCSEs) at the age of 16, merging the supposedly more academic General Certificate of Education

(GCE) O-levels and the more vocational Certificate of Secondary Education (CSE) examinations, substantially increased the pool of qualified applicants at 18. Ironically, it was a Conservative secretary of state, Keith Joseph, sceptical of the benefits of mass expansion, who took this momentous decision. Just as growth became the central goal of economic policy (at any rate until fears about global warming and environmental degradation in recent years produced the political, and moral, space to consider alternative paths), so expansion of student numbers became the pivot of thinking about the future development of higher education. Alternative scenarios, whether steady state or contraction, lost nearly all their credibility.

This focus on increasing supply was aided by a transformation in the climate for public expenditure. This period was bracketed by two economic crises, the UK's disorderly exit from the European Exchange Rate mechanism in 1992 and the banking crisis (and subsequent economic recession) in 2008. But the first proved to be a blessing in disguise, and the second was successfully managed by concerted international action in which the UK government played a key leadership role. In the intervening years, however, the legacy of 'cuts' from the Thatcher Government was replaced by the largesse of New Labour when public expenditure increased rapidly. Higher education benefited greatly from this change in the expenditure climate. Of course, New Labour's largesse came at a price, the acceptance of 'modernisation', a set of managerially inclined reforms emphasising efficiency, and an obsession with 'delivery', a new political buzzword that has lost none of its popularity. But the bottom-line remained that the state backed, and bankrolled, the development of an expanding system of mass higher education in the UK.

Even under John Major, Margaret Thatcher's successor as Prime Minister after her defenestration by her own party, the state adopted an increasingly activist approach to public policy – which led to growing scrutiny of, and interference in, higher education, its once 'private life' irreversibly invaded (Scott, 1994). This state activism became even more intense after the New Labour election victory, and the replacement of Major by Tony Blair as Prime Minister, in 1997. This creeping process of growing state 'steering', of course, went back all the way to Robbins' first articulation of the idea of a higher education 'system' 30 years earlier, and had also been a fixed feature of the years between. But during the 1990s and 2000s various forms of 'steering' were established as the standard mode of relations between higher education and the state.

The first, and most decisive, move was made by the Major Government when a new secretary of state for education, Kenneth Clarke, decided to end the binary division between universities and polytechnics, and the UFC and PCFC were replaced by a single body, the Higher Education Funding Council for England (HEFCE) (Department for Education, 1991). There has been much discussion about the reasons for what was regarded then as a sudden change. One relatively ephemeral reason no doubt was the focus on 'classlessness' as a general theme of the government's policy. The distinction between universities and polytechnics appeared superficially to be an egregious example of the class society. But, in retrospect, at a structural level the ending of the binary system appears inevitable. The differences between universities and polytechnics had become increasingly fuzzy. One driver of this convergence between the two sectors perhaps was 'academic drift' by the polytechnics, which sought to build up postgraduate courses and research at the expense of sub-degree courses. Less noticed was a reverse drift with the universities moving into professional and vocational courses. But the main driver was that, once local authority control of the polytechnics had been abandoned and the distinction between the 'autonomous' and the 'public' sector effectively dissolved, it no longer made sense to run what had become in effect two parallel national systems of higher education.

Another consequence of Clarke's ending of the binary system, which was almost as important although initially less visible, was that separate Scottish and Welsh funding councils were established. Up to that point, universities in both Scotland and Wales had been funded by the UGC and then the UFC, while in Wales non-university higher education remained within the domain of local government (except for church colleges), and in Scotland the central institutions, the broad equivalent of England's polytechnics, were funded directly by the Scottish Education Department (SED). In one sense the national/local differentiation of the original binary system was reproduced. The universities were firmly national – in other words, UK – institutions while the rest of higher education remained a local responsibility.

The so-called 'repatriation' of the Scottish universities to Scottish control had already been debated for more than a decade (Scottish Tertiary Education Advisory Committee, 1985). The universities were initially hostile to having their links with the UGC/UFC severed, although the 'cuts' of the 1980s softened their hostility. In 1998 this shift of responsibility acquired a new significance, and sharper edge, when a devolved administration was established and a Scottish Parliament re-established after a gap of almost three centuries. This differentiation of national systems within the UK set off a process of divergence which, to some degree, counteracted the convergent forces represented by the ending of the binary policy. In the 21st century the historical distinctiveness of Scottish higher education, the most obvious feature of which was a standard four-year undergraduate degree, was reinforced by policy divergences between the UK (in effect, English) government and the Scottish government (and its restored Parliament), notably on the fundamental choice between free tuition or fees. As a result, it no longer made sense to talk of a single UK higher education system.

The increasing power of the state was oddly highlighted by the limited impact of the National Committee of Inquiry into Higher Education chaired by Lord Dearing (Dearing Report, 1997). In most respects the Dearing Report in 1998 matched the standards established by Robbins a generation before. Its analysis was equally penetrating and the supporting evidence it marshalled was almost as impressive. Yet Dearing failed to match the magisterial authority of Robbins. One reason that has been suggested was the change of government gear with the shift from Major's Tories to Blair's New Labour. Another – less flattering – is that Dearing lacked the intellectual, and indeed moral, qualities so evident in Robbins; his report's recommendations were certainly disappointing – perhaps too technical – given the weight of its analysis and evidence. But perhaps the real reason was that the time when the main direction of higher education could be largely determined by a quasi-independent Royal Commission had passed – and gone for ever. In a mass system, with millions of students and budgets running into billions, this could now only be decided at the heart of government.

Despite these overall increases in public expenditure, key changes were made in the funding of higher education during the 1990s and 2000s. One of the most significant was the acceleration of the shift from student maintenance grants to loans. But the change that attracted all the headlines was New Labour's (re)introduction of tuition fees – initially at the modest level of £1,000 but increased to £3,000 in 2005. The second increase was approved by the House of Commons by a majority of less than 10, the largest backbench revolt experienced by the New Labour Government, which had a notional majority in the House of Commons of 160 in its years of office (a larger revolt than that against the invasion of Iraq shortly before).

But perhaps the long-term lesson of New Labour's spending largesse was that it stimulated the appetite for increased funding across all public services, intensifying competition between them. However fast spending was increased, needs and appetites increased faster. At the turn of the century the essential truth of Nye Bevan's remark that 'politics is the language of priorities' was underlined and even reinforced. This competition highlighted how higher education's stature had declined and its claims had slipped down the order of priorities, even though the additional income generated by tuition fees was initially truly additional. In the 1960s the universities had effectively been 'outside' (and 'above') the spending game. Forty years on they faced a defensive struggle as not-terribly-loved suppliants. This too was an irreversible change, and arguably an inevitable consequence of mass expansion which made higher education both more 'familiar' (and perhaps less to be deferred to) and also a much larger component of national finances. Revealingly the last act of New Labour was to establish a new committee of inquiry, not into higher education's broad direction but into alternatives to the current pattern of funding.

A higher education 'market'?

In 2010 a new Conservative-dominated government was elected, which received the report of the committee of inquiry into student fees and funding, chaired by Lord Browne (Browne Report, 2010). Soon 'Browne' acquired almost as much resonance as 'Robbins' although, like the Dearing Report a decade earlier, practically none of its detailed recommendations were implemented. Browne's fame, or infamy, was due to the fact that, on the back of the report, the new government proceeded to impose a set of market-like reforms in higher education (Department of Business, Innovation and Skills, 2011; Callender and Scott, 2013; Hillman, 2016). The centrepiece of that reform was a tripling of tuition fees to £9,000. This fee was capped. This was different from the ingenious system proposed by the Browne Committee, which envisaged greater freedom for universities to set fees levels,which, above a fixed point, would be progressively taxed to provide a general fund for support of universities and especially low-income students. It also bore no relation to the actual cost of provision, which varied substantially between subjects – a variation that had always been reflected in the funding formula used by HEFCE and its predecessors which required the allocation of subjects to four 'price groups'.

The decision to triple fees met with strong resistance, especially from students. This was ironic in the light of the claim made in the title of the White Paper initiating these market-like reforms that students were being put at 'the heart of the system' (Brown and Carasso, 2013; McGettigan, 2013). Labour's decision six years earlier to increase fees from £1,000 to £3,000 had been resisted not only by the Conservatives, although their opposition was discounted as rank political opportunism and caused them no damage, but also by the Liberal Democrats, who had nailed their colours to the mast of the total abolition of fees. As junior partners in the new Coalition Government, the Liberal Democrats decided to reverse direction and support higher fees. A decade later they have still to recover from what was seen by many as a betrayal of principle. After its second election defeat, in 2015, Labour abandoned the centre-left ground it had occupied so effectively in the previous decade and moved sharply to the left. This, combined with the collapse of the Liberal Democrats, led to an erosion of the base for progressive politics, which arguably led to a strengthening of the political right – including the decision to leave the European Union (Brexit). That shift is likely to influence the fortunes of higher education profoundly and perhaps irreversibly.

The 'market' that Conservative reformers wished for stubbornly failed to emerge. It encountered two obstacles. The first was the original intention that institutions would charge variable fees, up to the £9,000 cap, depending on the cost of provision (with the new fee they received more funding for classroom-based subjects than they had received in HEFCE grant) and also their reputation, was frustrated. All institutions, with trivial and very temporary exceptions, raised their fees to the new cap. Because students received loans from the Student Loans Company (SLC) to pay fees and faced no up-front cost, there was no effective price mechanism. Also, institutions judged, correctly, that any slight market advantage they might gain from charging lower fees was greatly outweighed by the reputational damage of appearing not to have full confidence in the quality of their 'products' (as well as leading to lower levels of income to meet rising 'consumer' expectations on the part of students). The second obstacle was that it was calculated, wrongly as it turned out, that less than a third of student loans would have to be written off and become a charge on public finances – the so-called Resource Allocation Budgeting (RAB) charge. The government also assumed, hopefully but eventually also wrongly, that any charge could be hidden off balance sheet rather as the cost of the Public Finance Initiative (PFI) for funding public infrastructure had been.

Yet, in the short run, the market-like reforms worked – up to the point. The fee income, funded by the state initially but not treated as routine public expenditure on the grounds that most of it would be repaid, allowed English higher education largely to escape the austerity that was imposed on other public services. This apparently favourable treatment did not go unnoticed by these other services (not least, further education) and probably eventually eroded still further higher education's place in the list of priorities for public expenditure. The scale of this comparative advantage can be judged by the comparison with the funding of higher education in Scotland, where none of these reforms were introduced and tuition remained free. A funding gap certainly opened up, although probably not on the scale routinely claimed by Scottish university principals.

But the short-term success of England's high-fee regime must be qualified in two important ways. First, these market-like reforms did not allow untrammelled growth to meet student demand, even after the cap on student numbers was eventually lifted, although this has been claimed as their key advantage. In fact, growth rates in the 2010s were significantly lower than in the 2000s, calamitously so in the case of part-time students, where numbers fell precipitously (mainly because no one in government had considered the impact of higher fees, not backed by loans for most part-time students, which perhaps underlined, once again, how peripheral part-time provision seemed to many policy makers). Second, these reforms, as a matter of deliberate intention, produced winners – typically the most traditional universities – and losers – typically the 'new' universities (despite their lower costs and more open student recruitment). The latter, which had been the engines of expansion in the previous three decades, were left out in the cold. A new discourse of our 'best universities' – and, by inexorable implication, our 'worst' ones too, although the weasel words 'underperforming institutions' were usually preferred – flourished. How much true differentiation of mission was produced by these market-like reforms is doubtful. But there is little room for doubt about the toxic divisiveness, which this discourse encouraged and legitimised, and which undermined the solidarity of the higher education system that had served it well in the past. United we stand, divided we fall …

In any case there was no attempt to consolidate these reforms. Instead, even more radical policies were introduced (Department for Business, Innovation and Skills, 2015). The removal of the cap on student numbers, with its predictably (and intentionally?) disruptive and divisive effects, has already been mentioned. HEFCE was replaced by a new Office for Students (OfS); thus died away the last echo of an arm's-length relationship between universities and the state. In the supposed interests of student-consumers, the OfS introduced a tough, and intrusive, regulatory regime. The time had come to honour the Mephistophelian bargain university leaders had naively struck with the government by supporting its market-like reforms. The number of 'alternative providers' rapidly increased. With some honourable exceptions, most were low-cost (and low-quality?) for-profit institutions exposed to frequent changes of ownership as profitability waxed and waned. A true market of monetised income streams, tradable globally, developed alongside the ersatz market of the traditional, if no longer fully public, higher education system.

But, even before the COVID-19 pandemic, this latter market had started to unravel. First, the Office for National Statistics (ONS) insisted that, because of the escalating RAB charge on student loans, the cost of unpaid loans could no longer be hidden away off balance sheet. Instead, a proportion of state-funded loans equivalent to the best guess of the percentage that would eventually have to be written off had to be counted as public expenditure when they were first paid out, and repayments only counted when they were actually received. The immediate impact was substantially to increase the deficit in public funding by many billions of pounds, and to reduce the scope for extra spending elsewhere. The longer-term impact, of course, will be again to expose higher education to competition from other publicly funded expenditure as its 'exemption' from austerity expires. Next, in response to the effective closure of universities by the pandemic (and their uncertain road to recovery), the government moved quickly to reimpose the cap on student numbers, although not in a way necessarily guaranteed to restore stability to the system. The decades-long trend towards greater state interference accelerated, with a flood of 'letters of instruction' from the Secretary of State to the OfS, duly transmitted onwards to universities. In tightening the screw, the government, sanctimoniously, ordered the OfS to reduce the 'burden of bureaucracy'. These most recent policy developments will be further considered in the final chapter of this book.

It seemed that research funding, a major focus, of course, for the most traditional ('our best') universities, was largely unaffected by the turbulence produced by high tuition fees. But that impression may have been misleading. The establishment of the OfS made it necessary to establish a new body to fund research (previously HEFCE, and all its antecedent bodies, had funded both teaching and research through a core grant to institutions). The government chose a radical solution, to establish UK Research and Innovation (UKRI) under which were grouped together the research councils, UK-wide bodies, and Research England, a special-purpose vehicle to distribute core, or quality-related research (QR), funding to English institutions. At a stroke, the so-called 'dual-support system', with a clear demarcation between core research funding as an unhypothecated element within general institutional grants, and project or programme funding by research councils, was abandoned. Also removed was the previous ability of universities to cross-subsidise research and teaching on a significant scale, except by using the surplus created by international student fees.

Finally, as has already been indicated in the example of the curious constitution of UKRI, the English reforms led to even greater divergence between the UK's higher education systems. In the particular case of research, the funding councils in Scotland and Wales continued to distribute QR funding, preserving the dual-support system and the scope for cross-subsidy. More generally, divergent pressures increased. Scotland continued to offer tuition-free higher education to Scottish-domiciled students, while Wales, because of its proximity to and close relationship with England, adopted an intermediate position on fees. The 'stories' of higher education in the UK nations diverged during the 2010s. While in England the 'story' was of fees and markets (and resistance to them), in Scotland it was of fair access, the drive to increase the representation in universities of students from more socially deprived backgrounds, and in Wales it was of, intriguing but still unconsummated, policies designed to promote a wider tertiary education system. In the process, UK higher education as a coherent system, in most important respects, ceased to exist.

Beyond the UK

This account of the development of higher education since 1960 has focused almost exclusively on the UK, a guilty confession perhaps of endemic national insularity (and, even more narrowly, an inexcusable Anglocentrism because the other UK nations also tend to be marginalised). This statement, of course, must be heavily qualified. In terms of science and scholarship, UK universities have always been open and international. The list of major intellectual figures and scholars from the rest of the Europe, and the wider world, who found sanctuary and success is proof enough –

Ludwig Wittgenstein, Lewis Namier, Karl Popper … Today, the vitality and productivity of research in UK universities depends more than ever on academic mobility from outside the UK, whether of postdoctoral students and early-career researchers or of senior professors.

Yet, in terms of policy borrowing, the UK has remained a largely closed system. The concept of mass higher education was imported from the United States, and in some university circles remained suspect because of its origins. 'Their' America was a land of Ivy League universities and a small number of Mid-West and Pacific Coast state universities, the exception, rather than a land of mass commuter universities and community colleges, the rule. Any borrowing was inevitably highly selective (Bocock et al, 2003; Shattock, 2012b). At times there has been some slight interest in Australia, mainly because of its development of a higher education contributions scheme which was seen as a stalking horse for the introduction of tuition fees back home in the UK. In general, policy borrowings have mainly been cherry-picked according to ideological preferences.

Europe and international students

There are two exceptions where UK higher education was decisively shaped by external policy. First, the UK was dragged into a closer relationship with the rest of Europe initially through its membership of the European Union (EU), and its participation in the Erasmus Programme and other student and staff mobility programmes and successive European research programmes, and later through the Bologna Process. The UK had always been part of a common European cultural and scientific space, of course, but these new relationships were now also political and structural. The Bologna Process initiated in 1999 led on to the development of the European Higher Education Area (EHEA) and the European Research Area (ERA).

But this closer relationship has always been dogged by a deep ambivalence. Although the UK, along with France, Germany and Italy, had the year before been a signatory of the original Sorbonne Declaration which anticipated the Bologna Process, the belief persisted that the UK had a lot to teach and little to learn from its European neighbours about the basic architecture of courses and degrees and on quality assurance, which were the major preoccupations of the Bologna Process. The core of the UK's collaboration with the rest of Europe was the enthusiastic, and successful, participation of UK universities in European research programmes: the successive 'Framework' programmes and the 'Horizon' programme. Their participation in the Erasmus student exchange programmes, although also significant, was undermined by the chronic imbalance between outward and inward flows. Brexit, of course, is likely to lead to fundamental changes in this European orientation. The UK has withdrawn from Erasmus, which is to be replaced by a scheme of Turing scholarships with a wider geographical focus. Continuing participation in European research programmes, except in the very short term, is no longer guaranteed. But the UK's role in the EHEA and the ERA, which are not EU initiatives, will presumably continue.

Second, as has already been indicated, the recruitment of international students became an increasingly significant income flow after Crosland's decision that they should be charged full-cost fees. Over the next 40 years international student recruitment became, literally, a 'business'. Elite universities used it to support their research capacity both by making good a deficit in the number of UK-based research and postdoctoral students, and by providing an income stream to match the supposedly more generous funding of their rivals and peers in other countries, notably the US. Other universities recruited international students to compensate for shortfalls in demand from UK students. Substantial investments in marketing, agent fees and support services were made.

But what is interesting in retrospect, beneath the internationalist rhetoric, is how limited the intellectual and cultural impact of this mass recruitment of international students seems to have been. The emphasis remained on their acquisition of a 'UK experience', without much attention to how that 'experience' might be changed by their presence (and also by the increasing recruitment of UK students from ethnic and cultural minorities). As a result, internationalisation of the student body has not been accompanied by a deliberate and systematic internationalisation of the curriculum on anything like the same scale. Over the past four decades UK universities have become increasingly financially dependent international students paying high fees, a risky dependence cruelly exposed by the COVID-19 pandemic.

World higher education systems

In 1960 the US system was – by far – the most important. It was the only true mass system, and the most productive in terms of science and scholarship. The state systems established during that decade and the next, notably as a result of the California Master Plan (still in business today after several revisions), established a model of system structure and coordination which remains immensely influential, still something of a gold standard in the architecture of higher education systems. The US system was already the home of public intellectuals with much wider influence, which the radicalism of student revolt magnified (ironically so, given its intention to challenge the established political and academic order). The supposed age of 'the end of ideology', reprised (also implausibly) as the 'end of history' in the early 1990s following the fall of communist regimes in Central and Eastern Europe, was briskly succeeded by ideological wrangling which has now exploded into full-scale 'culture wars'.

Finally, US higher education was not only a mass system but was also regarded as a key element in America's public life. The UK system was tiny in comparison, although also highly productive in research terms. The same connection between 'going to college' and the advance of democracy had yet to be made. Other European systems enrolled more students than in the UK but were still not yet truly mass systems. They too were important contributors to research and, especially, scholarship. The connection between universities and broader intellectual culture may have been more explicit in other European countries than in the UK where pragmatism still reigned, notably more so in France (again turbocharged by student radicalism?). Universities in the rest of the world barely counted. Higher education was essentially a North Atlantic game, firmly anchored in the US.

This was confirmed by the explosive growth of US higher education in subsequent decades. During the 1960s the number of students increased by 120 per cent, and subsequently by 45 per cent during the 1970s and 19 per cent during the 1980s. By 2018 there were 18.9 million college students in the US compared with only 6 million in 1960. However, the pattern of growth was different in the US from the pattern in the UK and the rest of Europe. As these figures suggest, the rate of expansion declined after the peak in the 1960s when mass higher education was established in the US. In the UK and most of the rest of Europe (and, in particular, Central and Eastern Europe) the peak came a generation later, during the 1990s and 2000s. In the 2010s enrolments actually fell in the US (from 20.4 million in 2011 to 18.9 million in 2018) at the time of peak growth on the opposite side of the Atlantic. In France the number of students almost doubled from 1.18 million in 1980 to 2.6 million in 2018. The pattern was similar in Germany, increasing from 1.9 million at the beginning of the 21st century to 2.9 million 20 years later.

So, by 2020 much had changed. The US system retained its dominance, especially in research. But the hopes of the mid-20th century have faded. State universities had to cope with dwindling state budgets, often the result of voter initiatives supporting fiscally conservative measures such as balanced budgets. As a result, no-fee and low-fee regimes were progressively eroded. It became routine to describe state universities as 'state supported', as other income streams increased in importance (although traditional forms of political – and often politicised – governance were maintained and even strengthened). Elite private universities often increased tuition fees at a much faster rate than either inflation or income, provoking growing political and public resentment. Other private institutions, often for-profit and online, had to struggle to defend themselves against low standards, high dropout rates and even allegations of misuse of funds. Long after the challenges of the New Left and student revolt in the 1960s and 1970s appeared to have faded, new culture wars intensified. As a result, the global leadership role of

US higher education, its solid occupation of the moral high ground, may have been weakened.

Over this period European higher education revived, with the UK sometimes a central player and sometimes occupying an awkwardly peripheral mid-Atlantic position. Playing catch-up with the US, most European systems became mass systems from the 1990s (Nybom, 2003). After the fall of the Berlin Wall, and collapse of communist regimes, higher education in Central and Eastern Europe belatedly embraced expansion (although much of the growth occurred in private institutions in contrast to the state-dominated model of Western, and Southern, Europe). Reforms, of course, had been undertaken in earlier decades, notably the structural reforms associated with the French Education Minister Edgar Faure in the late 1960s, which effectively recreated unified universities out of fragmented Faculties. From the 1960s onwards, a thorough-going reform of Swedish higher education was pursued, heavily influenced by US models. In most European countries west of the Iron Curtain, new universities were established, as they had been in the UK. Nanterre, Konstanz and Kassel were the equivalents of Sussex, Warwick and Stirling. Although many European higher education systems remained (and remain) binary in structure, with the formal distinction between traditional universities and higher professional schools maintained, increasing efforts were made to promote greater coordination between them.

But it was the Bologna Process that galvanised efforts to modernise Europe's universities. It provided a 'story' (and cover story) to justify intensified efforts to modernise European systems and acted a catalyst for major reforms in course structures and quality assessment regimes. In many countries the bureaucratic links between universities and state administrations were loosened, to be replaced by milder forms of state 'steering'. In the process, universities acquired increasing degrees of autonomy, and – inevitably – had to develop their own management capabilities. As a result, the organisational differences between UK and other European universities were progressively reduced. In another example of this convergence, stronger links were established between universities and independent research institutes such as Max Planck institutes in Germany and the CNRS institutes in France. Unlike in the US, tuition generally remained free, with the notorious exception of England although, as has already been said, private, for-profit institutions proliferated in post-communist Central and Eastern Europe (especially in Poland and Hungary). The idea that universities were essentially public institutions went unchallenged even as they took on more entrepreneurial roles. The strong emphasis on the 'social dimension' was reinforced as a key motif of European higher education.

But perhaps the most significant changes in world higher education during the period from 1960 to 2020, in particular over the last two decades, occurred in East Asia, although developments in South Asia and the Middle East should not be ignored. At the start of this period, China was shortly to be plunged into the chaos the Cultural Revolution, and India had been free of British rule for less than two decades. Japan had recovered economically from defeat in the war, but its ambitions had been curbed and its moral standing eroded. South Korea was still a poor country. Singapore and Malaysia had not yet gained their independence. Higher education systems were still confined to small elites.

In the present century, Chinese students in large numbers continued to be attracted to, and enrolled in increasing numbers in, universities in north America, Europe and Australasia. A stark example was provided by the fact that on taught Masters' programmes in UK universities there were as many students from China as from the UK itself. But it soon became clear that China was becoming a higher education powerhouse in its own right. The day would clearly come when it became a net importer of international students – and sooner than expected. An increasing number of Chinese universities were ranked highly in the, admittedly flawed, global league tables of top universities. China's growing geopolitical power, in terms of economic growth, technological innovation and political influence, was felt in higher education with increasing force. Over this period higher education participation rates in several East Asian countries, notably South Korea, exceeded rates in Europe and even the United States. A so-called 'Confucian' model of higher education came to rival the hitherto dominant US model as a global standard.

In 1960 UK higher education was among the world's leading higher education systems, despite its comparative underdevelopment in terms of student enrolments. It probably came second only to the US. In 2020, after more than half a century of sustained expansion it remained among the world's leading higher education systems, but its position was now not so assured. The model of world higher education dominated by a single system, the US system (with the UK perhaps in close but subordinate support) has gradually been replaced by a more pluralistic and distributed model. While the comparative influence of the US declined, higher education in many countries in the rest of the Europe was revived by institutional reforms that allowed it to match Anglo-American scientific and intellectual eminence while East Asian higher education systems emerged with new force. All these developments outside the UK will be considered further in Chapter 6, which discusses the state of contemporary higher education outside the UK.

4

Themes and transformations

In the previous chapter a chronology of the development of higher education between 1960 and 2020 was offered, almost entirely confined to the UK but with a brief coda about the development of higher education in the wider world. In the present chapter the focus is on four themes, or transformations. The first three transformations – on 'steering' and regulation; the coordination and funding of higher education; and institutional governance and management – are discussed almost entirely through the lens of the experience of the UK, although similar developments took place in many other countries. The fourth transformation – of the intellectual landscape – is of much wider application, although the focus is also on how this has played out in UK higher education. Again, there is a brief coda that looks more widely (both geographically and conceptually).

'Steering' and regulation

Since 1960 far-reaching changes have been made in how UK higher education is 'steered', funded, planned and regulated, at both system and sector levels. At the start of this period the University Grants Committee (UGC), first established in 1919, still – just about – acted as an effective buffer between universities and the state which provided the bulk of their funding, but on an arm's-length principle (Berdahl, 1959; Carswell, 1986). By the end of the period (in England, at any rate) arrangements for 'steering' the system had been completely changed. The Office of Students (OfS) had been established. As a regulator, like the bodies that regulated many other sectors such as broadcasting (Ofcom), energy (Ofgen) and standards in schools (Ofsted), which shared the 'Of-label', it was designed on quite different principles to the UGC. Yet, despite this, universities, although they had diversified their income streams, still received a high proportion of their funding from what would once have been called 'publicly planned' expenditure, both grants for high-cost teaching from the OfS and quality-related research (QR) funding from Research England, but also student fees initially bankrolled by loans provided by the state-owned Student Loans Company. It is difficult to imagine a more striking transformation of system governance.

From the late 1960s to its eventual abolition two decades later, the UGC adopted an increasingly interventionist approach towards universities, while preserving the principles of arm's-length funding and of a block grant for both teaching and research which universities could use at their discretion. 'Letters of guidance' from the UGC to universities proliferated and became more detailed. The most striking example came in its final years as the UGC (and, in particular, its last chairman, Sir Peter Swinnerton-Dyer) played with ideas of imposing an R-X-T (mainly research; mixed economy; mainly teaching) taxonomy of universities and, when it became clear that such a formal classification was not feasible, introduced the Research Selectivity Exercise that morphed into the Research Assessment Exercise (RAE) and now the Research Excellence Framework (REF).

The Universities Funding Council (UFC), in a brief interlude between 1988 and 1992, and, after the abandonment of the binary system in 1992, the Higher Education Funding Council for England (HEFCE) took this interventionism to a new level. The two other newly established funding councils in Scotland and Wales followed its lead, although perhaps more tentatively. The HEFCE became a 'steering' body in a way the UGC had never aspired to be, even in its last, most assertive period. The student numbers of individual universities were controlled, admittedly with a degree of flexibility, through a system of 'maximum aggregate student numbers' (MASNs) that imposed funding reductions in the case of universities which had either over-recruited or failed to recruit within a limited 'tolerance range' of plus or minus 10 per cent. Initiatives in a wide range of areas – such as widening participation and knowledge exchange – proliferated, all with dedicated pots of extra funding. Cynics criticised this growth of so-called 'jam jar' funding. At the height of the New Labour years in the early 2000s, HEFCE even aspired to be granted a formal planning role over English higher education, although this proved to be a bridge too far.

The OfS is an entirely different body from the UGC, and also from the UFC/HEFCE. It has (reluctantly) retained some direct funding responsibilities that could not be sloughed off – for example, for high-cost subjects particularly in science, technology, engineering and medicine (STEM), although this ceased to be formulaic and in 2021 was relabelled as a 'strategic initiative fund'. But its primary focus is as a regulator. Until the looming financial crisis created by the COVID-19 pandemic it had little interest in the financial stability of institutions, except to the extent that this might cause detriment to students (for example, by abrupt course closures or even sudden institutional collapses). The old language about meeting the 'needs of the sector' and its 'financial health' has fallen largely into disuse. The OfS has opened the door wide to 'alternative providers', private (and mostly for-profit) providers which, with a few exceptions, would previously have been barred from entry into the UK higher education system. Partly to guard against potentially wayward behaviour in this new group of volatile providers, but also in response to the growing politicisation of the governance of higher education (anti-radicalisation measures, protection of 'free speech' …), the OfS has imposed a detailed regulatory regime that would have been unthinkable in the days of the UGC, and even the HEFCE in its most imperialist moments.

In the non-university sector different governance arrangements applied initially. At the start of this period in England, the colleges that were about to become the polytechnics remained the responsibility of local authorities, although they were funded through the so-called 'advanced further education pool', a financial instrument designed to equalise the cost across all local authorities. A few of the larger local authorities, notably the London County Council (LCC) and its successor the Inner London Education Authority (ILEA), presided over what were in effect regional systems of further and higher education colleges. But frequent rounds of local authority reorganisation and restrictions on their financial freedom of action eroded the capacity of many local authorities effectively to coordinate their colleges except in narrow budgetary control and routine administrative terms. The colleges of education, whether local authority or voluntary, were tightly gripped from the start by the Ministry, then the Department, of Education, which determined student numbers according to (often flawed) projections of future demand for teachers. In Scotland, the central institutions, which later became 'post-1992' universities, were, as their label suggests, funded directly by the Scottish Education Department. In Wales, the Welsh Joint Education Committee (WJEC) acted as a loose coordinating body.

Over the next two decades these arrangements evolved rapidly. As has already been discussed in Chapter 3, the National Advisory Body (NAB) was created to try to ease growing tensions between the polytechnics, in particular, and their controlling local authorities and provide some degree of coordination across a rapidly expanding sector that was soon to match the universities in terms of student numbers (and which now embraced the colleges of education, or at least those that had avoided closure). Within the constraints imposed by very different, and more prescriptive, funding arrangements, the NAB attempted to behave rather like the newly interventionist UGC. This duopoly between the UGC and NAB was reproduced when both had been abolished and the polytechnics and other higher education colleges removed from local authority control, in the shape of the UFC and the Polytechnics and Colleges Funding Council (PCFC). Then, in 1992, unified system governance arrangements in the shape of HEFCE were established, with the important exception that responsibility for both the Scottish and Welsh universities passed from the UGC/UFC to separate funding councils.

How should these striking transitions in the system-level governance of UK higher education be understood in wider and more conceptual terms? A number of frames of reference are available.

The first relates to the transition from a welfare state, in which government takes direct responsibility for the provision of a wide range of public services, to a regulation state, in which the responsibility of government is largely confined to regulating the provision of 'public' services by a range of 'private' providers, whether for-profit companies or charitable organisations (Svallfors and Taylor-Gooby, 1999; Christensen and Laegreid, 2006). The fit between this wider conceptualisation and what happened to UK higher education is fairly good – but it is not perfect. In the UK, for example, unlike the rest of Europe, universities had never been directly controlled by the state, despite being overwhelmingly funded from taxation.

A second frame of reference emphasises the ideological rather than structural and organisational aspects of this transition. This second frame emphasises, in political and economic terms, a reduced focus on 'public goods' and an increased focus on 'individual (or private) benefits'. In more strident terms, this can be described as a shift from welfarist social democratic to entrepreneurial neoliberal values (Harvey, 2005). The fit between this conceptualisation and changes in system-level governance in UK higher education is not so good. The UGC was hardly a typical public-goods, social-democratic institution, even if the OfS is clearly a private-goods, neoliberal one.

A third frame of reference is of the decline of deference to high-status traditional institutions, such as universities, and also regulated professions and experts at large. A more virulently populist, although hardly democratic, culture has emerged. This culture is instinctively sceptical about traditional forms of autonomy because these are regarded with suspicion as defences against critical accountability (or, worse, bases for leftist ideas). It is also sceptical about taking professional expertise on trust. Its scepticism has been fuelled by the faux-populist mass media and also by a communicative revolution that has created an explosion of social media and an uncontrolled proliferation of rival 'experts'. Although this frame of reference has great resonance within universities, it is less clear that it offers a good explanation of changes in system-level governance.

A fourth frame of reference focuses on the effective nationalisation of public policy, the origins of which can be traced back to the 19th century when consistent national patterns of administration were imposed on a chaotic localism. This has taken many different forms – on the one hand, the drive to reduce the autonomy enjoyed by civil society institutions, including universities, and free professions in the supposed interest of greater efficiency (and 'relevance', a coming word throughout this period); on the other, the attenuation of local government as an independent focus of political power and the redefinition of local authorities as 'delivery agents' for the national state. Other strands within this process of 'nationalisation' are the long-term aggrandisement of administrative power by Whitehall Departments, but also more recently the increasing politicisation of public administration and ideological confrontation. The desire to distinguish 'us' from 'them' first emerged explicitly during the 1980s and has never disappeared. This frame of reference fits the transition in system governance of UK higher education rather well.

Coordinating and funding higher education

In the early 1960s, to the dubious extent it is possible to talk about there being a 'system' of higher education at all, it had six components (or maybe proto sectors).

- The largest comprised the universities, which were all funded through the UGC. In turn, the UGC was still responsible to the Treasury, a UK-wide Department, rather than the Ministry of Education, the responsibilities of which were confined to further, adult and school education, and its remit to England and Wales. The universities, therefore, comprised a UK-wide sector, although the imminent transfer of responsibility for the UGC from the Treasury, a UK Department, to the Ministry – later Department – of Education, the remit of which was confined to England, did create something of an anomaly. The Scottish universities were now indirectly funded through an England-only Department. This anomaly was only partially addressed by involving the Scottish Education Department (SED) in the Ministry's decisions with regard to universities.
- The second component consisted of the colleges of advanced technology (CATs) in England and Wales, which had been funded directly by the Ministry of Education since their designation following the 1956 White Paper *Technical Education* (HMSO, 1956). The later University of Strathclyde, originally the Royal College of Science and Technology, in Glasgow, is often assumed to have also been a CAT, because it was included among the so-called technological universities established following the Robbins Report; in fact, it was already funded through the UGC.
- Next were the colleges of education in England and Wales, of which there were 146 (98 had been established by local education authorities and the remainder were voluntary – that is church – colleges), and in Scotland (seven in total, and two Roman Catholic colleges, and funded jointly by the SED and local authorities).
- Then there were the regional and area colleges in England and Wales, some of which were amalgamated to create the polytechnics a decade later, and which continued to be maintained – that is funded and controlled – by local authorities.
- The final component was provided by the 15 central institutions (CIs) in Scotland which, as their name suggests, were directly funded by the SED.

Two decades later, within what had now irreversibly become a 'system' of higher education, the number of components, now sectors, had been reduced by one. They now comprised:

- universities throughout the UK, all funded through the UGC;
- what was now generally termed 'local authority higher education' in England, consisting of the polytechnics, local authority-maintained colleges of education and scattered provision of advanced further education courses across a range of other further education colleges;
- the remaining voluntary colleges of education;
- the CIs in Scotland.

In terms of overall student numbers, the universities were still the dominant sector, but growth had been rapid in 'local authority higher education' in England (principally in the polytechnics, and also the Scottish CIs, which had come increasingly to resemble the polytechnics). Many colleges of education had been closed or merged into polytechnics during the 1970s and the remainder now represented a vestigial sector.

The system as a whole was becoming much more coherent, bipolar in funding as well as binary in structure (and imagined mission). The number of funders had also been simplified. In England the Department of Education and Science (DES), the successor of the Ministry of Education, had largely ceased to be a direct funder with the redesignation of the CATs as technological universities and their transfer to UGC funding (although a few institutions continued to be directly funded, such as the Open University and the Royal College of Art). The field had been left to the duopoly of the UGC on the one hand and on the other the English and Welsh local authorities, although the latter now increasingly operated through the embryonic national framework provide by the NAB. This duopoly, of course, was never total. The SED continued to be a direct funder of the CIs. Also, there were other public bodies that made grants to universities – the Department of Health/National Health Service for clinical medicine and dentistry; other Departments for research contracts; and research councils for research grants.

Between 1987 and 1992 the architecture of UK higher education was fundamentally changed. First, the Education Reform Act 1987 stripped local authorities of their responsibility for funding the polytechnics and other higher education colleges in England and Wales, which were now established as independent 'higher education corporations' (HECs; as discussed later). For the next five years they would be funded nationally through the PCFC. However, despite the eviction of local authorities, the bipolar pattern of funding continued. The UGC was replaced by the UFC, which continued to fund universities throughout the UK. There had been a sustained campaign to 'repatriate' the Scottish universities. But, in the event, the anomaly of their being funded by a UK-wide body ultimately responsible to an English Department was judged to more acceptable than direct funding by the SED which was still the only alternative.

Then, in 1992, the dual structure of the system, the duopoly that had existed for two decades, was abandoned and a unified system (in each of the UK nations) was established. The UFC and PCFC were abolished and replaced by unified funding councils in England, Scotland and Wales – HEFCE, the Scottish Higher Education Funding Council (SHEFC) and the Higher Education Funding Council for Wales (HEFCW). The UFC had widely been regarded as a limp successor to the UGC, and there was little regret about its abolition. The PCFC was judged to have performed better, building on the semi-centralisation of polytechnic and college funding through NAB. HEFCE, therefore, was heir to both traditions of funding. In the 1990s there was some debate, and much speculation, about which tradition had dominated. The best guess then, and still now, was that it had absorbed the style (and many of the personnel) of the UGC/UFC but had an appetite for funding systems and methodologies more reminiscent of the operation of the PCFC/NAB.

Two big shifts took place in 1992. First, and most strongly emphasised, the funding and planning of higher education was, in effect, nationalised with the abandonment of the binary system. The diversity of funding, with a large component of local funding, that had prevailed at the time of Robbins was finally and irreversibly replaced by single-source national funding. Under consideration here, of course, is only the public funding of higher education; most institutions attracted other sources of funding, such as income from fees paid by international students, external contracts and, to a limited extent, endowments. They also received funding from other Departments and agencies, mainly for research but also teaching in nursing and other healthcare disciplines. This process of nationalisation, with a high degree of deliberateness was – and continues to be – disguised by emphasising the continuation of (formal) institutional autonomy. For the 'pre-1992' universities this rang hollow because their effective autonomy was plainly being eroded. For the polytechnics and colleges, which became the 'post-1992' universities, legal autonomy was still a comparatively novel experience and had more substance.

But in the second, and less emphasised, shift, three separate national systems were created, in England, Scotland and Wales. The appetite for such a change was greater in Scotland, where the 'repatriation' of responsibility for Scottish universities had been on the agenda throughout the 1980s and had been greatly stimulated by hostility in Scotland to the Thatcher Government. The explicit creation of a separate Scottish system, of course, was rooted in historical precedent; Scotland's ancient universities had always been key elements in Scotland's national identity and its education system had remained separate even after the 1707 Treaty of Union (Davie, 1961/2013, 1986). The creation of SHEFC made it possible for a separate Scottish system of higher education to be established while continuing some form of arm's-length funding through a funding council rather than direct subordination to the SED. It also allowed the CIs to be removed from this SED subordination and funded through the SHEFC. For the first time since the 19th century, a coherent Scottish higher education system was established under Scottish control. The appetite for a separate system of its own was more limited in Wales. But in both countries the re-establishment of a Scottish Parliament and the creation of a National Assembly in Wales as a result of the devolutionary settlement made by New Labour in 1998, and separate Scottish and Welsh Executives (later governments), gave impetus to this fragmentation of UK higher education.

Initially all three systems stayed broadly in sync. All three funding councils continued to make block grants to institutions for both teaching and research, preserving the dual support system for research (core grants from funding councils complementing programme grants from research councils). But divergences soon appeared, especially between England and Scotland. These divergences expanded and accelerated after the election of the Conservative-dominated Coalition Government in 2010. They were not confined to high-level policy on key matters such as tuition fees, which were effectively abolished in Scotland but increased in England. They also extended to structure. In Scotland SHEFC was made responsible for funding further as well as higher education and became the Scottish Funding Council (SFC), thus opening the door to progress towards establishing a tertiary education system in place of a higher education system (although progress was slow).

In 2018, as discussed in the previous chapter, HEFCE was abolished in England and replaced by the OfS. Because the OfS, unlike HEFCE, did not fund research (its role seen primarily as a regulator anomalously burdened with some funding responsibilities), a new agency had to be created in the form of Research England to distribute the core funding previously allocated through HEFCE. This in turn led to a new anomaly. Research England – as its name suggests, a body confined in its operation to England – became part of UK Research and Innovation (UKRI), which, again as its name suggests, operated throughout the UK, in particular taking responsibility for the UK-wide research councils as a successor to the Advisory Board for the Research Councils (ABRC). In Scotland and Wales core research funding continued to be included in the block grants made to institutions by their respective funding councils. The explicit encouragement for alternative providers, which are mainly for-profit, to enter the higher education market in England added a further element of divergence. In the two other countries higher education remained almost exclusively the domain of public institutions.

This process of fragmentation of UK higher education into three national systems (four, if Northern Ireland is included) has received less attention than the nationalisation of planning and funding implied by the end of local authority control of polytechnics and colleges in England and the ending of the binary policy. But over the longer term it may be more significant. The two processes also pulled against each other. The latter, nationalisation, encouraged convergence and greater uniformity. The former, fragmentation, encouraged divergence, at the structural as well as policy level. The events of the last two decades suggest that these divergences can only increase, with England moving towards a regulated market, topped by an elite university sector and tailed by a growing number of small-scale alternative providers, and with Scotland moving in the opposite direction towards a managing public system in which pathways through the whole of tertiary education are increasingly coordinated. In these circumstances it may become increasingly difficult to maintain the remaining elements of UK-wide architecture of higher education, notably the research councils but also jointly managed mechanisms such as the Research Excellence Framework (REF), even if the Union itself is upheld.

But these are questions that will be considered in future chapters. For the purposes of this chapter, the focus has been on the journey travelled over the past 60 years, and the transformation of the coordination and funding architecture of UK higher education. Three trends, or forces, were at work:

- The first was the drive towards systematisation, inherent in Robbins' original formulation of higher education's responsibilities and its whole-system approach. This involved a reduction in the number of (weak) coordination agencies and (traditional) intermediate funding bodies, as well as changes in the pattern of institutions.
- This drive towards systematisation was closely related to the second trend, a process of nationalisation, first the creation of an increasingly bipolar architecture then of a unified system …
- … or, rather, systems because the variety of coordinating and funding agents, characteristic of the time of Robbins, reasserted itself in the form of three distinctive, and increasingly divergent, national systems, which was the third trend.

Systematisation, nationalisation and fragmentation – together they make up the story of the transformation of the architecture of UK higher education in terms of coordination and funding.

Institutional governance and management

The transformation of institutional governance and, more widely, organisational culture has – if anything – been even greater than that of 'steering', regulation and governance at the system level. At the start of this period, the 'efficient' governance of all the then universities shared common features, despite detailed differences in their 'dignified' constitutions (to adopt Walter Bagehot's celebrated mid-Victorian terminology), with the perennial exceptions of Oxford and Cambridge. Typically, governance was distributed, in the sense that councils (or courts in Scotland) with their lay majorities and senates as representatives of the academic community shared decision-making powers (Moodie and Eustace, 1974).

The vice-chancellor, or principal, was regarded as *primus inter pares* with an authority that was as much symbolic as executive – although even in the 1960s there were increasing numbers of vice-chancellors who were beginning to have more strategic ambitions for the role (especially in the new universities which were in a state of dynamic growth and development). Other senior academic managers – pro-vice-chancellors (and vice-principals), deans and heads of department – were often elected and still generally appointed for fixed periods, were expected to rotate back into their roles as professors and were part-time. They were supported by a traditional civil service-style administration, as yet untainted by the cult of 'management'. Registrars and secretaries were best compared perhaps to permanent secretaries in government departments. This prelapsarian idyll was best summed up in the Oxford sociologist A.H. Halsey's arresting phrase, the 'donnish dominion' (Halsey, 1992).

In the non-university sector, the pattern was different, but equally traditional. Unlike universities, the colleges, and later the polytechnics, were not independent legal corporations. Instead, they were included in the wider bureaucracies of their maintaining local education authorities, which owned their assets and employed their staff. The authority of their governing bodies was limited in two senses – first, a majority of their members were, if not councillors, party-political appointees; second, most major decisions had to be approved by local authorities. Some key decisions, not simply policy decisions but also administrative decisions (and sometimes at a petty level), were not within the jurisdiction of governing bodies. Voluntary colleges were also subordinated to the authority of their parent churches. Within these strict limits, the principal, or later in the case of polytechnics the director, was all powerful. Deans and heads of Department were permanent positions, and answerable to the principal. Academic boards, the equivalent of university senates, which had often been recently established, played a highly circumscribed role. The polytechnics and colleges were later established as independent corporations now owning their own assets and employing their own staff, and local authority control was removed by the Education Reform Act 1987. But the essential balance of power within them, heavily weighted towards the principal/director and the managers responsible to them, remained largely unchanged. Indeed, their power was increased when local authority oversight was removed.

Even when the binary system was abandoned, important differences remained between the chartered universities (although, in exact fact, not all of them had royal charters), the so-called 'pre-1992' universities, and the 'post-1992' universities, the former polytechnics, and other higher education colleges. A formal distinction was between chartered universities – that is those with royal charters, and statutory universities – that is those established under legislation. The most important practical difference was that in chartered universities the corporation was usually defined as the wider university community in some sense (in a few cases including all students, present and past). In the 'post-1992' universities the corporation was defined as the governing body (the 'higher education corporation'). Another important difference was shared lay-academic governance between councils and senates. This had never applied in the non-university sector or later in the 'post-1992' universities and colleges, but it survived in the 'pre-1992' universities (somewhat precariously). However, even in these universities it is important to remember that the formal powers reserved to senates varied widely, and there was a sustained trend across this period towards those powers being eroded in practice.

Despite these differences, there was substantial convergence between the two types of universities after 1992 (and, to a limited extent, even before 1992). Institutional governance in 'pre-1992' universities had already begun to take on some of the features of governance in the then non-university sector. The 'management turn' was already apparent. After 1992 university councils and governing bodies, in particular, were increasingly urged to assert themselves, by taking active control of determining institutional strategies rather than simply reviewing and endorsing these strategies. This shift from an essentially fiduciary view of institutional governance to one that strayed beyond the strategic and verged at times on the quasi-executive represented a major change.

However, the main shift between the 1960s and the 2000s was the growing power of the third leg of institutional governance alongside lay councils and academic senates (or academic boards): the executive management headed by the vice-chancellor. Over this period most vice-chancellors were redefined, or redefined themselves, as chief executive officers. They were typically chief academic officers too, although revealingly much less emphasis was placed on that role. In the UK there has been little appetite for adopting the split between an executive – and outer-facing – president and an academic provost common in the US. The cult of the CEO became well established.

More recently the corporate-level salaries of vice-chancellors became a matter of acute concern and open controversy – and perhaps a key element in the erosion of the universities' reputation among politicians (and the wider public?).

Senior management teams cohered under the leadership of vice-chancellors, now composed not only of the most senior academic officers but also directors of professional services such as finance, information systems and human resources. Senior academic officers, pro-vice-chancellors and vice-principals (greatly expanded in number) but also deans and heads of department became largely full-time and permanent positions, often with enhanced salaries like vice-chancellors. Without the prospect of rotating back into professorial positions, their academic 'touch' sometimes weakened, and occasionally their academic credibility was eroded. In lockstep with the development of a senior academic managerial class with its own career track, the whole managerial apparatus of universities rapidly expanded.

The reasons for these far-reaching changes in institutional governance and culture were not only structural and organisational but also political and ideological. Determining the balance between these different reasons is difficult, but essential. The structural reasons are unlikely ever to be reversed because they are an inherent feature of mass higher education systems and institutions, and indeed of all large organisations. The political reasons may be more amenable to change. But the structural and the ideological are also deeply intertwined. As a result, disentangling them is equally difficult.

At a structural level, major reasons for this transformation of institutional governance and, more widely, organisational culture are, that as a result of mass expansion over this period, universities became much larger and more complex and, of course, had much bigger budgets. First, the change in scale was transformational. Where they once enrolled thousands of students and employed hundreds of staff they came to enrol tens of thousands of students and employ thousands of staff. Although the number of higher education institutions increased at least fourfold, their average size increased at an even faster rate. The next change, in scope, if anything, was more transformational. Even the most traditional universities came to engage in a range of non-traditional activities: continuing professional development (often focused in business, medicine and other health subjects, and engineering but common among all professional subjects); taught doctorates; blended learning (classroom and online); access and outreach; knowledge transfer; consultancy and the rest. In short, the once-periphery invaded the core. In newer and more innovative (and more entrepreneurial?) institutions, these 'peripheral' activities often became their mainstream provision. Finally, the change in budgets was exponential. By the end of this period the total budget of UK higher education was now upwards of £30 billion where at the start it had been in the hundreds of millions.

In the 1960s the legal framework in which all organisations, including universities, operated was primitive by the standards of the 21st century. Sixty years later they had become subject to a wide array of legislation and regulation – on accounting standards, on corporate governance, on procurement, on (equal) pay and employment rights, on race and gender discrimination, on health and safety (including, of particular relevance to universities, the use of embryos in research), on travel and building use and environmental issues, on freedom of information and data protection, and on a range of other matters. In addition, there was now an equally wide array of voluntary codes of good practice, notably on governance – for example the successive codes devised by the Committee of University Chairs (CUC). It is important to recognise the impact of these generic legal and regulatory requirements alongside the particular accountability requirements that apply to higher education on the evolving forms of institutional governance and management. Indeed, in terms of administrative burden these generic requirements probably weighed more heavily. To meet them, all universities needed sophisticated, and elaborate, management systems. Those who complain about the inevitable organisational consequences of all these legal frameworks and regulatory regimes need to be clear which they regard as redundant.

So, the transformational changes in institutional scale, scope and budgets ineluctably required universities to develop more professional management systems. This required the increasingly large-scale recruitment of specialist staff and the more elaborate development of expert systems, however alien MIS (management information systems), PIs (performance indicators) or 'dashboards' might appear to more traditional academics. The light-touch administrative processes supported by minimalist bureaucracy, which was adequate at the start of this period, were no longer fit for purpose by the end. The growing heterogeneity of the 21st-century mass university also tended to erode the academic, and even normative, coherence characteristic of the elite universities of the mid-20th century. Different disciplines, in terms both of their cognitive values and of their professional structures, came to have less and less in common with each other. Nor was this simply the result of a sinister replacement of an academic collegium (= good) by managerial culture (= bad). Equally, or more important, had been the influence of academic fragmentation, the advance of ever more fine-grain specialisms.

It is hard to see any of these structural and organisational responses by institutions to the development of mass higher education as anything else but inherent to this development – and also to wider changes in regulation and accountability in 21st-century society. Arguably, although undesirably, it might be possible to 'roll back' mass expansion. But it is barely possible to conceive of such a retrograde movement being possible in the face of powerful social and political resistances, which will be discussed later in this book. Instead, critics of mass higher education tend to pin their hopes on the re-creation of a well-guarded elite university sector within the wider system, in which collegial values can be reasserted. However, it is still difficult to imagine that higher education, or even a re-established elite university sector, could ever be exempted from the general trend towards regulation in wider society. To a large extent the transformation of institutional governance over the past six decades must be regarded as inevitable, and irreversible.

At the same time, there have clearly also been ideological drivers for this transformation, which are more contestable (and reversible?). From the 1980s onwards there was a strong current of belief that governance and management norms as well as practices in higher education, especially in more traditional universities, were somehow 'amateur' and even self-serving and self-indulgent, as well as chronically inefficient. Governance and management both needed to be changed to become more 'business-like', in other words aligned more closely with the norms and practice of the corporate sector. This critique was strongly endorsed by some more ambitious university leaders – perhaps on the Mandy Rice-Davies' principle 'They would say that, wouldn't they?'. It was the Committee of Vice-Chancellors and Principals (CVCP) – the more accurately labelled forerunner of Universities UK – which commissioned the Jarratt Report on university efficiency (Jarratt Report, 1985). Reading the Jarratt Report today it is difficult to be surprised, let alone shocked, by many of its detailed recommendations. However, its real influence was at the level of values as much as of practices. Fairly or unfairly, Jarratt was seen as kick-starting the creeping corporatisation of university governance and management, in an increasingly ideological sense.

Much (Too much?) has perhaps been written of the so-called 'New Public Management' (NPM), which was a normative equivalent of the 'modernisation' policies pursued with particular vigour by New Labour between 1997 and 2010 in the UK, but also in many countries. At one level NPM simply attempted to apply the new techniques that were being developed within the private sector, notably improved management information systems and systematic evaluation, to the public sector, including universities. So far, so unobjectionable. But within NPM there was always an ideological strain, partly derived from business school mantras (and how could universities object to the principles of management they so lucratively taught to others now being applied to themselves?) but also, with increasing force after 2010, derived from neoliberal belief in the quasi-moral superiority of market relations. Some accounts have gone further developing the idea of 'academic capitalism', bracketing together the transformation of the organisational culture of the modern university with the supposed commodification of knowledge (Slaughter and Leslie, 1997; Slaughter and Rhoades, 2004).

What mattered perhaps was not the proliferation of theoretical frameworks – Fordism, post-Fordism, neoliberalism … – nor whether these frameworks have always been used with proper academic rigour, but the impression left on the academic community. In the 1960s the forms of governance and (limited) management, in the university sector at any rate, went largely uncontested – with the brief exception of the assault mounted by leftist student radicals. By the end of this period the new forms of institutional governance and management had come to be sharply contested. Again, it did not matter that much of this opposition had been provoked by the ideological glosses placed on a largely inevitable transformation of institutional governance and management, or that it was misdirected because the real target should have been the 'market' policies pursued by the Conservative Government (in England) after 2010 to which institutions had little option but to respond. The degree of contest had become established, and with it a belief there was now a strong dissonance between core academic values and how institutions were now governed and managed.

New agendas

It is almost impossible to characterise, without caricaturing, the changing contours of intellectual culture (in the context of scholarship and science) between 1960 and 2020. But it must be attempted, because without some understanding of this overarching context more detailed changes in both the priorities, organisation and management of research in universities and also the courses, curriculum and wider ecology of student learning are difficult to comprehend fully. Without that understanding, the only credible explanation then becomes a version of a conspiracy theory, that they are just another manifestation of the growth and abuse of managerial power within universities and of politically inspired interventions from outside. 'Managerialism', when it is finally and properly defined, may be held responsible for many things – but not for everything (Deem, Hilyard and Reed, 2007). It is important to be open to at least the possibility that some of these changes may have been inherent both in the mass higher education project itself and the wider social, and intellectual, environment.

The development of mass higher education in the 1960s reflected, but also actively reproduced, two key intellectual currents. First, the extension of the higher education 'franchise' embraced new groups of individuals from outside the elite student base of the traditional universities (composed, of course, of both inherited and co-opted elites). This, in turn, stimulated new intellectual priorities and preoccupations. The most obvious linkage was between the increase in female participation in higher education, from less than a third to more than half of the total student population, and the growth of feminism both as an intellectual strand within research and more concretely as new curriculum. A similar alignment can be suggested between the increase in participation among Black and other minority ethnic (BAME) students and the interest in Black studies, post-colonial studies and world literature. Later other 'minorities' were given voice too by mass higher education, the emergence of universities as creative hubs of innovation and experimentation and the growing focus on 'identity', which has arguably been one of the most significant aspect of the extension of the higher education 'franchise'. Gay, or queer, studies developed in this broader context. Moreover, is it necessarily fanciful to imagine there were alignments between this widening of the social base and new fashions within more traditional disciplines – for example, the shift within history not only more to familiar social and economic themes but also to embrace new cultural and anthropological perspectives, which had long been familiar in France but much less so in the UK?

The second intellectual current which shaped, and was shaped by, mass higher education was the belief that mass universities could no longer imagine that they stood apart, or even a little aside, from society. Instead, they had become unambiguously social institutions. In the late 1960s, this idea was raucously and rancorously expressed by New Left student activists who saw higher education not as part of the apparatus of the growing welfare state being built by social democratic 'revisionists' but as a base from which radical revolt against such 'revisionism' could be organised. Like others before and since, they believed the mission of universities was not to understand the world but also to change it. Expressed in often juvenile and debased Marxist language, their challenge failed. Or did it …? Many of the rapidly expanding social sciences, even in their most analytical and empirical modes, never entirely abandoned a commitment to advocacy, whether of social reform or of free-market economics. And repurposed as 'social engagement' or 'impact', this idea that universities must be activist institutions operating in real time in the real world not only flourished but intensified towards the end of the 20th century and into the new century.

The expansion of higher education after 1960 had more practical impacts too. The growth in the number of undergraduates stimulated a similar growth in postgraduates. In particular, the increasing number of research students turbo-charged university research, especially in science and technology. The result was the creation of a research workforce, a pool of scientific labour, that transformed the quasi-artisanal character of university research into something closer to mass production. In terms of game-changing science – 'paradigm shifts' in the terminology of Thomas Kuhn – this may have made limited difference. But the impact of this quasi-industrialisation of research was more heavily felt in the routine production of routine scientific progress – Kuhn's 'normal science' – especially in less mature (and less prestigious?) subjects.

As a phenomenon, mass higher education is conventionally associated with teaching larger and larger numbers of students. But a collateral, and less noticed, effect of expansion was greatly to enhance the capacity of these mass institutions to undertake research. Expansion required the recruitment of many more academic staff. Most had a stronger research orientation than their donnish predecessors because they were themselves products of a more systematic process of professional formation and also because research productivity was a new element in new forms of appraisal of individual performance. As the years went by, a full and satisfying professional identity could no longer be derived solely from teaching students. Mass higher education inevitably stimulated the development of more research-focused institutions, and not simply in elite universities determined to retain their distinctive mission but across the whole system.

These, and other, impacts of mass expansion form the context within which more detailed changes in research and teaching can be discussed. Looking back from the over-regulated, over-audited and over-managed 2020s, it is easy to slip into the belief that the 1960s must have been some kind of lost Arcadia. But the research councils already existed; their mission to fund research that was not just 'promising' (in terms of scientific merit) but also 'timely' (thereby implying some imposition of external priorities) was already well established. The Royal Society, the British Academy and other scholarly and scientific bodies already policed a hierarchy of reputation, although more gently than later formal assessment regimes. The great success of science in demonstrating its usefulness, notably during the Second World War, was already feeding the appetite for more strategic direction. Seen in this light, the increasing coordination of research, first through the establishment of the Advisory Board for the Research Councils (ABRC) in the 1970s, the growing demand for guiding research themes and then the creation of ever more elaborate assessment instruments, the Research Assessment Exercise (RAE) in the late 1980s and finally the Research Excellence Framework (REF) in 2008 represents continuity not rupture.

A similar pattern can be observed with regard to teaching. Once again there had been no Arcadia, no 'secret garden' of the curriculum, at the start of this period. In 1960, as in 2020, many professional disciplines were subject to external regulation if their graduates were to be professionally licensed. The content of law, medical, engineering and other professional and vocational degrees was already prescribed by the relevant regulatory or professional bodies, sometimes even in greater detail than is now required. Outside the university sector, courses in local authority colleges were either university-franchised (often by the University of London) or approved by, and led to awards from, first, the National Council for Technological Awards (NCTA) and a parallel body in art and design and, later, the Council for

National Academic Awards (CNAA), its replacement. The polytechnics offered CNAA degrees almost up to their designation as universities in 1992, although within an increasingly loose framework not easily distinguished from being independently degree-awarding.

The oversight of courses and degrees in the non-university sector was initially a sign of subordination, on the grounds that these institutions were not sufficiently mature to manage their own academic standards and held out the promise of eventual emancipation from these controls. But as the 1970s and 1980s went by, it took on many of the characteristics of a process of systematisation, with college and polytechnic staff developing their own standards but on a collective basis. The universities were not immune from the pressure to systematise, and make more explicit and transparent, their own forms of academic regulation. A small start was made in the 1970s when the CVCP established an academic standards unit, to develop good practice, in particular on external examining.

After the abolition of the CNAA and the ending of the binary system, a Higher Education Quality Council (HEQC) was established with a broader remit on quality matters. The HEQC in turn was replaced by the Quality Assurance Agency (QAA), which took on more of a regulatory function conducting detailed Teaching Quality Assessments (TQAs) of individual subjects in institutions (later scaled back to less intrusive whole-institutional audits). Although the QAA also attempted to promote the enhancement of academic standards, its main focus remained firmly on audit. A further body, the Higher Education Academy was also created to raise standards in higher education teaching (now merged with the Leadership Foundation for Higher Education to form Advance HE). By the end of the period, the growth of the quality industry, with its proliferation of acronymic agencies, had become one of the most prominent features of UK higher education.

There were two other important strands in the development of the control and regulation of teaching and research between 1960 and 2020 – metrics and management (intimately related, of course). The increasing popularity of measurement, despite the known dilemma that what can most readily be measured is not always the most important (and vice versa), allowed the performance of universities, departments, subjects and even individuals to be assessed in terms of measurable 'deliverables' or quantifiable 'outcomes.' It also powered the creation of national surveillance and ranking regimes. The most prominent, and notorious, was the REF, which ceased solely to be an instrument for allocating QR funding between institutions and instead was used to rank reputation within an increasingly fractious and divisive hierarchy. But it was joined by the Teaching Excellence and Student Outcomes Framework (TEF), designed as an antidote to the bias towards research but rapidly evolving into a supplier of comparative data to provide raw material for the construction of more pervasive university rankings, which were developed and often exploited by commercial companies. In 2021 the Department for Education resisted the conclusion of the review of the Pearce inquiry that the main value of the TEF had been to promote enhancement not to inform student choices (Pearce Report, 2021). This lurch in the focus of system-level initiatives on teaching and research from limited goals, such as identifying good professional practice or allocating funding, to surrendering to full-blown consumerism was one of the most striking developments of the first two decades of the 21st century.

Finally, the impact of new learning technologies over this period cannot be overlooked. That impact was not confined to new modes of delivery of higher education, such as massive open online courses (MOOCs) or the facility to measure (some forms of) effectiveness– whether of individuals or of courses – by means of learning analytics. That impact is likely in time to extend through the development of new modes, habits and even cultures of communication to entirely new learning ecologies – and, in research, more distributed and reflexive forms of knowledge production.

Beyond the UK

As in the previous chapter, the focus of this chapter has been almost exclusively on the UK, although many of the developments touched on here – the general effects of mass higher education, the emergence of more coherent systems which needed to be 'steered', shifts in organisational cultures and in governance and management practice, the drive towards systematisation of good practice (and then, some more …), the rise of metrics and management, the impact of new technologies on student learning – were equally felt in other higher education systems. On looking back from 2020 to the 1960s, these trends and transformations appear to be more generic than the particular chronology of the development of UK higher education over that 60-year period.

The UK was perhaps exceptional in the consistent drive towards creating a national system of higher education (or, more accurately, national systems in England, Scotland and Wales). The United States, despite the rise and fall (and rise again) of 'master plans', was unable (and had no desire) to create such a system because of the fragmentation of US higher education into state institutions (all 52 of them …) and private institutions (also divided into charitable and for-profit institutions). In much of the rest of Europe, binary systems, divided between traditional universities and higher professional and vocational schools often within different legal frameworks, persisted, also complicating the emergence of coherent systems, although governments made increasing efforts to coordinate these different elements within common frameworks, at first legal but later extending to matters of governance and administrative.

In terms of organisational culture, the US appeared more advanced than both the UK and the rest of Europe, with a settled demarcation between 'faculty' (the academic staff) and the 'administration' (senior managers and professional staff). Outside a few elite universities it was also most advanced in accepting a strongly entrepreneurial, if not always market, orientation. Yet the US was also exceptional in tolerating overtly politicised patterns of management in state universities, and business-dominated patterns in the private sector. Within Europe, the UK at the beginning of this period appeared an outlier of Europe, having an 'autonomous sector' of self-managed and lightly managed universities, while in the rest of Europe universities remained public institutions firmly embedded in state bureaucracies – although it is important to remember that in the 1960s (and through to the late 1980s) half of UK higher education was equally embedded in local if not national state bureaucracies. However, by the end of this period, the gap between the UK and the rest of Europe was much narrower. Other European universities, as the price of increased distance from the state, had been obliged to adopt many of the same managerial practices with rectors, too, acting as chief executive officers, more professional and sophisticated administrative structures, institutional strategies and more managed academic staff.

Finally, in terms of the management of teaching and research, the UK may appear to be the leader and the US the laggard, although with important qualifications. The UK had been most active in building a national superstructure of quality agencies with oversight of teaching and academic standards, as well strengthening the responsibilities of coordination and funding agencies for overseeing teaching and research performance. The fragmentation of the US system precluded such developments, although at the institutional level the assessment and measurement of the performance of individual members of academic staff and departments, both teaching and research, was always fierce. In the rest of Europe, the move away from state qualifications, where standards were simply a matter of compliance, to institutional qualifications, which required more nuanced forms of professional regulation, led to an increased emphasis on what became generically known as 'quality culture', which revealingly became one of the pillars of the Bologna Process. As a result, other European higher education systems began to develop 'quality' architecture similar to, although not yet as intrusive as, that in the UK.

Beyond the North Atlantic world, similar trends could be observed. These included the elaboration of coordinated but tiered systems of different categories of institution, such as the various layers of 'key universities' in China; the development of organisational and managerial cultures (often with even more limited traces of collegiality); and the development of quality agencies and instruments (although often with no attempt to disguise their subordination to the state).

This convergence of broad trends in system architecture, organisational culture and learning and research economies is hardly surprising in the light of the fact that over this period the development of mass higher education systems became a global phenomenon, although at different rates and times, with the US always in the lead (at least until the 21st century) and Europe, including the UK, typically 20 years behind – and, of course, both are now in the process of being overtaken by the dynamic development of higher education in East (and South) Asia. However, hidden within this greater convergence there are important, and intriguing, particularities. These particularities are shaped both by the uniqueness of national experience and the character of national higher education systems. That experience and that character are the subjects of the next two chapters.

5

Higher education today

Higher education in the UK in 2020 is, by any measure, a mass system. It enrols 2.5 million students, one of only five systems with more than two million students in Europe (the others are France, Germany, Italy and Poland). This still comes as a surprise because of the deep-rooted prejudice that continental European higher education systems are sprawling, disorganised and wasteful, while the UK is selective, structured and efficient. In England half of all school leavers continue on to some form of higher education, and in Scotland the participation rate is approaching 60 per cent. In Martin Trow's classic taxonomy of elite, mass and universal stages in the development of higher education systems, the UK is on the brink of entering the third stage and becoming a universal system. The total budget is more than £40 billion, the majority provided directly or indirectly by the state. Expenditure on higher education is now a substantial element within the state budget, and also a significant item in terms of private spending. The largest universities, University College London (UCL) and Manchester, each have more than 40,000 students, the population of a medium-sized town. Several others have more than 30,000. Universities have become even more visible presences in urban landscapes, their expanding campuses now dominated whole precincts.

The scale, and timing, of this transformation has been discussed in Chapter 3. The past is very much 'another country' ... And yet, that past lingers on. For a higher education system on the brink of becoming a universal system, UK higher education has retained many of the characteristics, and consequently much of the 'feel', of an elite system. High student completion and low wastage rates; the sustained attempt to maintain uniform academic 'standards' by the twin means of academic peer review and bureaucratic policing instruments; stubborn resistance to any formal stratification of institutions (combined, of course, with widespread acceptance of an informal pecking order), which reflects a core belief in the unity of academic work – teaching, research and scholarship; an equally strong belief that a university education constitutes a 'rite of passage', although no longer (so) confined to a social elite; a system dominated by a monoculture of comprehensive universities traditionally formed – these, and other attributes, are some of the hallmarks of elite higher education.

These attributes cannot easily be regarded as residual features that time will wither, growing pains that reflect UK higher education's difficulty in adjusting to being a mass system. This has been comparatively recent change because the size of the system has doubled in less than a quarter of a century. The persistence of these elite attributes also exposes the limitations of conceptual (and linear) models of the development of higher education. Rather, UK higher education, along with most other higher education systems, is more like an archaeological site composed of many layers. The values and practices characteristic of earlier layers are still active and alive (and even dominant), and often at war with the values and practices of more recent layers of change. Sometimes the 'war' between these different layers is expressed in terms of nostalgia – for example, for the days when the state funded (of course, a much smaller) university system without asking many, if any, questions. At other times these tensions, and even contradictions, are reflected in policy dissonances – for example, working through the tension between upholding 'excellence' (a term more widely used than ever in the context of institutional and national rivalries) and promoting 'access' (or entitlement). These policy dissonances in turn reflect more fundamental normative and even cognitive dissonances – about the core purposes of higher education and even the nature of relative claims of social justice and economic efficiency in modern democratic societies.

Size and shape

Students

The standard taxonomy of higher education systems is still based on the model suggested half a century ago by the American sociologist Martin Trow: elite systems enrolling up to 10 per cent of the relevant age group; mass systems enrolling up to 50 per cent; and universal systems enrolling more than 50 per cent. There have been a number of difficulties with this essentially linear and quantitative model of the development of higher education systems. In recent years the label 'high-participation systems' has sometimes been preferred to 'mass' systems ('universal' systems have largely remained an empty category in analytical terms). Whatever label is preferred, the UK system is clearly a 'high-participation' or 'mass' system, with participation rates nudging or exceeding 50 per cent.

The current (2019–20) total of 2.53 million students in UK higher education marks an increase of 3 per cent on the previous year (HESA, 2021a). The total number of students has finally exceeded the previous peak, which occurred in 2010–11 just before the introduction of the UK government's reforms in England. The main reason for the decline from that peak in the intervening decade was that student numbers in England fell after the introduction of much higher tuition fees. The initial impact of higher fees was significant, especially on part-time student numbers, but since 2016–17 growth rates have recovered. Interestingly, the number of qualifications obtained fell to 800,335, a decrease of 28,000, between 2018–19 and 2019–20.

The most important characteristics of UK higher education may be summarised as follows.

- It predominantly caters for young, full-time students. Only 795,000 of the 2.53 million total are aged 25 or older, and students aged 30 and older make up less than half that number. The age profile of students enrolled with 'alternative providers', typically private (and largely for-profit) colleges, is different, with 37 per cent aged 25 or older, but the overall number of students in these providers remains very small. The student body is now even more skewed towards full-time study, mainly because of the disincentive to study part time created by higher fees in England.
- Most students study in universities or university-type institutions. The proportion of students on higher education courses in local colleges continues to decline, to 6.1 per cent (170,000 students). However, this disguises a sharp difference between England (5.7 per cent) and Scotland, where it is more than 25 per cent. This difference largely explains the much higher overall participation rate in Scotland. As has already been said, the number of students enrolled with 'alternative providers' is tiny – only 3 per cent, or 71,000 (2018–19). UK higher education, in effect, is a university monoculture.
- The overall balance of the study body has shifted 'upwards'. There has been a substantial decline in the number, and proportion, of students on 'other undergraduate' courses – by half in the case of Higher National Certificates (HNCs) and Higher National Diplomas (HNDs), and by a quarter in the case of Foundation Degrees since 2015–16. These students have been displaced into first-degree courses. The proportion of postgraduate students is also higher than it has ever been, despite impressive growth rates for undergraduate students. Postgraduates now make up a quarter of all students. The main area of growth has been students in taught postgraduate courses, while the number of PhD students has remained stable for the past decade.
- More UK students are on courses in the humanities and social sciences (1.96 million) than in the sciences (920,000), although the difference is less pronounced if international students are counted. More significant perhaps is that in both subject groups vocational subjects predominate. In the arts and social sciences, the most popular subjects, in order, are business and administrative studies, social studies, creative art and design, and education. In the sciences, the most popular subjects are those allied to medicine (which include nursing and other healthcare subjects), biological sciences, engineering and technology, and computer sciences. In one sense, this subject balance is unsurprising; it simply reflects the

weight of various economic and employment sectors. But the result is that UK higher education has a strong vocational bias.
- The social composition of the student population is also revealing. There are substantially more female students (1.44 million) than male students (1.1 million), although this overall female predominance conceals important differences between subjects. Some recruit disproportionate numbers of female students (for example, education) and others remain male strongholds (for example, most forms of engineering). The majority of students are also White but there is a growing representation of Black and other minority ethnic (BAME) students. Among UK-domiciled students there are 1.44 million White students and 226,595 Asian and 152,420 Black students. Again, there are important differences between subjects – with Asian students now dominating entry to many medical schools, and types of institution – with BAME students concentrated in post-1992 universities and colleges (in 'alternative providers' they make up 44 per cent of all students). Even after a generation or more of mass expansion, students remain predominantly middle class. School leavers from the top socio-economic quintile are more than three times as likely to participate in higher education than those from the least privileged quintile.
- Finally, there is a substantial presence of non-UK students in UK higher education, comprising more than a quarter of the total. The majority, 409,000, come from outside the EU, with the remaining 147,000 from other countries within the EU. The number of EU students has remained almost the same, no doubt a result of Brexit, while the number of other international students continues to grow, by just under 15 per cent in 2019–20. Other data suggests that more recently there has been a sharp decline in EU applications. Much the fastest-growing UK group is from China – 86,500 in 2018–19 compared with 29,000 10 years earlier. The presence of non-UK students is particularly marked on postgraduate courses, where the proportion of students from outside the EU is almost the same as that from the UK itself, with the remaining 10 per cent coming from other EU countries. There are substantial variations between institutions, with non-UK students concentrated in the most selective universities but also in institutions that have struggled to recruit UK students. As a footnote, there are 667,000 students on transnational education (TNE) courses, with 314,000 on courses leading to a UK award and only a small number (56,000) enrolled in high-profile overseas branch campuses. (These figures are from 2018–19.)

Institutions

Higher education systems typically organise institutions in three different ways.

- First, there are dual, or binary, systems that distinguish between traditional universities and other higher education institutions (usually with a strong focus on professional and vocational education). The UK system was such a system until 1992, although in an increasingly dilute or fuzzy form through the 1980s. Many other European systems remain dual systems, although here too the barriers between universities and other institutions are becoming more porous.
- The second organising principle is to have stratified systems whereby institutions are organised according to a formal division of labour (or mission) – typically research universities awarding doctoral degrees; other universities awarding bachelor's and master's degrees; and open access institutions principally engaged in two-year associate degrees and vocational courses. This is the pattern in many US states.
- The third organising principle is to have unified systems in which institutions have common characteristics, although with different balances, between research and teaching; academic (or scientific) education and professional and vocational education; selection and wider access; residential and commuter students; full- and part-time students; and so on. In unified systems there is no formal differentiation of roles or missions. Since 1992 the UK system has been a largely unified system.

As a result, as has already been emphasised more than once, the institutional landscape of UK higher education is dominated by multi-faculty universities. This has been true since the abandonment of the binary system 30 years ago, with its division into universities and polytechnics. The non-university sector now comprises a collection of specialist institutions especially in art and design (although many of them have full university status, even if it is not reflected in their titles); further education colleges that offer higher education courses; and, increasingly, private or independent colleges (usually categorised as 'alternative providers', although a small number now have full university status too).

But this predominance of the universities tends to obscure the fact that there is a variety of institutional types in UK higher education, including differences between types of university. These differences can be categorised in various ways.

In a formal, and legal, sense, universities either have Royal Charters or they have been established as higher education corporations (HECs). The first group comprises the universities established before 1992, hence the label 'pre-1992', and the second the universities that have been established since that date. Any changes in the charters and statutes of the 'pre-1992' universities formally must be agreed by the Privy Council, although in practice this means the relevant government (the Department for Education in England, and equivalent Departments in Scotland, Wales and Northern

Ireland). The 'post-1992' universities have, in effect standard off-the-peg, instruments and articles of government approved by the relevant Secretary of State or equivalent in the four UK nations. Other non-university institutions in the public sector are also HECs. These legal differences between chartered universities and HECs, which are fewer in practice than might be supposed, will be discussed later in this chapter.

There is a second formal sense in which higher education institutions can be distinguished. All universities have full degree-awarding powers; chartered universities always had these powers. 'Post-1992' universities were awarded these powers *en bloc* in 1992. But other institutions have limited or no degree-awarding powers. Some have the same powers as universities, while others only have bachelor's and master's degree but not doctoral degree-awarding powers. Further education colleges and most 'alternative providers', even when they teach degree-level programmes, must have these programmes validated by or franchised from degree-awarding universities. The power to award both taught and research degrees is presently exercised by the Quality Assurance Agency (QAA), which will be discussed in greater detail, alongside other agencies, later in this chapter. In addition to degrees, many institutions award professional qualifications regulated by professional bodies, which make no distinction between different institutional types although they typically impose detailed conditions and ration the number of institutions they permit to award their qualifications (whether to maintain quality or to restrict supply).

Moving on from legal, and formal, distinctions between different institutional types, UK higher education is split into a bewildering set of sectoral bodies and so-called 'mission groups'. The sectoral bodies are relatively stable. The main body is Universities UK (UUK), of which 137 universities (in effect, all public universities, plus two private universities, the University of Buckingham and Regent's University) are members. Within UUK there are two regional groups: Universities Scotland representing universities in Scotland, and Universities Wales representing Welsh ones. Universities UK is often regarded, and likes to be regarded, as the voice of UK universities.

But that claim is limited in two respects. The first is that another body, Guild HE, represents non-university institutions. Because some specialist institutions, notably in art and design, have now been granted full university status, there is some crossover of membership with UUK. The second, and more important, limitation is that UUK represents not universities (despite its title) but university vice-chancellors and principals (in other words, the management). Governing bodies, councils and courts, which have the overall authority unambiguously in the case of HECs and predominantly so in the case of chartered universities, are not involved. The chairs of these bodies come together in a third body, the Committee of University Chairs

(CUC). In practice, UUK and CUC work closely together. But increasing emphasis on the need to make a clear distinction between management and governance could lead to significant divergence in future.

It is the 'mission groups' that are most often seen as representing a stratification, or hierarchy, of UK higher education institutions. There are three main groups:

- The first is **the Russell Group** which represents, in its own terms, 'the 24 leading UK universities'. It was founded in 1994, in direct response to the supposed levelling effects of the abandonment of the binary distinction between universities and polytechnics two years previously, and incorporated in 2007. Its members are: Oxford; Cambridge; the five big London universities (four of which are still technically Schools of the University of London); the big civic universities in England; Glasgow and Edinburgh in Scotland; Cardiff in Wales; and Queen's University Belfast in Northern Ireland. The only 'new' university of the 1960s to be a member is Warwick.
- The Russell Group's main rival was – and is – **Million Plus**, established at the same time to represent the former polytechnics and assert their distinctiveness, and place, in the newly expanded university sector. Its claim is to be 'the association of modern universities'. Despite losing some of its initial university members, its 22 universities still enrol 1.05 million students, hence the name, and the majority of BAME students and students from more socially deprived backgrounds.
- The third name group is **the University Alliance**, which began life as the 'non-aligned' group occupying the middle ground between the Russell Group and Million Plus. It now describes itself as the 'voice of professional and technical universities'. It currently has 19 universities as members. It once had more, but it has found it difficult to dispel the impression of being neither one thing nor the other, reflecting its origins as a group of 'non-aligned' institutions.

There are even more groups – **Guild HE** also acts as a mission group as well as a sectoral group, while the universities that had their origins as church colleges have their own club, **the Cathedrals Group**. Some other groups have been disbanded. The most significant casualty was **the 1994 Group**, which was made up mainly of smaller 'pre-1992' universities without medical schools that were not members of the Russell Group. Several of its members have now joined the Russell Group. The 1994 Group was disbanded in 2013.

In their early days these mission groups amounted to little more than vice-chancellors' clubs. Even the Russell Group initially focused on specific and common interests, the most important of which was the interface between their medical schools and the National Health Service. But, as they have evolved, they have taken more substantial (and symbolic) roles.

The first is that within a unified university system the need to distinguish between different types (and ranks?) of universities was perceived to have increased, which was in sharp contrast to the previous instinct of UK universities to emphasise their common feature and to minimise differences. As there was little appetite to develop a formal stratification of universities along lines familiar in the US, and certainly no political will to do so, mission groups became proxies by suggesting an informal differentiation of missions. At best, this has been arbitrary; at worst, misleading. Despite the claim of the Russell Group to represent a superior cadre of research-intensive universities, many non-Russell Group members had equally impressive research reputations. It is also difficult to distinguish between the universities in other mission groups on the basis of their academic and student profiles.

The second role is that the mission groups have come to provide the basis for 'branding' in UK higher education, especially important in the marketised English system. They have been played, willingly or unwillingly, into a new discourse emphasising, confusingly, both traditional hierarchy and institutional competition. In this clashing environment the Russell Group has often come to be lazily glossed as 'our best universities'. The turbulence in membership of mission groups can partly be explained by the manoeuvring of universities to avoid ending up in the – logically necessary – other category of 'our worst universities'. UK universities have also been eager participants of global league tables despite their well-known flaws, conceptual (and moral) and methodological.

However, the most important differentiating element within UK higher education is not legal status or mission group membership but institutional size. The median size of a UK higher education institution is now more than 20,000 students, a total only exceeded by a handful of universities a generation ago. The largest is the University of Manchester, with many other civic universities not far behind. Even Oxford and Cambridge, overtaken as the UK's largest universities in the 1960s and reluctant to expand, have grown significantly, mainly among postgraduate students. At the same time, the number of institutions with small numbers has also tended to increase as a result of the growing number of 'alternative providers', most of which are small. As a result, the range of institutional sizes has widened.

Two consequences have flowed from this increasing variation in the size of institutions. First, mass universities tend to be either the most elite in terms of student recruitment and research concentration – the members of the Russell Group and a few others – or the most open in terms of student participation – largely big-city 'post-1992' universities. Both now operate on a very different scale than smaller institutions, whether 'alternative providers' or specialist colleges in subjects like the performing arts. In organisational and management terms they have much more in common despite their different educational missions. Second, these differences in institutional scale are not reflected in terms of regulation, oversight, funding, accountability and governance. With a few exceptions, all institutions, regardless of size, are treated alike. This 'one-size-fits-all' approach has led not only to a disproportionate burden on smaller institutions but also the imposition of over-detailed and intrusive regulatory and accountability conditions on larger institutions – a 'medium' that is anything but 'happy'.

Income and expenditure

Overall income and expenditure on UK higher education is both difficult and easy to measure. It is difficult to measure as a percentage of gross domestic product (GDP) for two reasons. First, measuring a nation's GDP is not straightforward. If the measure is nominal GDP, the UK has the sixth-largest economy in the world; if the measure used is purchasing-power-parity GDP, the UK slips to ninth; and in terms of GDP per head, the UK slips further still, to 23rd. Second, expenditure on education (and other services) is conventionally split into public and private expenditure, malleable categories as the way in which expenditure on student loans has ping-ponged between the two depending on accounting practices has highlighted. In most comparative statistics of expenditure on tertiary education (of which higher education is a variable component, a further complication) as a percentage of GDP, UK public expenditure is ranked low – 0.6 according to most Eurostat figures, compared with an EU27 average of 0.8. But overall UK expenditure on tertiary education (including private expenditure) is usually ranked between 1.6 and 1.8 per cent. So, the only safe conclusions to draw are, first, that total expenditure on higher education in the UK as a share of GDP is in the middle range compared to other developed countries and, secondly, that it has increased at a faster rate than the overall GDP growth rate.

Overall income and expenditure on UK higher education is easy to measure in cash terms. In 2018–19 total income amounted to £40.8 billion (HESA, 2020a). The largest component was income from tuition fees – £19.9 billion, or just under half. However, this total includes both fees paid by UK-domiciled students, funded by loans from the Student Loans Company (SLC), and fees paid by other students, principally international students, which is truly private money. Of the £19.9 billion, 60 per cent (£11.8 billion) was fees paid by UK students and 29 per cent (£5.8 billion) fees paid by international students.

A total of £6.6 billion came from research grants and contracts, again a mix of public and private money. The Funding Councils provided

£5.3 billion. The largest contributor was the Medical Research Council (MRC) (£342.9 million) and the smallest the Arts and Humanities Research Council (AHRC) (£629,000). Gifts and donations (£700 million) and investment income (£394 million) made up comparatively small proportions of total income. The remainder (£7.7 billion) was an omnibus category ('other income') but included income from conferences and lettings – higher education's 'hotel business' – and also from university companies and the proceeds of patents and licences. The major shift over the past decade has been from Funding Council grants to tuition fees.

Six universities had annual incomes of more than £1 billion. Top came Oxford with £2.5 billion and Cambridge with £2.2 billion, although these figures are misleading because they include income from their respective university presses. Oxford University Press, of course, is a global publisher, and in commercial and operational, if not legal, terms a separate entity. As a result, 'other income' at both universities was 45 per cent of their total annual income. Both universities also have gifts and donations out of proportion to any other UK university, although a substantial proportion of these were made to individual colleges rather than the parent universities. The other billion-pound-plus universities are University College London (£1.5 billion), Manchester and Edinburgh (£1.1 billion) and Imperial College (£1.07 billion). At the other end of the scale, 60 institutions had incomes of less than £100 million, including more than 30 universities.

The expenditure of UK higher education in 2018–19 amounted to £44.3 billion (HESA, 2020b). This total was higher than the total income, but it covered some non-cash items which do not appear on annual profit-and-loss accounts. Overall, UK higher education had a small surplus, although many individual institutions had deficits, some considerable. Expenditure was 36 per cent higher than five years before. The largest element was staff costs (£26.1 billion), followed by 'other operating expenditure' (£14.6 billion) and depreciation (£2.7 billion). Interest payments amounted to £843 million, or 1.8 per cent of total expenditure, which demonstrates the relatively low indebtedness of the system.

Some broad conclusions can be drawn from this brief survey of income and expenditure. The first, of course, is the size of that total amount. In comparison, public expenditure on the National Health Service in the same year was £129 billion. There is likely to be some double counting because of the overlap between medical schools and the NHS. But the comparison shows how big the business of higher education has become. The second is that most of the funding continues to flow from the state, either direct grants from funding and research councils or tuition fees funded by state loans provided by the SLC. As current estimates are that about 50 per cent of the total amount lent to students to pay tuition fees will not be recovered and will be written off, £5.9 billion of loans to UK students need to be counted as public expenditure. The third conclusion is that some funding streams on which considerable emphasis is placed, for example gifts and endowments, contribute comparatively small amounts. Even fees paid by international students amount to slightly over 10 per cent of total income (although the proportion is much higher for some institutions). Finally, in financial terms the disparity between institutions is even greater than in terms of student numbers. UK higher education is truly a system comprising both giants and minnows.

Academic profession

The academic profession in the 21st century is very far from being the self-governing guild of cherished (and false?) memory. Possibly false, because it is important to remember that many of today's higher education teachers are employed by institutions that never had anything approaching academic guilds on the Oxbridge model, and also that many teachers and researchers on non-permanent contracts were never admitted to the guild, real or imagined. But there still remains a powerful nostalgia for a lost Arcadia of almost complete academic freedom and professional autonomy. That nostalgia has fed into a narrative of decline and fall that emphasises control, surveillance and casualisation, which in practice may be exaggerated.

In 2019–20 there were 223,245 members of academic staff in UK higher education institutions, up from 201,770 five years earlier (HESA, 2021c). The rate of increase has been slightly greater than the rate of increase among students. The shape of the academic profession remains relatively traditional, compared with, for example, the greater diversity of that profession in the US. But it is broadly similar to the pattern in most other European countries.

An example of this traditional structure is that the largest group in the profession comprises academics employed to carry out both teaching and research (44 per cent), a reflection on the preference of most universities for employing 'standard' academics, despite the diversity of institutional missions. However, as a proportion, the number of those on teaching-only and research-only contracts has tended to creep up. The number of full-time teaching-and-research staff in 2019–20 was fractionally lower than the year before, while the number of teaching-only staff increased year-on-year by almost 3,000. Despite the assertion that the academic profession is becoming increasingly casualised, the great majority of academics are still in salaried posts – 192,910, compared with 30,335 who are hourly paid. But 33 per cent are on fixed-term contracts.

Ten per cent of all academic staff (22,810) are professors, which is probably an underestimate because heads of department and other senior managers are not included. There continues to be a substantial gender disparity among senior academics which is being eroded only gradually. Less than a third

(28 per cent) of professors are women, although women make up almost half (48 per cent) of all academics. Female academics are also much more likely to work part time, and are concentrated in certain disciplines, such as subjects allied to medicine, and the traditional humanities and social sciences. The ethnicity balance is better. Three-quarters of academics are White. Asian staff are the next largest group (22,055), while only a small number are Black (4,725), a lower proportion than the proportion of Black students. Finally, almost a third of academics in UK higher education (31 per cent) are not from the UK, with the largest number coming from the EU. This demonstrates the heavy dependence of UK higher education on imported academic talent.

Governance and management

All UK higher education institutions are free-standing legal bodies that own their own buildings (and other forms of property including 'intellectual property'), employ their staff, make contracts and borrow money. This is in contrast (still) with many other European universities which, despite now having a high degree of operational autonomy (and academic freedom), are more constrained in legal terms; with many state universities in the US, which operate within similar constraints; and with public universities in many other parts of the world, where they are still incorporated legally within state bureaucracies.

The relative legal autonomy of UK institutions has given rise to a lively debate about how best to describe their status, with a few arguing that in reality they are private organisations. More widely they are often described as public, but not state, institutions. This implies two things: first, that they receive large sums of public money; second, that across a wide range of their activities they serve the public interest, or public good, even if they also engage in entrepreneurial or directly commercial activities. But their status as 'public' institutions in these two senses, and the limits of their legal autonomy, remain ambiguous. While UK universities are able to 'fail', and go into liquidation, because they are not underwritten or guaranteed by the state, they are treated as public bodies, and *de facto* state institutions, in other contexts, for example their obligations under Freedom of Information legislation.

The principal legal responsibility lies with governing bodies, councils or (in Scotland) courts. 'Pre-1992' English universities often have 'courts' too. But these courts are much more representative bodies encompassing local and regional leaders in industry, education and the professions. Although they may even be, in a strictly legal sense, the supreme bodies within universities, in practice their powers have been permanently delegated to councils. Another wrinkle is that in many, but not all, chartered universities their charters and articles of government reserve some powers, over academic strategy and scrutiny, to senates (or academic boards) under arrangements typically labelled 'shared governance'. In the case of HECs, 'post-1992' universities and colleges, all powers are possessed by their governing bodies. A few public universities are companies limited by guarantee, that is they have no shareholders. All public institutions are treated as charities, which confers on them significant financial benefits, but they are consequently subject to regulation by the Charity Commission. Private institutions, of course, may be commercial companies subject only to company law and registration requirements imposed, in England, by the Office for Students (OfS).

In HECs the size of governing bodies is limited to 24, although many now have fewer members. In chartered universities councils used to have more members, but now approximate in size to that of governing bodies in HECs. In both types of university, and in colleges, a majority of members on council/governing bodies are lay people, that is they come from outside the university although some may be alumni/ae. In the case of HECs these lay members are generally described as 'independent members' to distinguish them from staff or student members. The chair is always a lay member. Crucially, in both chartered universities and HECs, councils and governing bodies themselves select new lay or independent members, usually with the help of nominations committees, although their freedom of choice may be constrained by convention or determined by criteria they themselves have chosen. Councils and governing bodies operate through a series of familiar committees – audit, finance, employment, nominations, remuneration and so on. As always, two universities do not conform to this pattern. Oxford and Cambridge have very limited lay involvement in their formal governance.

A number of questions and issues have been raised about the formal governance of UK higher education institutions (Shattock and Horvath, 2020). The first is the independence of the council or governing body from the executive management, particularly with regard to the information on which they base their decisions. While in the US boards of regents and other state-wide coordinating bodies, and boards of trustees in individual universities, typically have their own staffs to service their needs, UK governing bodies rely on the institutions themselves (and, crucially, their senior managers) for administrative support. The head of the university administration usually acts as the secretary of the governing body, although some governing bodies have appointed outside lawyers to undertake that role, in an effort to achieve some 'distance'. Another, related, issue is the extent to which chairs of governing bodies and vice-chancellors should work together in close partnership. In one sense this is essential; in another it may create the potential either for a confusion of governance and management responsibilities, which should be kept separate, or for the effective exclusion of other, perhaps more independent or critical, members of the governing body.

The second issue is the extent to which governing bodies are representative both of their universities and their wider communities. As has already been pointed out, they largely choose their own members, which has led unkinder critics to label them self-perpetuating oligarchies. As a result, questions have been asked both about what constitutes adequate representation of the university community (some councils and governing bodies have reduced staff, although generally not student, representation to streamline their operation); and also about a lack of diversity among their members, particularly in terms of age, gender and ethnicity. Most members currently are aged over 55 and very predominantly White, although the gender balance is better with 40 per cent women (HESA, 2021b).

To be fair, most councils and governing bodies have made considerable efforts to recruit new members from a more diverse backgrounds, by developing clear criteria for appointment and through public advertisement. However, members are nearly always not paid, which has restricted the pool of available members. Also, in terms both of wider representation of the university community and of diversity of membership, a more fundamental question remains unresolved: is a university governing body a quasi-executive board, similar to the board of an NHS trust if not that a private company; or is it better regarded as a more representative and collegial body?

The third issue concerns the efficiency, and competence, of governing bodies. As has been described in an earlier chapter, there has been a shift in their role – from being bodies with largely fiduciary responsibilities to bodies that play a much more active part in developing strategy and assessing performance. To some degree, this shift of roles was inevitable, as universities became much larger and more complex organisations with much more heterogeneous missions and subject to much higher levels of external regulation and accountability. Most recently, the responsibility of governing bodies for (academic) 'quality', latent in the past, has been explicitly reaffirmed. It is no longer possible, even in chartered universities, for them in effect to subcontract that responsibility unconditionally to senates. Although this is perhaps the best example of a deficit in relevant expertise and competence, similar deficits have arisen across a range of other responsibilities. Once again, a more fundamental question is raised – do governing bodies play an active, strategic and at times even quasi-executive, role in addition to their oversight and fiduciary responsibilities; and, in either case, what is the threshold of knowledge and expertise necessary to be effective in discharging either these activist or more traditional roles?

Many efforts have been made to improve standards of governance in UK higher education. The CUC has developed a code by which it expects governing bodies to abide (CUC, 2020). Compliance with the CUC code has come close to being a standard requirement in the eyes of most regulators. The code represents best practice but, understandably perhaps, it starts from the premise that the basic structure of governance is sound. There have been few root-and-branch experiments in reconstructing university governance on a different basis, although a more radical approach has been taken in Scotland where the chairs of university courts are now expected to be elected (Von Prondzynski Report, 2012). Although the mode of election and the make-up of the electorate have yet to be authoritatively defined, however imperfect, this reform does highlight the democratic deficit at the heart of university governance. In addition, governing bodies are expected to undertake regular effectiveness reviews. These reviews have created a useful market for consultants but, again, are not usually designed to address more fundamental issues of legitimacy, representation and competence.

The second pillar of governance is provided by senates or academic boards. In the past senates were often regarded as an expression of the academic collegium. They had large membership, for example, in some chartered universities all professors were nominally members of senates, even if they rarely attended. When councils regarded their primary responsibilities as fiduciary, and consequently were relatively passive elements within governance structures, senates substituted as the primary focus, acting to some degree as academic 'parliaments'. Although some senates continue to aspire to a wider institutional strategic role, the day-to-day business of most is now largely focused on academic regulation such as the approval of new courses, course reviews and quality assurance, although they also play a part in approving some sub-strategies for learning and teaching or research. Their membership has also been curtailed, partly because they had been too unwieldy to operate effectively but also partly to reflect this narrower, more professionalised and less 'political' role.

In most chartered universities, senates have a formally assured place alongside councils in university governance. Governance is 'shared'. In HECs, in contrast, academic boards are only advisory to vice-chancellors. In the past the conventional assumption has been that chartered universities have senates while HECs have academic boards. But this nominal distinction has tended to become blurred. Some 'pre-1992' universities have always had academic boards, for example UCL and the London School of Economics; several 'post-1992' universities have relabelled their academic boards as senates (an innocent example of 'academic drift' perhaps). However, this distinction between chartered universities and HECs remains potentially important. In chartered universities, there have been example of major strategic initiatives, for example the establishment of overseas campuses, which have been blocked by senates despite the support of councils and senior managers, although there are other examples of senates, or academic boards, in chartered universities struggling to have their voice heard on key initiatives. But academic boards in HECs cannot overrule initiatives taken by the executive management, although vice-chancellors may be persuaded to modify policies if it is clear the bulk of academic opinion is opposed to them.

In day-to-day practice, senates in chartered universities and academic boards in HECs tend to operate in similar ways. With very few exceptions, vice-chancellors chair senates and academic boards in all institutions. Although they include members elected to represent academic staff in colleges, faculties and departments and also professional staff, they often have a majority of 'payroll' members, that is senior managers who are *ex officio* members. Senates and academic boards are also typically serviced by secretariats based in academic registries, which reflects the nature of most of their business but also raises the same issues about their access to information that has not been filtered by the executive management. In general, senates/academic boards have received limited policy attention. Although they too have been the subject of effectiveness reviews, typically this is not in their own right but as part of a wider review of university governance.

The third, and most powerful, pillar of governance is provided by executive management. Vice-chancellors, once the only full-time academic managers whose authority was as much symbolic as executive, are now buttressed by ranks of pro-vice-chancellors (PVCs). Most PVCs have become executive managers on permanent or long-term contracts rather than rotating part-time appointments. The number of PVCs has also substantially increased in most universities. They are responsible for areas such as learning and teaching, research and enterprise, and students. In some universities the role of PVCs is restricted to policy, and they chair the relevant university committees, but in an increasing number of institutions PVCs are also responsible for managing staff and budgets in their respective areas.

At the same time heads of college, faculty deans and heads of department are now also mainly appointed as full-time executive managers. This practice, once confined to 'post-1992' universities and colleges, has now become close to universal. As a result, a substantial class of full-time academic managers has now developed in the great majority of UK universities. Where once the general pattern of university management had been a form of quasi-cabinet government, supported by a civil service-style administration, now it is focused on executive boards or senior management teams composed of full-time academic and professional managers. The role of administrators is now to support the executive board, not to provide a civil service for the university community. Like the civil service, they are increasingly focused on delivery.

Critics argue that, in the words of the famous House of Commons resolution in 1780 on the power of the Crown, the power of vice-chancellors and other senior managers 'has increased, is increasing and ought to be diminished'. A particular object of scorn has been vice-chancellors' salaries, which are widely regarded not only by academic staff unions but also by most politicians as excessive. Although in substantial terms a trivial issue, in symbolic terms senior managers', and in particular vice-chancellors' salaries have acquired a deeper resonance. Resentment of these supposedly excessive executive reward packages may, indeed, have played a not insignificant role in universities' loss of political and public support, which is one element in the 'general crisis' that is the overall theme of this book. Wiser heads among vice-chancellors, of course, have recognised the value of restraint and forgone high salaries and generous pensions. Mindful of the painful contrast between their remuneration and the pay and conditions of most academic staff, they recognise how this issue has poisoned industrial relations inside universities and established the damaging stereotype of vice-chancellors as 'fat cats' more widely.

Excessive salaries for vice-chancellors and, more generally, the growth of a new senior management class are often called up as clinching evidence to support the charge that universities have abandoned the sunny uplands of 'collegiality' (an Arcadian myth, of course) and been bewitched by the dark forces of 'managerialism'. Another piece of evidence is the suggestion that universities have been especially open to the (poorly misunderstood and much exaggerated) 'new public management'. In fact, there are deeper structural reasons for the changing nature of executive management in universities than a self-interested enthusiasm for neoliberal ideology. By most standards, universities were under-managed in the past. Even by contemporary standards, they remain under-managed compared with, for example, the NHS. Also, most senior academic managers continue to define themselves as academics (and even aspire to be entered in the Research Excellence Framework (REF) as active researchers), while many US university presidents would be happy to define themselves as belonging to the 'administration' rather than the 'faculty'. For most senior university managers, apart from those in professional services such as finance and human resources, an academic career is a prerequisite. Remarkably few have come from a general management background. For better or worse, the senior management class is still deeply acculturated in academic ways.

But the main reasons for the growth of this class are: that institutions have become much larger and more heterogeneous; that the burden of external compliance requirements and accountability has sharply increased (and is going on increasing); and that mass higher education is now more deeply embedded in the fabric of society, the economy and culture, greatly increasing the number and intensity of interactions that must be managed. To say this is not to defend the self-importance of some university leaders. Overemphasising their role as 'chief executives' may reflect their insecurity about the power they exercise as much as their arrogance, and show evidence of weakness as much as strength. If changes need to be made to the executive management of UK universities in the 21st century, they are more likely to take the form of more open and democratic styles of leadership rather than a reversion to traditional, and largely mythical, ideas of a lost 'donnish dominion'.

Funding, 'steering' and regulation

Once again, higher education systems can be sorted into three broad types, this time in terms of whether their principal focus is on:

- **funding**, in cases where state grants have remained the primary source of income for universities, which continues to be true in much of Western and Southern Europe, Latin America, Africa and large parts of Asia;
- **'steering'**, the coordination of the activities of different sectors of higher education and the institutions within them, sometimes by legal and sometimes by less formal means; or
- **regulation**, the setting of rules and establishment of parameters within which institutions are allowed to operate (and the policing of these rules and parameters through more or less detailed accountability regimes).

Of course, all systems combine elements of all three – funding, 'steering' and regulation. The allocation of state funding to universities cannot be done without some form of 'steering' – the identification of desired outcomes, or of regulation – accountability for this funding. Equally, systems that focus on regulation necessarily involve some kind of 'steering', because no regulation can be context-free and agnostic as to desired outcomes; regulation-focused systems also often still allocate substantial elements of public funding, typically for research and student support.

Historically the UK university system was once an almost purely funding system, with very limited 'steering' (except in terms of the creation of new universities and more expensive capital development) and equally limited regulation in terms of accountability. As has been shown in earlier chapters, this rapidly changed from the 1960s onwards as the University Grants Committee (UGC) took to publishing letters of guidance (and governments published White Papers on higher education) and university accounts were opened to greater scrutiny. In the two decades between the late 1980s and the late 2000s the UK system, now extended to cover all higher education, was very much a system focused on 'steering', as HEFCE in particular attempted to shape, if not directly plan, the system. Since 2010, in England at any rate, the system has become increasingly focused on regulation. But both the OfS and Research England have retained substantial responsibilities for funding, and since the onset of the COVID-19 pandemic the OfS has acquired a new appetite for 'steering' in terms of a perceived need to 'restructure' the system to cope with the challenges posed by the pandemic – an appetite that history suggests is unlikely to be lost when more normal conditions return. In addition, the UK government has added new responsibilities on the OfS to carry out greater surveillance of English institutions, which will be discussed further in Chapter 8.

However, it may be misleading to focus too much on the OfS at the expense of other elements in complex systemic architecture of UK higher education. This architecture is complex, with at least four levels.

UK and devolved administrations

The first level comprises Departments in the UK, the Scottish and the Welsh governments, and in the Northern Ireland Executive. The division of responsibilities between these different governments is itself complex, and not always coherent because of the incomplete state of the arrangements for devolution in the UK. For example, the research councils are UK-wide bodies, but the allocation of QR (quality-related research), or core research, funding is the responsibility of the four separate UK nations. This explains why UK Research and Innovation (UKRI), which oversees the research councils as a successor to earlier coordinating bodies going back to the Advisory Board for the Research Councils (ABRC), has had to create within it a special-purpose body, Research England, to distribute QR funding to English institutions.

To add to the complexity, unlike the Higher Education Funding Council for England (HEFCE), the OfS is not responsible for research funding; hence the need to establish Research England. But the Scottish Funding Council (SFC) and the Higher Education Funding Council for Wales (HEFCW) continue to give their institutions block grants comprising both teaching and research allocations. Other UK Departments also have responsibility for key aspects of higher education across the UK. The Treasury has a direct role in setting overall funding levels for the research councils through the UKRI, and an indirect role in determining the total funding available to the devolved administrations through the application of the Barnett formula (devised in the 1970s to determine their shares of UK-generated taxation). Visa and immigration policies are set by the Home Office which directly impact on the recruitment of international students (and employment of non-UK academic staff). Other UK Departments – for example, the Foreign Office or the Ministry of Defence – have more shadowy but important roles.

Clearly, a lot of 'steering' is taking place, although it is rarely joined up. The UK government itself does not appear to have a comprehensive strategy that extends across higher education, research and innovation.

Two separate Departments – for Education and for Business, Energy and Industrial Strategy – share direct responsibility as parents of the OfS and UKRI, respectively. But it is far from clear that any sustained attempts have been made across the UK government to coordinate policies that impact on higher education and research, except on a 'needs must' basis. In contrast, both the Scottish and Welsh governments have developed systematic strategies for higher education. The latter, in particular, has been active in promoting institutional mergers.

Intermediate public agencies

The second level comprises intermediate public agencies. In England these are the OfS and the UKRI, both established under the Higher Education and Research Act 2017. The title of the OfS describes its role. It is an 'Office' because it is a regulator like the other 'Of-' bodies that now litter the UK bureaucratic landscape; and its title highlights 'Students' (not, for example, higher education) because its primary focus is on the needs of customers, which is how students are regarded in the new English higher education quasi-market. It no longer has any formal responsibility for looking after the interests of institutions, which was a major responsibility of the HEFCE (and its antecedent bodies, the UFC and PCFC, and the UGC and NAB). Of course, it is more complicated in practice. First, it is impossible to safeguard the interests of students/customers without accepting some responsibility for safeguarding institutions, at least to the limited extent of ensuring that students are looked after in the case of institutional collapses. Secondly, the OfS continues to allocate several billions of pounds of public money to institutions and, as a result, it has a responsibility to ensure that that money is spent for the intended purposes (and, of course, according to agreed policies, which clearly involves a significant degree of 'steering'). Arguably, providing funding for institutions which it also regulates represents a conflict of interest at the heart of the OfS's mission. When the fact that institutions also receive even more substantial income from state-regulated (and, initially, state-funded) fees is also taken into account, the lines of responsibility and accountability become even more confused.

The UKRI is a more straightforward body, apart from its anomalous appendage Research England. In effect, it is a holding company for the research councils and some other bodies such as Innovate UK, although that label may understate its strategic role. The extent to which the additional bureaucratic burden it represents is compensated for by its successful coordination of its constituent councils is not yet clear. In Scotland and (for now) in Wales, conventional funding councils have been retained which continue to make block grants to institutions. Both also continue to operate according to some form of the arm's-length principle. In Scotland funding allocations are informed by outcome agreements between institutions and the SFC which, it has been suggested, are both too detailed and too 'light touch'. In response to such suggestions the Scottish government has argued that these agreements need to be 'intensified'. In Wales the relatively small scale of the system has sometimes made it difficult to distinguish clearly between the role of the HECFW and that of the Welsh Government itself which, as has already been said, has been active in promoting mergers between smaller institutions to promote greater sustainability.

In both Scotland and Wales the scope of these intermediate agencies has been different from in England. Although the OfS regulates and funds further education colleges that are also higher education providers, it has no responsibility for further education as a whole. The demarcation between higher education and further education has been preserved. In Scotland the SFC funds both higher education institutions and colleges (lower-level further education as well as higher education courses), although it has retained separate systems of funding and regulation for higher education and for further education. In Wales the government has given serious consideration to establishing a single body to oversee the whole of tertiary education.

A further layer of complexity, and potential confusion, is added when some of the major policy interventions deployed by intermediate agencies are considered. The most significant, perhaps, is the Research Excellence Framework (REF), which has had more impact on the behaviour (if not the shape) of UK higher education institutions than any other policy intervention. The very first version of a formal research selectivity exercise was undertaken in the 1980s by the UGC, a UK-wide body, although it applied only to the traditional, that is 'pre-1992', universities. Today the REF remains a UK-wide exercise, now extended to all higher education institutions. But it is jointly managed by the devolved agencies, Research England, the SFC and HEFCW. Although the assessment by expert panels is based on UK-wide criteria and produces common 'scores', the weight attached to these 'scores' with regard to QR funding allocations is determined by each of these agencies, leading to a significant divergence of outcomes. In contrast, the Teaching Excellence and Student Outcomes Framework (TEF) is solely an English policy instrument because it is primarily designed to enable applicants to make informed choices, and the stimulation of good practice in learning and teaching is a secondary objective. But institutions in Scotland and Wales are free to submit to evaluation to obtain a TEF 'score', and many do. The TEF is now to be simplified, in effect downgraded, in a decision taken by the UK Government for English higher education, which will be discussed further in Chapter 8.

Other agencies

The third level of systemic architecture comprises other agencies, many of which are 'sector agencies' because in terms of their governance they are 'owned' by the sector, even though they may have important public responsibilities, and even regulatory responsibilities. They include the Higher Education Statistics Agency (HESA), a recognised national statistical authority despite being owned by the sector (although government departments and intermediate public agencies have a privileged status as 'statutory customers'). Although its work is entirely neutral and uncontentious, HESA nevertheless provides much of the data on which more controversial activities such as generating key performance indicators or constructing league tables and rankings are based.

A second, also relatively uncontentious, agency is Advance HE, formed by a merger between the former Higher Education Academy (HEA), which promoted good practice in learning and teaching (and offered an accreditation scheme for individual teachers), and the Leadership Foundation for Higher Education (originally conceived as a kind of Civil Service College for university leaders). Other agencies include the University and College Admissions Service (UCAS), which manages centralised admissions (and has also begun gently to intervene in wider policy issues) and the University and College Employers Agency (UCEA), which represents institutions in collective bargaining over salaries and conditions for many of their employers. In another example of the informality of many relationships that characterises the UK higher education system, individual institutions are not bound to implement agreements made by the UCEA on their behalf, and the extent to which the UCEA is empowered to agree changes in conditions of employment, as opposed to salary levels, has never been fully clarified.

However, the most significant agency is the Quality Assurance Agency (QAA). The QAA is contracted by the intermediate public agencies to assure on their behalf the academic quality of UK higher education, a crucial and powerful role within a more extended system. The QAA has two grandparents: the Council for National Academic Awards (CNAA), the body established in the 1960s and responsible for awarding degrees in the polytechnics and colleges; and the Academic Audit Unit (AAU), the traditional universities' first faltering attempt to promote sector-wide academic standards, established a decade later. The QAA's parent was the Higher Education Quality Council (HEQC), established in the 1990s. The QAA had adopted a bewildering variety of instruments to undertake its work – initially detailed subject, or Teaching Quality Assessment (TQA), reviews, and more recently whole-institution audits. In England its work remains focused on quasi-inspectorial quality assurance, while in Scotland it has shifted to more collegially inspired quality enhancement. But, despite these differences over time and space, the QAA has successfully surfed the 'quality wave' that has swept up most national higher education systems. Today it still occupies a pivotal role, in effect acting as the gatekeeper for the granting of teaching and degree-awarding powers. But the emphasis on 'customer information', especially in England, and increasing use of metrics to assess performance and standards (entering grades, continuation rates and graduate outcomes) may hint at its longer-term decline.

Sector and interest groups

The fourth level of systemic architecture is provided by a wide variety of other agencies and organisations, which fall into five main groups:

- **representative bodies** like UUK, the CUC and Guild HE, and also the 'mission groups', which have already been discussed in terms of their claims to represent a stratification of the system or differentiation of institutional missions;
- **scholarly and learned societies**, for example the Royal Society and British Academy, both of which have important policy and even (minor) funding roles, but also a wide variety of subject associations, which play an important role in the identification of academic merit and reputation;
- **professional bodies**, such as the Law Society and the Bar Council (or Faculty of Advocates in Scotland), the individual Royal Colleges in Medicine, and the engineering institutions, and also other state regulators which license members of key professions;
- **charities**, some of which, like the Wellcome or the Leverhulme Trusts, are important founders of university research;
- **trade unions**, such as the University and College Union (UCU), which represents most academic (and senior professional) staff in higher and further education, and also a flock of think-tanks and research institutes, such as the Higher Education Policy Institute (HEPI), management consultants, and lobbyists of all kinds.

This complexity of government departments (UK and devolved administrations), intermediate public agencies, other agencies and other groups and organisations is a prominent feature of the systemic architecture of UK higher education today. This fragmentation even raises an important question – to what extent is it possible to talk of a UK 'system' (not simply in the sense that individual institutions have very different missions but in the context of its systemic disorganisation)? It has also produced a confused landscape of policy commonalities, policy borrowings and policy divergences. It even casts doubt on the usefulness of the typology of higher education systems – focused on funding, 'steering' or regulation – outlined at the start of this section.

Teaching and research

The 'core business' of higher education, a regrettable but now inevitable label, is teaching and research. Too often, it is simply taken for granted, or as a given, in discussions of the development of higher education systems. Instead, these discussions are absorbed by issues of structure, governance and management, and funding. Of course, it should be the other way round. The waxing and waning of disciplines, changes within subjects, new ways of teaching, trends in research – these are the engines of change in UK higher education. Any account of contemporary higher education has at least to acknowledge the importance of learning and teaching and of research. The last section of this chapter aims to do that, but only in the most sketchy and provisional manner.

The academic landscape

As has already been said, the most popular subjects in UK higher education are now vocational and professional subjects (HESA, 2021a). The most popular subject among all students, and among male students, is business and administration studies (413,000); the most popular among female students are those subjects allied to medicine (healthcare disciplines including nursing) (296,000). These two subject groups – the first practice-oriented and vocational and the second specifically professional – make up more than a quarter of all students (28 per cent). Elements of business and management education, barely recognised as a university discipline in 1960, also pervade a wide number of other applied subjects, many of which do have an important 'management' or 'enterprise' strands. Nursing and healthcare, although hardly new in terms of education and training, were only incorporated into higher education from the 1980s onwards. Both have naturally developed substantial research presences to match their weight in terms of student numbers.

However, the academic landscape has not simply been transformed by the growth or incorporation of new, generally vocational, subjects. All subjects, even the most academic and traditional, are in a state of constant flux – partly as a result of the evolution of scholarship and research, and partly in response to changes in wider society, the economy and more broadly intellectual culture. For example, history has been deeply influenced by several other disciplines, notably social sciences such as anthropology but also more exact sciences such as demography or climate science. At the same time, the changing status of women in society, and feminism as an intellectual or ideological analogue, and new attitudes to Black and other minority ethnic groups, and intellectual movements such as post-colonial or Black studies, have deeply influenced priorities within history as a discipline. In law, traditional forms of jurisprudence have been complemented, even rivalled, by new interests in social aspects of justice. In economics, econometricians, once dominant, now confront new rivals espousing alternative approaches to the discipline, sometimes a resurgence of Keynesian ideas, at other times in more radicalised forms. Engineering has been deeply penetrated by legal and environmental themes. And so it goes on ... There is no discipline taught or researched in the contemporary university that is not in a state of almost permanent ferment or constant movement. It is this ferment and movement that are the true drivers of change in 21st-century higher education.

Learning and teaching

Generalisations about the major characteristics of learning and teaching culture(s) and practices of UK higher education have always been difficult to make – and, at first sight, may have become even less credible. One of the most striking features of mass higher education, alongside the explosive growth of student numbers and the diversity of types of institution (and their missions), is that it has appeared to reinforce the separateness of 'academic tribes', which has always been pronounced. Once, despite their differences, these tribes appeared to be bound together by allegiance to a shared academic culture, which in turn provided a normative framework for thinking about the purposes of a university education. One component of that culture was a broad commitment to critical and scientific enquiry, often uncontaminated by considerations of immediate social or economic utility. Another less attractive component was the acceptance of a degree of academic (and social?) elitism. Both have been eroded by the development of mass higher education, to the extent perhaps that any sense of a shared academic culture has become difficult to sustain.

On the other hand, it can be argued that, because learning and teaching practices may also have tended to be extracted from their disciplinary cultures, some more generic characteristics have developed. Subjects as different as the traditional humanities and the vocational social studies or engineering and technology, which have little in common in terms of their intellectual norms, nevertheless may have adopted similar approaches to how the curriculum and teaching should be organised and perhaps even how progress and achievement should be assessed. As a result, although still a hazardous ambition, some generic trends in learning and teaching in contemporary higher education can be identified. These trends include:

- a shift towards what might be termed 'practice-based learning' – for example, problem-solving, project work, study placements – with less emphasis being placed on traditional forms of pedagogy. A parallel shift may also have taken place in how students' work should be assessed. In part, these shifts reflect the respective weight of subjects across higher education, and the preponderance of applied and vocational subjects. But they also reflect the widespread infiltration of applied elements into more traditional academic subjects. Another aspect is the increasing emphasis on employability skills, either embedded in courses or as standalone components of student learning;
- the growing popularity of 'active' learning on the part of students. Of course, informal peer learning has always been a feature of university study. In traditional universities it was always supposed that students were 'reading' for a degree, which implied a high degree of self-study rather than simply being 'taught'. But the shift from teaching to learning has not simply been a nominal one. Many subjects now employ techniques such as joint presentations as both a learning and assessment tool. Students themselves are more active in helping to shape the curriculum – or, by critiquing traditional authority (male, White, middle class, Eurocentric, elitist …), challenge it;
- a shift towards multi-disciplinary courses and, even more frequently, towards plurality within apparently single-discipline subjects. Although the number of students on combined subject courses has not increased disproportionately, and by some measures may even have declined, many of the applied and vocational subjects that now predominate are themselves inherently pluri-disciplinary. Their content is not so much determined by any 'inner' logic of cognitive coherence but defined broadly in terms of social, economic and culture change and specifically in terms of professional and occupational categories;
- a further shift, which has been produced by the impact of new information technologies on student learning. For at least a generation, learning management systems with curated links, online material and chatrooms have played a key role in the teaching of most subjects. Student learning has become partially detached from the constraints of time and space. Now the widespread use of social media has further radicalised this shift. All student learning today is to some extent 'blended', combining online and face-to-face teaching. A powerful effect of technology has been to encourage a more homogeneous approach to designing not just learning and teaching and assessment but also the organisation of the curriculum;
- the systematisation and professionalisation of learning and teaching in higher education institutions, evidenced by a proliferation of new role-labels (directors, leaders, coordinators …) and of dedicated units. The organisation of the curriculum, and how it is delivered and assessed, are

no longer essentially private matters locked in the 'secret gardens' guided by academic disciplines. Instead, they are governed by general principles that apply across all disciplines. Academic staff are also now expected to be 'trained to teach', another indicator of their professionalisation as teachers as well as being members of 'academic tribes';
- a final, and closely related, generic shift produced by the greater need to manage learning and teaching in a mass system. The objectives of courses, and their desired learning outcomes and assessment criteria, now have to be explicitly identified. Students themselves increasingly expect such transparency. Institutional managers use these to manage the performance of academic staff, not least to satisfy the requirements of external accountability instruments such as the TEF. And these objectives, outcomes and criteria, although they may differ in detail, must have sufficient commonality to allow for this transparency and accountability.

Research

The character of research has been shaped by both internal structural and external forces – both by the evolution of the cognitive cores of disciplines briefly alluded to earlier in this section; and by the organisational forms taken by research, such as changing career patterns among researchers, new strategies and priorities both at national and institutional levels, stricter assessment regimes and more formal hierarchies of reputation. At a conceptual level, various attempts have been made to describe this dynamic. One example has been the attempt to frame academic-scientific change, economic (and business) needs and political imperatives within a so-called 'triple helix' (Etzkowitz and Leydesdorff, 1997). A second has been the argument that traditional forms of scientific and scholarly enquiry, largely determined and policed by scientific and scholarly communities ('Mode 1'), are being complemented, and occasionally superseded, by more open and distributed, reflexive and contextualised, forms of knowledge production ('Mode 2') (Gibbons et al, 1994). Inevitably, in later work the 'triple helix' has acquired a fourth, or even fifth, strand, while new 'modes' have been added. These conceptualisations, however open to critique (and even demolition), are interesting because they highlight the urge to make sense of an increasingly complex research environment.

Part of that complexity has been produced by the internal dynamics of disciplines and by the proliferation of new subjects in the contemporary university with contrasting cognitive structures. This volatility and heterogeneity have led to new organisational challenges. Part has been produced by the large-scale increase in the volume of research activity. The development of mass higher education systems, with much larger number of students and staff, has generated this increase in volume. As a result, their research capacity of contemporary mass higher education systems far outweighs that of the elite university systems of the past. Most academic staff in UK higher education still have contracts requiring them to both teach and research. Many of those on teaching-only contracts also aspire to, and do, engage in research, through their active choice but also because it may be required if they hope to secure permanent academic employment. The system's research capacity has been further increased by the more than 50,000 academic staff on research-only contracts, who do much of the heavy lifting in key scientific disciplines. More academic staff means more research outputs. To a significant extent, research productivity is driven by these numbers.

Two characteristics of the UK higher education system have intensified this general effect that has influenced the development of all systems. First, the bulk of research is concentrated in higher education institutions, with independent research institutes playing a much smaller role than in many other countries such as France and Germany. As a result, teaching and research careers are more closely coupled. Second, UK higher education is a unified rather than a dual system, which has encouraged the spread of research practice across the whole system rather than restricting it to the elite segment.

But part of the complexity has also been produced by attempts to steer research priorities, and to assess research not simply in terms of scientific quality but also of its 'impact'. Although all higher education and research systems aim to 'pick winners' and create sustainable centres-of-excellence, these attempts have been pursued with exceptional vigour in the UK. They have become pervasive at all levels:

- For **individuals**, the quality and productivity of their research are managed to maximise departmental (and institutional) reputation (and funding).
- **Institutions** compete for reputational advantage through the REF, seeking to increase their core and external research funding, and also compete in the 'bragging' competition encouraged by global league tables.
- **Nations, and supra-national groupings** such as the EU, develop research and innovation strategies, which they link explicitly to hopes for faster economic growth and enhanced well-being.

At every level, profound behavioural changes and significant organisational adjustments have been made which are still poorly understood. Viewed through one lens, these behavioural changes and organisational adjustments have been a success, strengthening the position of the UK in key scientific fields (at any rate as measured in global rankings); viewed through another lens, they have distorted the natural evolution of disciplines, stifled their natural creativity and in the long term may have weakened their capacity for innovation. There is a serious danger of 'over-trading', not simply in the usual sense of pursuing unsustainable funding strategies but in the deeper sense of denying individuals, and research teams, the creative space they need.

The changing academic landscape is the fundamental condition of institutional and systemic change. The permanent revolution in disciplinary structures (and cultures), the emergence of new intellectual and scientific agendas (produced in part by this permanent revolution and in part by wider social, cultural and economic forces) and the development of more open research systems with multiple participants and stakeholders – these have all influenced, and are aspects of, that changing academic landscape. But in the case of UK higher education these naturally occurring and dynamic changes have been mediated through two processes. The first has been the systematisation and professionalisation of student learning and teaching. The second has been more assertive, and top-down, efforts to manage research priorities and performance. Both processes have been shaped and policed by a more aggressive use of elaborate assessment instruments than is typical in many other higher education systems. There is clearly a risk that both these processes, despite their appearance as neutral and technocratic interventions, in practice embody beliefs about values such as excellence and competition that are, and should be, sharply contested.

6

A further gaze

So far this book has focused on the UK. But higher education in the UK system is not exceptional. It shares many features with other Northern and Western European higher education systems, notably in Scandinavia and the Netherlands. The paradox of Brexit is that it has come at a time when the UK and other European systems have been converging rather than diverging, despite the belief (boast?) that England's high-fees experiment represents a radical rupture from the general European model of state-funded free-tuition higher education. Nor has this convergence been all been one way, from the rest of Europe towards the UK, as some believe. A better way to describe it may be as a shared effort to build a common European higher education (and, in particular, research) space.

The influence of the US higher education system remains powerful. That influence is expressed in conceptual terms; the world's first mass system inevitably produced some of the most influential conceptualisations of mass higher education, through the work of Martin Trow, Burton Clark and others. It is also expressed in terms of personal connections and experience, particularly in terms of traffic between elite universities. Anglophone solidarity, however frayed and diminished, still counts, implying there are greater social, cultural and political affinities between the UK and the US than with the rest of Europe, despite compelling contrary evidence. Post-imperial and post-colonial relationships with both 'old' and 'new' Commonwealth countries, although no longer subordinate or deferential, also remain important. As a result of these multiple interactions between the UK and other world systems many of the characteristics of, trends within and challenges to UK higher education are shared with many other higher education systems.

Nevertheless, it is important to raise our sights beyond the UK. This chapter is an attempt to offer, an inevitably brief and sketchy, comparative gaze. It is divided into three main sections. First, the shape and trajectories of global higher education are considered. Mass higher education, after all, is a global phenomenon, active in every country and on every continent. The second section focuses on the process of internationalisation in its various aspects: flows of ideas, of staff, of students and of reputation. The third, and longest, section discusses in more detail three world regions: Europe (including, of course, the UK); North America, in particular the US; and East Asia, the home of so-called 'Confucian' higher education systems. The choice of these three regions, by implication if not intention, suggests they are the most dynamic in terms of the development of 21st-century higher education.

But a note of caution. At the start of the period covered by this book the academic world seemed to be unipolar not tripolar, with the US system regarded as the exemplar for all to follow, although in the chapter in the Robbins Report on non-UK systems the former Soviet Union was also considered in that brief post-Sputnik dawn of reformed communism. Few people then believed that other European systems had much to offer as organisational models, despite their acknowledged eminence in science and scholarship. Higher education in East Asia was still largely seen through post-colonial eyes, and not even post-colonial in the case of Hong Kong, which remained a UK colony until the end of the 20th century. A possible exception was Japan, but it was still sullied by wartime memories. So it is by no means impossible that by the middle of this century this tripolar world of Europe, North America and East Asia could appear equally anachronistic, with new centres of influence and excellence developing in other parts of the world – Latin America perhaps or Africa, the continent with the fastest population growth.

Global higher education

Reporting international data is difficult, especially so in the form of comparisons across countries and over time, even when standardised definitions are used. So, a simple question like 'How many higher education students are there in the world?' can be tricky to answer. Higher education is typically included in the wider category of 'tertiary education' in OECD and World Bank statistics. The World Bank's count of tertiary education students was 224 million in 2018. UNESCO statistics, quoted in a study by Angel Calderon of the Royal Melbourne Institute of Technology (RMIT) published in 2018, counted 214 million students in 2015. The broad picture is clear. The number of students has doubled since 2000. Calderon projected a total of 377 million by 2030 and a staggering 594 million by 2040 (Calderon, 2018). If this projection is correct, the growth in the number of students will be even faster in the first four decades of the 21st century than it was between 1970 and 2000, the age that supposedly saw the development of mass higher education. Despite the projected increase in the world's population, the proportion with a college degree is expected to increase from 7 per cent to more than 10 per cent.

The total annual production of tertiary education graduates has also rapidly increased. According to UNESCO, top comes China (12.9 million) followed by India (8.4 million). The UK is ninth with 755,000 tertiary education graduates. Another way to measure the scale of impact of this rapid growth since 2000 is to compare the number of people in a defined age group who have completed tertiary education, defined by OECD as the 'highest level of education', with the total number of people in that age group. As a result of the historical pattern of expansion, the proportion is highest in the youngest age group and progressively declines with older age groups. The most recent statistics from OECD show that the average percentage of 25- to 34-year-olds who have completed tertiary education among OECD countries is 44.5 per cent (OECD, 2019, 2020). At the top comes South Korea (69.6 per cent) with Canada and Japan next (both just over 60 per cent). The proportion in the UK is a fraction over half (50.8 per cent), ahead of the US with 49.4 per cent.

The bulk of future expansion will inevitably take place in countries still with comparatively low overall participation rates, notably in Africa and some countries in Asia. Other Asian systems, notably South Korea, are already high-participation systems with little room for further growth in student numbers. Most systems in Europe, Australasia and even North America are mid- to high-participation systems, with limited room for further growth. Of course, these mature systems still have considerable room for growth at postgraduate level. But most of the expansion at undergraduate level will take place in the less mature higher education systems. A small part of that growth will be siphoned off into more mature systems, especially those currently with comparatively small numbers of international students (principally in East Asia, although geopolitical, cultural and language barriers may act as inhibiting factors), which explains the even more explosive growth projections for internationally mobile students. But most of the growth will have to take place 'at home'. The result is likely to be a fundamental rebalancing of global higher education, along the lines suggested in the introduction to this chapter.

Internationalisation

At first sight, the focus on internationally mobile students is puzzling. Although, as for all tertiary education students, their number has doubled since 2000, it is still only 5.3 million. Why should such a small fraction of students attract so much attention? One reason, of course, is that counting internationally mobile students is also problematical. For obvious reasons, the count is determined by national boundaries, which do not always correspond to language and cultural zones. For example, many of the 'international' students in Russia are students from former Soviet republics (in particular, the Central Asian republics, but also Ukraine) who before 1990 would have been regarded as national students. In several of these countries Russian is widely spoken and remains the 'metropolitan' or elite language. A more extreme example is Luxembourg, which has an exceptionally high proportion of incoming and outgoing students, even though many may live within commuting distance.

A second reason is that the expansion of mixed modes of study ('at home' and 'abroad'), institutional partnerships (such as two-plus-two course arrangements), blended learning (online and on-campus) and in-country branch campuses have also made counting internationally mobile students increasingly difficult. Some counts exclude 'study abroad' students, because they continue to be registered by their home institutions, and some exchange students, which may be a particular issue within Europe. To some degree, the focus on physical mobility is also restricting. A student following an online course at a foreign university may be receiving more of an 'international' experience than a student on a foreign campus but surrounded by a large number of compatriots in a *de facto* enclave Both these reasons suggest that the available data on international students may be an underestimate.

However, there are three more substantial reasons that explain what appears at first sight an excessive focus on international students. The first is that flows of international students often serve as a proxy for wider internationalisation, when staff mobility (whether early-career researchers or senior scholars and scientists), international research collaboration (of which academic tourism is only a small element) and even global alliances of like-minded universities may be more important. To rank nations, or institutions, in terms of their shares of international students is at best a crude measure of their degree of internationalisation in this wider sense. The second substantial reason is that both the presence of international students and internationalisation in this wider sense have important strategic, geopolitical and 'soft power' dimensions. For institutions in importing countries, they confer significant reputational advantages and financial gains, and also enhance their research productivity and performance. And for individuals in 'exporting' countries, whether members of traditional (and new) elites or of the expanding middle classes, study abroad confers both social and cultural prestige and advantages in the employment market.

The third substantial reason is that the internationalisation of higher education is only one component of a wider process of globalisation. This process is reflected in the growing importance of international organisations and associations (from the United Nations to FIFA); of international companies, the formal domicile of which is dictated by pragmatic reasons concerning legal and regulatory framework and tax advantages rather than any sense of national rootedness; of global divisions of labour and worldwide just-in-time supply chains; and of global consumption of mass media, producing hybrid cultures that blend native and cosmopolitan elements. Seen through this lens, internationally global students often become globally mobile elites. As a result, the loud resonance of the internationalisation of higher education is simply re-echoing these wider movements.

In 2019 more than four out of five international students were enrolled in universities in G20 countries. Eight countries recruited three-quarters of all internationally mobile students. Top (still) comes the US with 1.1 million, although during the 2010s that number first stabilised and then, while Donald Trump was US president, fell slightly. Next comes the UK, with fractionally under half a million, although that too was a slight fall on the previous year and represents a declining market share. Third – surprisingly, perhaps – is China, because it is also the highest-volume exporter of international students. The others are Australia, France, Germany, Canada and Russia. Overall, almost half (48 per cent) of international students are studying in Europe, followed by the US with a fifth (21 per cent).

The number of countries from which international students come is almost as limited. China and India head the list. Other Asian countries, too, notably Korea, Malaysia and Hong Kong, are important sources. The US is also a major exporter of students, although some are 'study abroad' and exchange students. More detailed examination of international students flows demonstrate the importance of geopolitical considerations and cultural affinities. Three quarters of international students in Russia, as has already been mentioned, come from Kazakhstan, Uzbekistan, Turkmenistan and Ukraine. Much the largest number of international students in Poland come from Ukraine (the western part as opposed to the Russophone east). In France students from Morocco and Algeria make up almost half the total. In the UK India, Hong Kong and Malaysia are among the largest sources of international students.

This analysis raises a number of questions for the future. The first is the direct impact of the COVID-19 pandemic, which has at least the potential to disrupt the pattern of internationalisation, scale and distribution that has developed over the past half century. In the short run, travel restrictions will have a serious impact. Over the longer term, fundamental behavioural changes may reshape flows of international students and staff. It has been suggested that one effect of the pandemic might be to encourage mobility in the 'near abroad' (to adopt the rather menacing phrase sometimes used by those who regret the demise of the former Soviet Union) and discourage longer intercontinental travel. Others, perhaps on securer ground, have argued that virtual mobility might feature more prominently in national, and institutional, strategies for internationalisation in the future. On the other hand, the impact of the pandemic could be short-lived, with existing patterns and trends reasserting themselves within a few years.

The second question concerns the post-pandemic state of the global economy. In the short run, a major recession on a scale not seen since the 1930s (although possibly of shorter duration) is inevitable. The market for highly skilled labour is likely to be disrupted, with important implications for graduate employment. In the longer term, it is possible that significant changes in economic policy, such as a revived respect for the role of the state as opposed to the free market and also measures to build in greater resilience, will take place, which could lead to the process of globalisation (of which the internationalisation of higher education is a component) being viewed in a more critical light. Such speculation provokes an important question – whether the projected rates of growth in the number of international students will need to be substantially revised – downwards. The safest answer is probably that they may have to be trimmed, if only because some already appeared to be extravagant and over-ambitious.

A third question is whether the current pattern of importers and exporters of international students is likely to survive, whatever the longer-term impact of the pandemic. Is it likely by the middle of the century, or even by the end of the decade, that international student recruitment will continue to be dominated by the G7 nations, and that East Asia will remain the major source of international students? China is already an important destination for international students, and it is difficult to imagine it will continue to be such a large-scale exporter. China has already embarked on an impressive programme of university building. Post-imperial links may also weaken still further as the century progresses, which might erode the positions of France and the UK as favourite destinations for international students. The UK could suffer disproportionately because post-Brexit nationalism (and xenophobia) might appear to have created a less welcoming environment.

On the larger canvas of internationalisation similar trends are also likely. The centre of gravity of the global economy will continue to shift from the North Atlantic world to the East Asian world. Left unchecked, geopolitical tensions could increase if a new 'cold war' develops between China and the US (with Australia and the UK in tow). China, South Korea, Hong Kong, Taiwan, Malaysia and Singapore have already followed Japan to develop centres of research excellence, and these can only expand. Increasing opposition to 'elite' knowledge traditions in the US and Europe may undermine the prestige of Western scholarship in some key disciplines on the wider world stage, although it is also possible to argue that multiculturalism at home could actually strengthen internationalisation by making these host countries more welcoming environments. The links once almost universally assumed between modernisation – the development of advanced economies and structural reforms – and modernity – the values developed following the Enlightenment (principally in Western Europe and America) – have frayed, perhaps beyond repair. In the light of all these trends the most plausible scenario, therefore, is of a significant rebalancing of both staff and student flows around the world.

Key to understanding the likely future scale, and patterns, of international student flows is a careful assessment of motives and drivers. As has already been said, some factors will continue to favour the currently dominant shares of international students enjoyed by a small number of – Western – countries. For example, the demand for higher education among the growing middle class in many countries once labelled 'developing' will continue to outstrip efforts to increase capacity within national higher education systems – although perhaps by a decreasing margin. Their increasing wealth, and desire to access university brands that continue to command prestige, will continue to make studying in a Western university attractive – but, once again, by a decreasing margin as 'world-class' universities develop in other world regions.

But there will be countervailing forces that tend to erode Western universities' current dominance. All countries will intensify their efforts to develop high-tech knowledge-based economies, placing growing emphasis on the strength of their higher education and research systems. But the consequent transformation of a community of world science and scholarship, built on principles of universalism and altruism, into an arena in which countries compete for technological supremacy and economic advantage will inevitably lead to far-reaching changes in how the internationalisation of higher education is perceived. At an institutional level it seems likely that individual universities' stake in internationalisation – numbers and shares of international students, staff, research collaboration and research networks – will continue to be a mark of prestige. But, once again, the increasing popularity, and impact, of global rankings (in which internationalisation is typically a key element) has intensified competition, and over time is likely also to produce greater volatility. If world regions outside North America and Western Europe are successful in developing more of their own 'world-class' universities, this will inevitably disturb the current balance of prestige.

The incentive of universities in the North Atlantic world to import academic and scientific talent will continue to be strong. Their scientific success depends crucially on 'brain drain' from other countries. This dependence could only decrease if the production of home-grown researchers were to be substantially increased. But this seems unlikely because of the comparative attractions (and rewards) of academic and scientific careers and other high-status jobs. A more homogeneous scientific workforce could be counterproductive in terms of both creativity and productivity. But, if demand will remain strong, the same cannot necessarily be said of supply, which will be influenced by geopolitical considerations and economic rivalry, as well as the need to strengthen higher education and research capacity in countries that have been the source of many academic staff and researchers in Western universities.

Higher education outside the UK

The final, and most substantial, section of this chapter considers the development of higher education outside the UK. It focuses on three world regions – North America, with particular emphasis on the US; Europe, which of course includes the UK; and East Asia, widely regarded as the most dynamic region outside the North Atlantic world in terms of the development of higher education (and in many other respects, not least economic development and technological advance).

But, before embarking on consideration of these three regions, two preliminary comments are necessary. The first is an apology and an explanation. Major developments have taken place outside these regions – in South Asia, in particular India; in the Middle East, in particular the Gulf States and Saudi Arabia; and in Latin America. The decision in Chile to abolish student fees had a global resonance, and students in many Latin America countries remain a direct political force in ways no longer familiar in Europe or North America (or indeed other world regions). The second is that many national higher education systems have common features and shared experiences – of expansion (and massification); of attempts to articulate more successfully the various elements within tertiary education systems, in particular the differences between universities and higher professional and vocational education; of efforts to balance the sometimes discordant demands of teaching and research functions; of difficult debates about how best to fund these extended higher education systems; of efforts to maximise the contribution of universities to economic development without eroding too much their crucial role as educational institutions promoting critical enquiry, and also to maximise their social impact, by widening access, while protecting academic standards. These are powerful forces of convergence.

The United States

By most measures the US still has the world's leading higher education and research system. Although participation is now higher in some other systems, the US system remains the archetype of a mass higher education system. The 'language' of mass higher education was first invented in the US, and the concepts and categories first developed in the 1960s and 1970s remain influential half a century later. The funding, regulatory and organisational dilemmas created by mass expansion were first confronted in the US, and its solutions to these dilemmas – whether stratified systems, building sophisticated student-facing structures or increasing tuition fees – have come close to be recognised as globally relevant issues.

Long before the advent of mass higher education, US colleges and universities were regarded as models. Outside Europe, and the colonies of European powers, they provided the dominant model. Even in Europe the influence of this model was strong, especially in the UK, where the new universities of the 1960s had so much in common with new US campuses being developed at the same time, for example at Santa Cruz and Santa

Barbara in the University of California. This influence was felt not only in visual and spatial terms but also in the aspiration to develop a broader multi-disciplinary curriculum. In East Asia too, the home of supposedly rival so-called 'Confucian' systems, many universities drew their inspiration from the model of the US college. Today in terms of science and (much) scholarship the US system remains pre-eminent, even if the first signs of a loss of dominance are becoming apparent. US universities dominate all the global rankings. Indeed, the very concept of a 'world-class' university is openly derived from the model of a US research university (to the unfair detriment of the standing of world systems organised on different principles).

Currently there are almost 20 million students in just over 4,000 US degree-awarding institutions of higher education. Three-quarters are studying in public institutions and a quarter in private institutions. Higher education is the responsibility of state governments, with the role of the federal government focused on student aid (which is also provided by the individual states) and, of particular importance, research. The states 'own' their own public institutions, with responsibility for making arrangements for their governance and providing some of their funding. They also license private institutions. But it is misleading to talk of a US 'system' of higher education. At best there are 51 state 'systems', and some states make only limited attempts to coordinate even the public institutions within their boundaries. In many states responsibility for community colleges, for example, typically rests with local government boards. Only a minority of larger states attempting to coordinate state-wide 'systems' of a kind familiar in many parts of Europe.

This decentralisation is compounded by almost bewildering variety. At first sight the distinction between public and private institutions is key. But in practice some 'private' universities receive almost as much 'public' money, principally through student aid and research funding, as 'public' universities. Although nearly all students apart from those enrolled in community colleges pay tuition fees, fees are lower in public institutions. But since the 1980s free or low-cost tuition has been abandoned in most major state university systems, mainly because of voter-approved initiatives on low taxes and balanced state budgets. Private institutions are also very diverse, divided into not-for-profit foundations (for example, Harvard University) and for-profit companies (for example, the University of Phoenix, owned by the Apollo Group). They also range from those with large-scale historic endowments – Harvard's is as large as the GDPs of some nations – to those entirely dependent on tuition fee income (and, therefore, highly vulnerable to fluctuations in enrolments). There is almost a significant number of faith-based institutions, a model that spread to some other countries heavily influenced by the US from the 19th century onwards but is much less common in Europe, where universities, with few exceptions, are secular institutions.

This variety makes it difficult to categorise US higher education. One possible categorisation can be derived from the chronology of higher education in America, giving, first, the colonial colleges led by Harvard (established in 1639 and so one of the world's oldest universities), which have morphed into the Ivy League, although this now includes some later post-colonial foundations. A second group, often with similar historical origins, are liberal arts colleges. Some liberal arts colleges like Dartmouth are very eminent and, in practice, may also have impressive scholarly profiles. The third big group are the land-grant universities established by the Morrill Act of 1862, which allocated land owned by the federal government to support education in agriculture and other useful occupations. Included in this group, again with a few inconsistencies, are the large state universities like Wisconsin, Michigan and California. These three groups of universities today still constitute the heartland, or powerhouse, of US higher education. Later foundations followed in the late 19th and 20th centuries, with the two-year community colleges emerging in their current form after 1945.

A second possible categorisation is to adopt the semi-official Carnegie classification dating from 1970, which divides institutions into five main categories: doctorate-awarding universities (418 institutions enrolling 7.3 million students, and including the 'Ivy League' and big land-grant universities); master's degree-awarding colleges and universities (685 with 4 million students); bachelor's degree-awarding colleges (575 with 900,000 students); bachelor's and associate's degree-awarding colleges (262 with 1.3 million students); and associate's degree- awarding colleges, that is two-year colleges (1,000 with 5.8 million students). There are three other residual categories.

A third, and simpler, categorisation is to use that devised by several of the larger states that have attempted to construct effectively coordinating systems. Typically, these comprise a major research university, often with several campuses, which has a monopoly of doctoral programmes (and most of the research); a multi-site state university, or state universities, which are usually confined to master's and bachelor's degrees but often aspire to offer doctorates (sometimes successfully); and a third tier of community colleges offering two-year associate's degrees and other professional and vocational qualifications. The model most often quoted is the California Master Plan, which was first articulated in 1962 but has been frequently revised. In practice, few state systems are as tidy as their headline 'plans' suggest. The historical pattern of institutions, geography and local politics and the presence of private institutions often get in the way. However, a key feature of these state 'systems', and indeed of all US higher education, is the ease of transfer by students from one level to another, a novelty (and rarity) in most European higher education systems.

Despite all these achievements and advantages, there is a pervasive sense of crisis in US higher education. Many elements have come together produce this sense of crisis. One element is the impact of the uneven and, by international standards, unimpressive performance of high school graduates who enrol in college. A second is endemic culture wars in which colleges and universities are under constant attack from right-wing populists and critics on the left especially among Black and other minority ethnic communities. Indeed, such has been the polarisation of American politics that these culture wars are approaching pandemic proportions. A third is a slow-burn anxiety that the US is ceasing to be such an attractive destination for international students – and, in particular, the foreign-born scientists on whom the research system depends for its global dominance. A fourth is growing concern about high drop-out rates, particularly in for-profit private institutions (which often over-rely on online learning), graduate underemployment, or unemployment, and the declining efficiency of the system despite massive investments in new learning technologies.

However, the most immediate crisis is a fiscal one, from the point of view of institutions, and an affordability crisis from the perspective of potential students. In the long retreat from no- or low-cost tuition, institutions, including public universities, have become increasingly dependent on income from tuition fees. While state funding declined by more than a quarter between 1987 and 2012, tuition fees increased by 260 per cent between 1980 and 2014. Both trends have continued in more recent years. In private institutions differences in endowment income have widened. The median is $65.1 million, hardly adequate in proportion to the annual budget of the average institution. But a significant number of private colleges effectively have no endowment income and must survive instead solely on tuition fees paid by their students. At the other end of the spectrum, 10 private universities have endowments in excess of $10.8 billion, headed by Harvard, with an endowment of $39 billion ($10 billion more than the next university on the list, Yale).

Although there is widespread agreement that the inflation of tuition fees cannot continue at the present rate, and acknowledgement that the financial viability of some institutions was already threatened before the COVID-19 pandemic, there is little evidence that a consensus about how to tackle these deep-rooted issues can be addressed. Building such a consensus is an almost impossible task in a 'system' responsibility for which is fragmented between the federal, state and local governments, trustees and corporations. What remains is that pervasive sense of crisis. The titles alone of some recent books reveal how widespread this feeling now is: *The College Dropout Scandal*; *The Impoverishment of the American College Student*; *Lower Ed: The Troubling Rise of For-Profit Colleges in the New Economy*; *Indebted: How Families Make College*

Work at Any Cost ... (Kirp, 2019; Koch, 2019; McMillan Cotton, 2018; Zaloom, 2019).

Europe

The original home of the university was in Europe. It was during the Middle Ages that higher academic learning took on something resembling, however remotely, its current organisational form, in the shape of the *studium generale* or *universitas* bringing together different arts and sciences, as they were then understood, in a common institution that was deeply entwined with secular and religious power but nevertheless distinct (and even autonomous). Of course, there were other models of advanced learning, notably in the then intellectually and culturally superior Muslim world. But it was the European model of the university that became the world standard. It was exported, often through imperial and colonial expansion, to other world regions and, outside the orbit of European domination, universally emulated. Europe was the original source of the university, however uncomfortable it may be today to adopt a Eurocentric viewpoint.

Europe remained the heartland of the university until well into the 20th century, although increasingly complemented by and even in competition with universities in other regions (in particular the United States). But two world wars, global depression, the rise of fascism, genocide and communist rule not only destroyed much of the physical and human fabric of Europe's higher education but also undermined its moral standing. The European civilisation to which the European university had so powerfully contributed appeared to be close to collapse. Scholars and scientists fled – mainly westwards to the US (although in a more limited sense to the UK). After 1945 there was nothing to match the dynamic effect of the 1944 GI Bill (the Servicemen's Adjustment Act) on American higher education. Although Western Europe quickly recovered, and indeed reached new heights of social and economic development, the reform of universities was a slow and muted process. It was only near the end of the 20th century that European higher education really began to regain its poise, which is why the essentially technocratic Bologna Process has acquired its wider resonance.

Despite the fact that in many European countries secondary school leavers who had passed the *baccalaureate, abitur* or equivalent examination were entitled to university places, Europe's encounter with mass higher education came a generation later than in the US. It came later still in Central and Eastern Europe, which had to wait until the collapse of the communist regimes at the end of the 1980s. Despite the increase in student enrolments and expansion in the number and size of universities across Western Europe, reforms were often focused on issues such as better representation of students (almost as if they represented a political estate). Large-scale structural reforms on the scale of those associated with French Education Minister Edgar Faure were the exception. Systematic and structural reform on a Europe-wide basis picked up momentum with the Bologna Process begun in 1998 and elaborated regularly since then – for example, the creation of first a European Higher Education Area (EHEA) and then a European Research Area (ERA).

At first sight, the Bologna Process is not very exciting, consisting of the reform of course structures on the bachelor's/master's pattern and the development of what has come to be called a more robust 'quality culture'. What gave Bologna its impetus was, first, that it was only one element within a wider European project, the development of a collaborative (even integrationist) post-conflict culture which appealed in particular to younger people; and, second, that it provided individual countries with political 'cover' for long overdue national reforms. Alongside Bologna, the EU's ambitious research programmes – beginning with successive Framework programmes, then Horizon 2020 and now Horizon Europe – have had a transformative impact on research in European universities. As a result of the implementation of Bologna (and the development of the EHEA/ERA), national reform initiatives and the impact of EU research programmes, European universities have undergone far-reaching modernisation, promoting both their cohesion and their competitiveness.

However, that modernisation process is far from complete:

- Reform has been most rapid, and far-reaching, in Northern and Western Europe. In Sweden a thorough-going reform of higher education, heavily influenced by US models, had taken place in the 1970s. The pace has been slower in Southern Europe, while in some Central and Eastern European countries the reform impulse has been partly expressed through the development of private institutions. As a result, Europe's universities enjoy substantially different degrees of effective institutional autonomy and demonstrate different degrees of dynamism.
- Despite efforts at improved coordination, many European higher education systems remain institutionally fragmented – into *grandes écoles* and universities in France; into universities and *Fachhochschulen* (or equivalent higher professional schools) in Germany, the Netherlands and several other countries; into universities and separate research institutes including CNRS Institutes in France, the German Max Planck and other research institutes and residual Academy of Sciences institutes further east. The fracture lines between Humboldtian and 'Napoleonic' (and, indeed, liberal education) models of the university have not entirely disappeared.
- The diversity of higher education systems across the EU28 (now EU27 with the departure of the UK) and the 48 countries that now comprise

the EHEA makes it difficult to identify common features which in turn distinguish Europe from higher education in other world regions, notably North America and East Asia. It is sometimes asserted that the 'social dimension' is emphasised more strongly in Europe, often code for justifying the continuation of state funding of universities and low-cost, or free, tuition. But, although influential rhetoric, it is perhaps too general to serve as a truly distinctive feature (Scott, 2021). Despite the increasing burden of tuition fees in the US, most American institutions, apart perhaps from the most elite private universities, are equally socially engaged or more so.

But the cumulative effect of reforms has gone a long way to restoring the reputation of European universities, not simply in terms of science and scholarship (which had never been seriously questioned) but also in terms of policy and organisation. Today the US and European systems – although in practice, of course, both have multiple 'systems' – have equal weight in global higher education. There are approximately the same number of higher education institutions in Europe as in the US – more than 4,000 – and also similar numbers of students – 19.8 million tertiary education students in the EU28 (when the UK was still included). Sixty per cent are studying for bachelor's degrees, 28 per cent for master's degrees, 4 per cent are on doctoral programmes – and 7.4 per cent on 'short-cycle' higher education courses (broadly equivalent to associate's degrees in the US). Of the 4,000 institutions, 900 are universities, which are equivalent to research and doctoral degree-granting universities in the US (the first category in the Carnegie classification). Among these universities, 800 are members of the European University Association, which covers not only the EU28 but also other countries that are not members of the EU, including Russia and Turkey.

The main challenge facing European higher education is the danger that the wider European project will falter – partly as a result of the departure of the UK from the EU and the economic difficulties (and political tensions) produced by the COVID-19 pandemic; but mainly because of the threat to the open, democratic, communitarian and liberal values at the heart of that project posed by the rise of nationalist and quasi-authoritarian governments in some European countries, and a wider crisis of confidence and identity across the continent. Not only might the integrationist trends within the EU27 be inhibited but also the attraction of the idea of 'Europe' that has powered the wider EHEA reduced, both weakening the drive to develop a distinctively European model of higher education. The attempts to root that distinctiveness in terms of progressive reform and modern, forward-looking values rather than elite academic culture and even nostalgia for the historic achievements of the European university could be compromised. But there may be grounds for hope. The European 'project' is probably too advanced to be reversed; yet still sufficiently malleable to meet new circumstances. To a greater extent than in the two other world regions considered in this chapter, the cohesion and distinctiveness of European higher education, and so its success, are wrapped up in these wider futures.

East Asia

The third world region discussed in this brief survey of higher education outside the UK is East Asia – in particular, China (and Hong Kong), Japan, South Korea, Malaysia and Singapore. As has already been indicated, East Asia is a major source of international students enrolled in North American, European and Australasian universities. However, these countries have now developed mature and dynamic higher education systems of their own which rival those of the West – in terms of overall participation, number of students (and institutions) and, increasingly, scientific quality and productivity. The platform on which these systems have been built has been rapid economic growth in the region. But it has also been argued that their success can also be attributed to the Confucian values that most of them share, although this may require a high degree of flexibility in defining 'Confucian'.

The dominant East Asian country, of course, is China. In 2018 there were 30 million students in higher education institutions, and several million more on vocational programmes. Half of all 18-year-olds are now enrolled in higher education, and the proportion of graduates among 25- to 34-year-olds is slightly higher than the OECD average. According to the Ministry of Education in 2018, there are 5,769 higher education institutions; the exact total depends on how institutions are categorised. Of these, 815 are research universities offering postgraduate programmes. Private higher education plays a significant role, although two important qualifications are necessary. First, there are almost no private institutions in the top tier of universities. Second, and more important, all institutions, private as well as public, are subject to effective direction by the Chinese Communist Party. In effect, Chinese institutions are subject to dual governance, by the regular administration (appointed by either central or regional ministries) but also by Communist Party committees. This party control is reinforced by the fact that all students must take compulsory courses in subjects such as Marxist ideas and the history of China.

Japan was the first East Asian country to modernise along, broadly, Western lines. This modernisation was a deliberate act of state policy, not imposed by external powers. Within little more than three decades of the 1868 Meiji restoration Japan was already recognised as a great power by the Western nations, however reluctantly. As a result, its trajectory has been different from those of China, where after failed attempts in the Qing period modernisation had to wait until the establishment of the People's

Republic in 1949 (and inevitably remains dominated by totalitarian state structures), or Hong Kong, Singapore or Malaysia, where it was initially based on colonial templates.

At the apex of the Japanese higher education system are the 90 national universities, including famous universities such as the University of Tokyo, established in 1877 less than ten years after the Meiji 'restoration, and the University of Kyoto. The next layer is composed of 100 public universities established by provincial and prefectural administrations. However, almost three-quarters of Japanese students attend the 600 private universities, which also include famous institutions, such as Waseda University. This proportion far exceeds the proportion of students in private institutions in the United States. Beneath the national, public and private universities are a large number of special schools (*Senmon Gakko*) and 'short-term' universities offering two-year and vocational courses. Much of the interest in East Asian higher education in North America and Europe in recent years has focused on China, partly because of geopolitical rivalry but mainly because large numbers of Chinese students are enrolled in their universities. This may have led to a lack of a similar focus on the equally important Japanese university system, although its scientific quality (buttressed by the successes of Japanese technology and industry) has never been questioned.

In other, smaller, East Asian countries the development of higher education, if anything, has been an even more dynamic process. Taiwan and South Korea have among the highest higher education participation rates in the world, both exceeding 85 per cent. Hong Kong and Singapore have been equally successful in building high-participation systems on the foundations laid down during the colonial period. All contain what are recognised to be world-class universities – Seoul National and Yonsei in Korea, and the University of Hong Kong and the Chinese University of Hong Kong. Malaysia, outside the zone of Sinic culture, has been almost as successful. Even in less wealthy countries such as Vietnam there have been important developments in higher education.

The success of East Asian higher education has created, in effect, a tripolar configuration of North America, Europe and now East Asia. There has been much debate about the reasons for East Asia's remarkable success in reconciling still resilient national traditions with dynamic modernisation rooted in Western science. Clearly the engine has been the growth of national economies in this world region. One explanation is simply an inverted version of the 'decline of the West': it is now (East) Asia's turn. However, this is difficult to square with the many positive trends in the development of European systems, and the attraction of the US and Canadian systems remains very powerful. The most common view tends to emphasise the core values, beliefs and habits associated with 'Confucianism'. As a result, East Asian systems have come to be labelled 'post-Confucian'.

There are a number of difficulties with this explanation in a precise form. First, 'Confucianism' (post-, or not) at times seems to have been used loosely to describe a highly diffused (and attenuated?) Sinic culture. What did the imperial values of Japan in the first half of the 20th century really have in common with the Communist ambitions of contemporary China? Second, Western influences have been strong in East Asia, whether mediated through colonial regimes (Britain and France), imperial reach (the US) or Marxism (Soviet communism). Perhaps a more satisfactory explanation is to emphasise the growth of hybrid forms of modernity which, in this particular case, can be described as East-West. The links between modernity as it has been understood in the West, essentially the values of the Enlightenment, and modernisation – the development of economies, the advance of technology and the growth of new social structures (and, of course, higher education) – were once regarded as rigidly causal. Today they are recognised to be more reflexive, and even contingent. The value of regarding the success of East Asian higher education in this wider framework may be that it opens up the possibility of other forms of hybridisation involving other world regions as the 21st century progresses.

Conclusion

This brief, highly selective and inevitably unsatisfactory account of higher education outside the UK nevertheless demonstrates the degree of convergence and commonality among all higher education systems. They have very different histories. In Europe universities were established by monarchs (with a little help from popes) and later by nation states, and most remain predominantly funded by public expenditure. With very few exceptions, they are unambiguously secular institutions. Even in England (though not, of course, the rest of the UK) the struggle to slough off the 'public' label has at best only half succeeded. In the United States the history is a little, but not radically, different. The impression of greater diversity is produced partly by the multiple layers of government – federal, state and local – and partly by the presence of a minority private sector which is focused on the most elite and also the most entrepreneurial parts of the US system. In East Asia private higher education is more prominent not only in status but also in quantitative terms. This reflects a past history of missionary and colonial activity as well as a more market-oriented present and future. However, states and governments continue to play key roles, an overweening role in the case of China. The primary causes of these, and other important, differences are varying patterns of state development, contrasting social structures and occasionally tighter (and more collusive?) relationships between political and corporate power, which are then reflected in these different trajectories of higher education development.

However, the challenges facing all higher education are remarkably similar – how to satisfy the rising demand to participate (typically, on a more socially equitable basis); how to square the circle between student preferences, often heavily influenced by cultural norms and traditions, and the demand for highly skilled workers in key economic and social sectors; how to improve the fit between university research priorities and the development of economies based on advanced technologies; how to organise what have become sprawling systems of tertiary education in the most sensible way (whether through an enforced stratification or by encouraging institutional competition; the usual result is an uneasy and messy compromise); how to monitor quality in these sprawling systems without dis-incentivising innovation; and, of course, how best to fund these systems, which raises both tactical issues – how best to dissipate, even conceal, the cost – and also fundamental questions – who are the beneficiaries of higher education, and what is (are) its essential purpose(s)?

Closely linked to these forces of convergence and differentiation within and between higher education systems is the issue of hybridity, which has just been mentioned in an East–West form. Hybridity embraces elements of both convergence and of diversity and differentiation. In the first respect, hybridity brings different values and traditions together in new creative combinations, an aspect of convergence. In the second respect it highlights differences in the intellectual and cultural domains, just as differentiation reflects divergence in an organisational context. All higher education systems are now engaged in creating new hybrid forms – not just between the West and other world regions, but between elites and wider social (and multi-ethnic?) strata, between 'world-class' science and more distributed forms of knowledge, between supposedly 'universal' and cosmopolitan values on the one hand and local and national traditions on the other. Hybridisation, therefore, is as much a 'domestic' as an 'international' issue. It shapes both the development of national systems – for example, fair access and affirmative action, and also decolonising the curriculum – as well as the future balance, and pattern of relationships, between higher education systems in different world regions.

7

The UK in the 21st century

Just as Chapter 4 attempted to place the development of mass higher education in the wider context of developments in politics, society and the economy since 1960, so this chapter attempts to place the current condition of UK higher education (and of global higher education, and higher education in other world regions) in the wider context of contemporary society, economy and culture. Again, with regret, the primary focus is on the UK. The only defence is that the UK, for all its Brexit-y claims to be exceptional, is in fact a fairly standard example of an early 21st-century society and economy, at any rate in the developed world.

Introduction

Over the past 60 years UK society has changed in fundamental ways, some of which could be measured in quantitative terms but others which have been more qualitative, even suggestive or speculative. First, the total population has increased substantially. In 1961 it was 52.4 million; by 2020 the total is estimated to have grown to 67.9 million; and it is projected to increase still further to 74.1 million by the middle of the 21st century (ONS, 2019). The growth is explained by increasing life expectancy, natural increase (in other words, the excess of births over deaths) and net migration, which in the mid-2010s amounted to more than 350,000 people a year compared with less than 50,000 as recently as the 1990s. Second, the UK population is older. In 1975 people aged 65 and over made up 14.1 per cent of the total, and by 2025 this proportion is expected to be over 20 per cent. The profile of the UK population reflects three demographic 'events': the postwar baby boomers (now in their seventies), their children (now in their forties and fifties) and their grandchildren (now in or approaching their twenties). These three peaks in turn are reflected in striking social realities: the political blocking-power of pensioners and the significance of the 'grey pound' in the cultural and leisure sectors; the ambitions, and insecurities, of the middle-aged and middle class; and the exuberance of a youth, and young adult, culture which is key to constructing novel lifestyles and also drives key economic sectors.

Third, the UK population is much more multicultural than it was in 1960, when the UK was still a predominately White and culturally homogenous society (its divisions still largely determined by social class). In the 2011 Census 13 per cent of the population were non-White, a proportion that certainly will be shown to have increased over the next decade, when the results of the 2021 Census become known. The largest group is people of South Asian origin, highlighted by their prominence in Cabinet posts (or as Mayor of London). In the five years before 2018 the fastest-growing local districts were all in London: Tower Hamlets (16 per cent), Camden (14 per cent) and Westminster (13 per cent), all areas with high non-White or immigrant populations. The rebound of London, of course, in population, economic and cultural terms is also a major feature of 21st-century UK society. In the 2011 Census 85 per cent of the UK's total population were UK-born; the largest non-UK born group was from Poland, although the headlong expansion of Polish immigration since the accession of Poland to the EU has faltered following the 2016 referendum in which the UK voted (by that wafer-thin majority) to leave the EU.

The UK, of course, had always been an immigrant society, with large inflows in the 19th and early 20th centuries from Ireland, Eastern and Southern Europe. But these earlier immigrant groups had been quickly assimilated, disguising the essential pluralism of the UK population. They were seen in a similar light as internal immigrants, for instance those migrating from rural English counties to the urban centres, or from Highland Scotland to the central belt (Irish immigration, of course, was internal until 1922). Their presence did not coalesce into a sharp-edged narrative of 'otherness'. Immigration in the last half century has had a more intrusive impact, not in terms necessarily of scale but of (perceived) cultural difference. In 2020, it is plain that the UK has become a multi-ethnic, multicultural and even multilingual society. This has created the scope for constructing alternative identities to those rooted in social class, and notions of community based on these alternative identities, and has also framed new (and often alarming) political narratives.

Fourth, the structure of UK society has changed radically. Some of the drivers of these changes reflect changes in the economy, and the occupational structure – for example, the decline in jobs in manufacturing industry and the rapid rise in the number of people employed in service industries. But that is not the whole story. These social changes have taken on an independent life of their own. In the 21st century social identity is more loosely associated with economic roles and job titles. The UK appears to have become a more 'middle-class', or 'classless', society in two different respects. First, there were fewer traditional working-class jobs and more (approximately) middle-class ones. Second, habits once characterised as 'middle class' have become more widely shared, while distinctively 'working-class' cultures have been eroded. An alternative way to describe this second shift is to say that social identities are now as much determined by consumption habits, very much influenced by mass media, as by roles in production, which has created a much greater fluidity of identities. This may help to explain why an appearance of 'classlessness' has emerged at a time when income differentials have actually widened.

The fifth change is a fluidity, and variety, of identities. The titles of two books, both first published in the 1990s, by Zygmunt Bauman (*Fluid Modernity*) and Manuel Castells (*The Power of Identity*) highlighted this new quality (Bauman, 1999; Castells, 2009). More rigid social identities based on region, class or gender have been overlain, although not superseded, by new identities. Some of these, like perceived ethnic origins, are still comparatively rigid, although eroded by a growing number of mixed families. But others are more pliable, in particular, gender (as opposed to biological sex) and sexuality more broadly (being gay or trans, for example). These more fluid identities have merged into wider lifestyle choices. Closely linked is a sixth change, the impact of new communication technologies which have reshaped communities by loosening them from physical constraints and allowed them to become more fluid (under the watchful gaze, and influence, of the high-tech companies, of course). The same technologies have also reshaped the practices (and etiquettes) of communication. The UK is now composed of many digital 'tribes', but also of one whole digital environment.

This chapter focuses on three particular themes – society (in particular, social class); culture (in particular, the clash between supposedly cosmopolitan and 'populist' cultures); and the economy (more specifically, the impact of the mass production of graduates). All three, of course, are interwoven to an extent that may make their separate treatment seem artificial and contrived. Whatever other 'identities' are constructed, they are still powerfully shaped by changes in the occupational structure. Globalisation is a common theme across society, culture and the economy. It may also be that mass higher education is another common theme. Experience of higher education is a significant ingredient in many of the post-class 'identities'; it is also a primary source and spreader of cosmopolitanism; and the mass production of a highly skilled graduate workforce is a key element in the 21st-century economy.

Society

There are almost too many theorisations of the essential character of contemporary society available. An early example was Daniel Bell's theory of 'post-industrial society' first developed in the 1970s (Bell, 1973, 1976). An enduring element in his theory has been the emphasis placed on 'knowledge' as a key economic resource and social good, although Bell could not have anticipated the explosive growth of data and information technologies. Half a century later, the label 'knowledge society' has become a commonplace description in political circles, even though in terms of more rigorous analysis it requires extensive unpacking to distinguish between data and 'knowledge', between technical processing and social and economic uses and cultural impacts, and between owners (and arguably exploiters) and beneficiaries (and sometimes victims). Some of this complexity is hinted at in other common labels: 'network society', whether collaborative utopia or dystopian web; or 'audit society', which introduces a much-needed emphasis on control and surveillance (Power, 1997; Castells, 2000). Other ingredients in these theorisations include 'risk' and 'self-organisation'. All have something to offer in terms of understanding the key characteristics of 21st-century society.

The decline of social class?

A familiar argument is that social class now plays a less significant role in shaping individual identities than it did for much of the 20th century. However, both broader concepts and more exact definitions of social class are artificial constructs. In the UK the Office for National Statistics (ONS) in its gold-standard Socio-Economic Classification (NC-SEC) emphasises that the classes it has derived are analytical categories not 'social classes' in a wider sense (ONS, 2020d). Its eight classes, from higher managerial, administrative and professional occupations (divided into two) through to routine occupations, have sometimes been collapsed into three broad categories: higher managerial, administrative and professional; intermediate; and routine occupations. This has created the temptation that these categories can be aligned to broad-brush characteristics such as upper, middle and working class. But it is a temptation that should be resisted. Although social class identities are influenced by occupational backgrounds, they have always been more fluid and nuanced – and perceptions, and so definitions, have evolved over time.

Since the 1990s the idea of classlessness has gained greater currency (Kingston, 2000; Turner, 2013). It is especially common in political circles and the wider commentariat. This idea has – conveniently perhaps – served to distract attention from increasing inequality of income and life-chances. In more expert and academic circles this argument has been treated with greater reserve. Greater emphasis has been placed not only on this increase in inequality, in terms of the growing gap between low and high earners (and rich rentiers), but also on the decline in social mobility. Both trends are difficult to reconcile with the argument that social class is in decline whether as an organisational category or a personal identifier.

Indeed, the second of these two phenomena, the stalling of social mobility, in particular, suggests that the meritocratic principle has been increasingly subordinated to the aristocratic principle (an aristocracy of wealth, both earned and inherited). Political circumstances, first during the Thatcher Government and then under New Labour rule, and once again after a decade of (in effect) Conservative government, have made it easier for the wealthy and privileged to protect their wealth and privileges, and to resist any serious downward social mobility. At the same time, the uncertain state of the economy (and its lopsided development) has made it more difficult to generate a sufficiently large increase in high-status and well-paid jobs.

Other reasons have been suggested for the decline of class which, on close examination, are unsatisfactory and essentially circular – for example, the argument that overall social status has become less important, because our concept of 'society' itself has been eroded with the supposed triumph of individualism. This fails to explain why patterns of social stratification remain so strong. Individuals may now be defined more in terms of their patterns of consumption than their role in the production of wealth. But this also fails to explain the persistent disparity in economic resources which fund consumption.

Despite these – essential – qualifications, there appears to be little doubt that 'social class', as it was understood in the 19th and for three-quarters of the 20th century, has become a less significant element in forming individual identity. The qualification 'as it was understood …' is key. In one sense, this is a truism. 'Social class' was moulded by specific socio-economic and historical circumstances. In the UK (and many other European societies) the idea of social class has been strongly related to the traditional 'proletarian' industries in extraction (especially mining) and manufacturing (shipbuilding, steel, auto production and so on). These industries were characterised by high levels of trade union organisation, and by geographically identifiable working-class communities. The working class was a real, and physical, presence. The apparent dominance of the industrial economy by these 'proletarian' industries, although it never came close to being the majority component of the UK economy, may have had the effect of drawing attention away from other meanings of 'working class', for example in personal services, which employed more people. But these industries have declined. As a result, it was inevitable that this particular meaning of 'social class' would become much weaker.

Gender, ethnicity, language and religion

And yet … Social class now has to compete with other forms of identification, more so perhaps than in the past. Of course, it has always had to compete. The hope that the solidarity of the proletariat would override national loyalties was proved to be an illusion, by the outbreak of the First World War in 1914 at the very latest. Today nationalism and xenophobia, misleadingly labelled 'populism', are again on the march, although contrary to many media analyses there is no clear evidence that these ideas are especially attractive to any particular social class (or, if it is preferred, any particular income group). More recently, in addition to traditional forms of nationalism, two other rival identifications to class have come to the fore. The first rival is characteristics such as gender, ethnicity, language and religion, which have already been discussed; the second is levels of formal educational attainment.

Gender, ethnicity, language (closely aligned, of course, with national identity) and religion can hardly be described as new. Occupations, habits and even language have always been highly gendered. Arguably they are becoming less so, paradoxically perhaps as a result of increasing assertiveness of women. The subordination of minority ethnic groups is also lessening, and for similar reasons. Nevertheless, it is argued that these other forms of culturally formed identity have become more influential than social class in 21st-century society. One – perhaps the – major social movement of the past half century (suggestively correlated with the advance of mass higher education) has been the trend towards the equalisation of male and female life-chances which, of course, is very far from complete. This has been expressed in terms of a shift in the male–female occupational structures, with female graduates invading once male-dominated professions, and also a shift in ideological orientation, feminism broadly defined, creating new forms of identity.

Biologically determined gender, of course, has always been a determinant of personal identity, so it cannot be reasonably be offered as evidence to support the claim that a new post-class society is emerging. What is new is a changed and more assertive consciousness among women – and not just among the more educated and socially advantaged. Paradoxically, one of the effects of this heightened consciousness, and greater ambition, among women may have been to reduce the traditional differences between male and female roles and life-chances. This convergence may cast some doubt on the argument that gender has become progressively more elemental in shaping identity, at any rate in concrete empirical terms.

There is evidence of the emergence of new and more fluid forms of sexual identity. For example, the – admittedly very high – proportion of the UK population defining themselves as heterosexual has tended to decline and stood at 94.6 per cent in 2018. In contrast, the proportion self-identifying as lesbian, gay or bisexual has increased to 2.2 per cent (and is double that in London, and also higher among younger people). Once again, there is perhaps a suggestive connection with mass higher education, and the urban cosmopolitan environments in which it is embedded and which it fosters. Most recently the arguments about trans rights, and their awkward relationship with feminist-inspired assertions of female 'spaces' (originally intended as protection against male encroachment), are evidence of the growing importance of these more fluid forms of sexuality in shaping personal identity (ONS, 2020a).

Ethnicity is also now regarded as an increasingly powerful source of personal identity (ONS, 2015). According to conventional accounts, first-generation immigrants are anxious to fit into host cultures, while subsequent generations are more determined to celebrate their differences, although a more accurate account may instead emphasise the role played by the growth of hybrid multicultural cultures across all ethnic groups. Participation in higher education has become a key arena for the advancement of Black and other minority ethnic (BAME) communities, as was explained in the previous chapter. But, as with gender, it is not clear why what is. after all. a process of assimilation into elite culture can at the same time be interpreted as an assertion of distinctive identity. It is unclear whether BAME graduates are less or more likely than other members of their communities to assert a distinctive, and potentially separate, identity.

Perhaps this is yet another demonstration of the complex relationship between social and cultural homogenisation and differentiation in modern societies. Overall, as again was indicated in the previous chapter, BAME students are overrepresented in universities compared with their share of the general population, even when the different age profiles of different ethnic groups are taken into account. Once again, two qualifications are essential – first, there are very significant variations in higher education participation rates among different minority ethnic groups; and, second, most BAME students are concentrated in newer and arguably less prestigious institutions.

Data on religion and language, two characteristics closely related to ethnicity, do not support straightforward conclusions. A quarter of the UK population has no religion, while almost 60 per cent still describe themselves as Christian. The next largest group is Muslim, at 4.8 per cent, followed by Hindus at 1.5 per cent. Other religions trail behind – Sikhism at 0.8 per cent and Judaism at 0.5 per cent (ONS, 2015). It is true that Muslim believers tend to be younger, while both Christians and Jews are skewed towards older people. But the impression is left of a loose fit between ethnicity and religion, with the clear implication that those of 'no religion' come from a variety of faith backgrounds. As with sexuality, the age differences suggest that youth is a significant indicator of identity. But that is a truism. It has always been so.

A similar picture emerges from the data on languages. English is the first language of more than 92 per cent of the population, and Polish is the next most widely spoken language (although that might be changing in the wake of Brexit). There are strong but not exact correlations between language and ethnicity. In, predominantly White, Redcar and Cleveland, English is the first language of 99.3 per cent of the population, while in the London Borough of Newham, a much more ethnically mixed area, this figure is only 58.6 per cent. But less than 2 per cent of the UK population admit to not speaking English very well or not at all.

However, despite these ambiguities and obscurities, it is reasonably clear that as a result of mass expansion participation in higher education is now a significant ingredient in shaping identity in 21st-century UK. To label the UK a 'graduate society' would be going much too far, because it runs the risk of exaggerating one particular shaping influence at the expense of others that may be equally or more important. But it is not yet clear the extent to which participation in higher education, and 'graduate-ness', can be seen in a progressive light, as a process of emancipation, as shaping a new kind of more open society 'open to the talents' in Napoleonic terms; and the extent to which these features should be seen in a less favourable light, as contributing to consolidating existing social differences initially determined by other forces, such as family or wealth. Any reform of higher education in the UK must directly address this dilemma.

Educational attainment

As has been pointed out earlier in this book, there is a strong correlation between educational level and political and social attitudes – and, presumably therefore, social and personal identity. In broad terms, the better educated tilt towards the left in politics and are more socially progressive, with substantial and significant exceptions. In particular, it is argued that experience of higher education, and the status of being a 'graduate', create a powerful form of identity that is an alternative to social class, in terms of access not simply to higher-status and better-paid employment but also particular lifestyles (and the social and cultural values they embody). But what are the mechanisms that explain these connections between, broadly speaking, liberalism and being a graduate?

It is true that for some individuals access to higher education offers new opportunities for self-realisation and even self-invention; the emancipatory potential of a university experience cannot be underestimated at the individual level. But across wider social groups and in aggregate, participation in higher education appears to reflect, and even consolidate (and, worse still, may legitimate), existing inequalities. For all the writing about the 'democratic intellect' in Scotland or about 'scholarship boys' in the post-war UK, the differences in rates of participation between the least and the most socially deprived remains little changed. A gulf remains. The absolute gains made by the latter have been largely the result of mass expansion – which, of course, should be properly recognised – rather than any serious reduction in comparative advantage between the more and the less socially privileged. These worrying differentials remain and are further compounded by the even greater differentials in participation rates in the elite universities which offer higher levels of social and cultural capital that is readily translated into economic advantage.

As a result, rather than treating levels of formal educational attainment as a rival to, or even an independent variable from, social class as a basis for social and economic stratification, for allocation of cultural capital or for individual identification, both educational attainment and social class are perhaps better understood as just a different expression of enduring social class distinctions – except at the, honourable, margin for selected individuals (Bukodi and Goldthorpe, 2009). The skewed social base of higher education is important because of the substantial economic advantages enjoyed by the 14 million graduates in the UK, 54 per cent of whom are employed in occupations at the top end of the NS-SEC scale, compared with only 12 per cent of non-graduates. Among 22- to 29-year-olds, 90 per cent of graduates are in employment, compared with 78 per cent of non-graduates in the same age group. And graduates in their twenties are much less likely to be categorised as 'economically inactive' – 6 per cent, compared with 17 per cent of non-graduates. They are also likely to have substantially increased earnings, an advantage that has not been significantly eroded by mass expansion, although the major factor has probably been the comparative depression of non-graduate earnings rather than the elevation of gradate earnings.

The overall impression from the data is that non-graduates are being pushed downwards in the occupational hierarchy or to the margins of the jobs market, which makes the continuing alignment between social advantage and participation in higher education even more alarming. It certainly makes it difficult to argue that participation in higher education is a discrete, and more hopeful, element in shaping social identity genuinely independent from social class. In this respect, the idea of a classless (or less class-ridden) society appears to be a myth.

Summary

The overall impression that is left is that the contemporary UK is far from being a classless society, or even moving towards a society in which class differences are significantly reducing. Social class, in the double sense of having a job in the higher or lower categories of the NS-SEC classification and residing in an area of comparative advantage or deprivation, still appears to be a (or even the) major determinant of individual identity, social status, income and life-chances. Other potential determinants are either congruent with class, as with levels of formal educational attainment, or relatively minor in their collective effect, however important they may be for selected individuals, as with gender and sexuality. It follows that talk of a 'graduate society', certainly as a replacement to 'class society', however appealing (and flattering to higher education), is almost certainly overblown.

Culture

The four-year (and continuing) anguish over Brexit has encouraged an unhelpful binary view of contemporary UK politics, society and culture: on the one hand, a metropolitan elite that is better educated, more progressive in political and social terms, more enthusiastic about innovation (whether technological or cultural) and less patient with more traditional social norms; on the other, the 'left behind', in smaller towns and hollowed-out industrial communities, suspicious of change, which they experience as invariably disruptive (and often destructive), who are more attached to traditional values. This binary account is beloved of the commentariat. It has also clearly seeped into party political tactics (the Conservatives' focus on breaching the 'red wall' in the 2020 UK general election and similar strategies, and Labour's new emphasis on 'patriotism').

It has also received some support within higher education, intellectually and in terms of policy. Ideas of 'clever cities' brimming with tech entrepreneurs and social experimenters, or of universities as 'anchor institutions' mobilising creative resources within their communities, command widespread attention. The assumption, shaken by Brexit but still intact, is that the UK is on a journey – from tradition to innovation and enterprise, from provincialism to cosmopolitanism, from darkness to life. And, despite present discomforts, higher education is a key life force. Whig habits go deep. History will vindicate.

However, under close and detailed examination, this binary account crumbles. Revealingly, on headline 'moral' issues such as cohabitation in place of marriage, abortion, gay rights (and marriage), the culture wars so apparent in the US have been largely absent in the UK, and most other Western and even Southern European countries – despite the best efforts of transatlantic zealots to ignite them. The supposedly Brexit-voting 'left behind' do not appear to be significantly less socially liberal on these issues, although some modish issues such as trans rights may be more closely associated with the metropolitan or leftist 'elites'. And, in any case, these supposed 'elites' hardly possess the influence and resources that real elites typically enjoy; rather, it has become a term of disapprobation (employed, of course, most frequently by politicians, journalists, academics and other commentators who do enjoy such influence and resources). Distinctive accents, linked to social class or to particular regions, have been smoothed away by a common exposure to the mass media. By many indicators, the forces of convergence in terms of social habits and cultural preferences have been much stronger than the crude binary divide between the educated metropolitan 'elites' and others variously described as the 'people', the 'left behind' to which commentators and politicians are fashionably addicted.

But this disapprobation has had an effect. Post-modernism may now be a concept that appears to be past its sell-by date, but it has been succeeded as a target by so-called 'woke' culture. Yesterday's anything and everything-goes relativists, accused of asserting that all knowledge was socially constructed and culturally contingent, have curiously morphed into today's 'cancellers' of history. It is also interesting that characteristics of graduates once defined in overwhelmingly positive terms – for example, lower crime rates or higher levels of civic involvement or participation in civil-society organisations – have now been redefined in much more negative terms – elitism, condescension, arrogance, a lack of empathy for fellow citizens, generally being out of touch. This also suggests that the modish post-Brexit cultural narrative is rather an aspect of right-wing politicisation rather than being based on serious social analysis. The trite sound-bite phrase of a former prime minister, Theresa May, in which she contrasted (bad) 'citizens of nowhere' with (good) 'citizens of somewhere' illustrates this aspect of the debate about cosmopolitanism. Even today only a tiny stratum of truly global citizens, inhabiting the corporate stratosphere, really belongs to 'nowhere' (their West Indian islands, French Riviera mansions, London town houses or New York apartments). But they are clearly not the target the radical-right opponents of cosmopolitanism have in mind. Many are key sponsors and allies of this populism even though they decline fully to live by it themselves.

In fact, most studies of cosmopolitanism emphasise the complex interactions between 'nowhere' – global brands, culture and science – with 'somewhere' – local and national traditions. Hence ugly neologisms like 'glocalisation'. In one (flattering) perspective, universities with their mass student populations are treated as key mediators between global and national cultures. They act as conduits through which global knowledge is applied in – and, of course, extracted from – local contexts. They also promote the large-scale mobility of students and scholars and scientists, creating in the process multiple diasporas. But just as (or more) decisive is the role played by multinational companies. The logos of Apple and Google and other global brands are much more part of the visual, and mental, furniture of the modern world than those of the even the most globally renowned university.

In any case, drawing too sharp a constraint between global and local knowledge and culture can be misleading. All knowledge and culture is, to some degree, hybrid. In the past anthropologists remarked how everyday objects in some cultures could easily become cult objects in other cultures. Similarly, intellectual and artistic movements leap across national and cultural boundaries, with more or less adaptation. This process of hybridisation has accelerated in the 21st century. For example, the Black Lives Matter (BLM) movement, which burst into life in the summer of 2020, was both stimulated by images of police violence in the US – so, in some respects, global events

– but also rooted in the daily social realities experienced by BAME people in the UK and other countries – arguably, local circumstances.

Alongside the continuing debate about cosmopolitanism, globalisation and hybridisation there has been a revolution in communicative culture in the UK and across the world, poor as well as rich. This revolution has been experienced, above all, as individual empowerment, the Pandora's box of the internet. Its economic impacts are many and varied, but generally well understood. They include the irresistible advance of advertising, brands and lifestyles; the use of information technologies with a greatly enhanced potential for data analytics; the hollowing-out of the high street by online shopping. The political impacts too are becoming more apparent. These include 24/7 always-on real-time politics (with obviously detrimental effects on traditional forms of political deliberation, except as a theatrical backdrop); new modes of media engagement, mass and social; and fierce consumer-like targeting, and stoking, of political fears and prejudices.

However, the social and cultural impacts are potentially more fundamental. The old fear that the 'cry in the poem is more real than the cry in the street', the distancing and displacement of emotions by literary culture, has greatly increased with the ubiquity of the mass media. 'Imagined' communities have been transformed into 'virtual' communities, with an enticing but often spurious intimacy. New knowledge and information, once mediated through scientific peer-review and at least semi-professional media channels, are now disseminated through 'open access' pre-prints or unmoderated 'fake news'.

The role of mass higher education in these various forms of cultural change is complex. Of course, it continues the role played by more elite university systems in the propagation of expert knowledge, whether scientific or more broadly cultural. But there may be an important difference. The reproduction of social and political elites, still performed by elite universities, has been diffused into the spread of a more diffuse 'graduate' brand through mass access. To characterise 21st-century universities as largely cosmopolitan institutions, promoting an expert scientific culture and initiating students into that culture, is misleading. They have become intellectually more reflexive and socially more highly contextualised institutions. Orthodoxies have been replaced by heterodoxies, not simply and most obviously within academic disciplines, but in terms of wider social and cultural practices. But not everything goes within these more reflexive and contextualised environments. Just as attitudes across different social classes have tended to converge and older regional and class-based differences such as accents or clothing have been smoothed away (even though inequality has increased), mass higher education has played an important role in creating a new and more generic 'graduate' culture but nevertheless still with shared, if not uniform, values, at any rate for the near-half of the population it recruits.

In some other respects, higher education has been a victim rather than a moulder of cultural change. Universities have been the source of clashing rival 'experts'. Debate and contestation, once regarded benignly as the primary means to make scientific advances and even refine 'truth', are now more closely associated with threats, uncertainties and discord. This shift has tended to destabilise the authority of higher education – while ironically generating even greater demands for experts and evidence. The revolution in communicative culture has also deeply affected traditional forms of teaching. Once, new learning technologies were largely seen as just that – technologies. Now that top-down learning management systems have been supplemented by more disruptive social media it is recognised that more is at stake than simply the technological enhancement of traditional forms of student learning. These more fundamental changes are partly benign – the promotion of active learning; but there are less benign consequences – the erosion of authority and even the trivialisation of learning. However, agent or acted upon, mass higher education is at the interstices of many of the major cultural shifts of the 21st century.

The economy

The evolution of the UK economy over the past 60 years has been sketched in Chapter 2. Three main characteristics of this evolution are:

- *De-industrialisation*: Manufacturing industries have declined and the economy is now dominated by services, in particular, financial services, retail and hospitality, and the creative and cultural industries. This process was partly inevitable but partly accelerated by deliberate state actions.
- *Marketisation*: This has come about not simply (or mainly) because the public sector has 'shrunk' but because commercial market practices (and players) have become increasingly important in the shaping and delivery of 'public' services.
- *Increasing inequality of income*: The erosion of the moral economy has reduced inhibitions about excessive salaries. Taxation policies have enabled the accumulation of wealth and its preservation across generations. The reduction of trade union power has depressed wages.

Having said that, the UK has enjoyed high levels of economic growth, a characteristic shared with the economies of all advanced countries regardless of their structural features, as would be expected in a globalised world economy. In the last quarter of 2019, the UK's GDP was £557,935 million, compared with £401,282 million in the first quarter of 2008, just before the banking crisis and subsequent recession (ONS, 2020b). At the start of the century, its GDP was £270,402 million. All these figures are at market prices as reported by the Office for National Statistics and, therefore, must be adjusted for inflation. Although there have fluctuations between quarter-by-quarter growth rates at constant prices since 1960 from 7.3 to −1.9 per cent, the highest rates were recorded in 1970s. This is at sharp variance with conventional historical remembering of comparative economic success, once again demonstrating the rather loose correlation between economic growth and political rhetoric (or remembrance) (ONS, 2020c).

Although the domestic consumer market is the driving force of the 21st-century UK economy, it is highly dependent on international trade – much more so than the US economy. A high proportion of consumer goods are imported, either from the rest of Europe and East Asia or from low-cost (and sweat-shop) economies elsewhere. To pay for these imports the UK relies partly on tourism, which makes the 'heritage industry' and cultural industries especially important, but mainly on a dynamic, high globalised (and disproportionately large) financial services sector. Although the UK has some world-leading high-technology industries, especially pharmaceuticals, they are locked into complex global research, manufacturing and supply chains which comprehensively transcend national boundaries (and undermine nationalist bragging rights). In relative terms, the UK lacks a similar advanced engineering sector to Germany's. As a result, the UK economy is especially exposed to the rise of protectionism and the retreat from free-market globalisation which was already apparent even before the COVID-19 pandemic (making Brexit even more an incomprehensible act of self-harm).

Like all modern economies, the UK economy floats on an ocean of credit, a centuries-old characteristic but greatly magnified in a hyper-financialised global economy. Personal levels of debt have exploded since the early 1990s. One, relatively technical, explanation is provided by shifts in payments systems (which have affected all payments but have been associated with the easy availability of available credit). But another explanation is that the ready availability of credit has partly compensated for restrictions on increases in real wages, as demonstrated in the extreme case of the growth in payday unsecured loans. Because trade union power has been curbed in the UK more than in many other European countries, the latter effect may be particularly pronounced. Four out of five new cars are leased, and these forms of financing are a major source of profit. A similar pattern applies to many other consumer goods – from mobile phones to furniture. Older practices of straightforward purchase, let alone saving up to pay for goods, are increasingly rare. This financialisation of consumption, of course, has major social and psychological effects.

Corporate structures have also been transformed by the activities of hedge funds and other arm's-length financial institutions, which have often leveraged takeovers by loading companies with very high levels of debt, producing short-term profit but sometimes at the cost of longer-term instability. In this respect, the UK is also more exposed than the two other major European economies, Germany and France. In Germany the larger proportion of companies still, in effect, consists of family-owned companies, while in France (lightly disguised) forms of state control have persisted. Also, more regulated forms of corporate governance in both countries have built stronger defences against the most predatory forms of financial capitalism. Ironically, and contrary to media stereotypes, the UK state itself has been a cautious borrower, although a lower proportion of current public expenditure in the UK is covered by tax receipts than in some other economies, notably in Scandinavia. The top rating still enjoyed by state borrowing as opposed to the junk debt of some over-leveraged companies is proof enough of the judgement of the markets.

Finally, like all advanced economies, the UK in 2020 faces two quasi-existential challenges. The first has been the shock of the COVID-19 pandemic. Interestingly, the explosion of compensatory government spending to wartime levels has highlighted the essential creditworthiness of the UK (and other major) states, and also the greater-than-imagined scope for Keynesian economic policy. Perhaps more challenging is the impact of global environmental change, which calls into question the whole emphasis on economic growth. In the 20th century, the social limits of growth, particularly with regard to so-called positional goods, were often emphasised. In the 21st century, the emphasis has switched sharply to the environmental limits of growth. The foundational belief in all modern economies, that the aim of state policy, and indeed corporate objectives and individual ambitions, is to promote economic growth is now severely challenged, with unknowable consequences because of its runaway consequences across politics and society.

The role of higher education and science

How central have higher education and research been to the growth of the UK economy? In terms of the introduction of new technologies in manufacturing and service delivery, in information and data handling, and in health improvements, universities have been key sources. However, market confidence and social organisation have played at least equally important roles in shaping economic success (or failure) as new technologies. Increased efficiency has come from a variety of sources. Improved productivity produced by scientific and technological innovation has certainly been one. But lower labour costs as a result of depressed wage levels have also been another, if less heroic, driver. It is important, therefore, not to be blinded by the brilliance of the idea of a high-tech economy. Technology is one enabler; its potential economic benefits depend on a wide range of other enablers. It is also important to recognise that the basic science from which most new technologies are derived is a public good, freely available and therefore resistant to national 'capture'.

The impact of the long educational revolution that had led to universal participation in secondary education and high levels of participation in tertiary education has typically been discussed more in terms of its social contexts and effects than in terms of its economic impacts. It was certainly true that the main driver of this revolution has probably been rising social aspirations and increasing standards of educational attainment. But investment in education has often been justified in terms of satisfying the demand for a more skilled workforce (despite the uneven results of detailed attempts at forecasting future patterns of work). Economists have long argued about whether 'pull' factors – the demand for labour – have been more important than 'push' factors – the greater availability of a more educated workforce (Wolf, 2002; Machin and Vignoles, 2018). Some, maybe mischievously, have even argued that countries had elaborate (especially higher) education systems largely because they have become rich enough to afford them. But the more common view, crystallised in theories of post-industrial or knowledge economies and more influential among most politicians, is that investment in education increases, and improves, the stock of human capital which has become an even more crucial input into economic development than financial and other more traditional forms of capital.

Perhaps the safest way to discuss the impact of the educational revolution on economic growth was to emphasise the interplay between supply and demand, 'push' and 'pull', within a dynamic regime of accumulation, rather than to highlight, or prioritise, any particular element. It might not be apparent that the growth of the financial services industry depended crucially on the development of a more highly skilled workforce, except in terms of the technical experts who design the information systems on which its successful operation now depended. It was at least as likely that the expanding proportion of managers and administrators in the workforce across all sectors had stimulated an increasing demand for business and management education as the other way round, whatever claims might have been made for the value of the MBA (Master of Business Administration) and other qualifications.

However, the development of some economic sectors would have been impossible without a better-educated workforce. The success of high-technology products and services in the UK economy (and an increasing proportion of material production and service delivery now depends on advanced technologies) has clearly been based on a constantly increasing supply of those with more advanced scientific and technical skills. Similarly, the health economy too has depended on the large-scale production of both highly skilled professionals, clinicians and managers, but also much larger numbers of so-called 'associate professionals', in healthcare and administration. An advanced economy has gone hand in hand with an advanced education system within a reflexive pattern of change.

The labour market

These changes in the structure of the UK economy are broadly similar to the changes that have taken place in all advanced economies but with some particular local features (and vulnerabilities to global influences). A common characteristic is the polarisation of wealth, which has been most effectively and dramatically highlighted by the French economist Thomas Piketty, who has analysed in great detail income differentials across most major countries over the past century or more (Piketty, 2014, 2015, 2020). He has emphasised the role played by the two world wars and intervening depression in the destruction of traditional wealth, the role post-war reconstruction rooted in civic values of solidarity played in generating a strong trend towards income equalisation, and the reversal of that trend from the 1980s onwards (especially in the US and, among European countries, the UK). He has also proposed reforms, notably the imposition of wealth as well as higher income (and corporate) taxes that place him firmly in the radical camp. Similar ideas have been expressed by other scholars (Dorling, 2018a, 2018b).

These disparities in income and wealth, and wider indicators of social inequality, have been especially pronounced in the UK compared with most other European societies, although not as marked as in the US and some fast-developing Asian countries. They have both reflected and been produced by far-reaching changes in the labour market. These changes have not happened only in the UK but are a global phenomenon (Brown and Lauder, 2012). One of the most prominent features has been a polarisation of the labour market. A seminal paper summed up that differentiation in its title 'Lousy and lovely jobs' (Maarten and Manning, 2007). Political discourse, especially on the left, has castigated what is seen as the triumph of a new class of the super-rich, bankers with bonuses and senior managers on seven-figure salaries (who, in a further incitement, have often made use aggressive use of tax avoidance schemes and offshore scams further to maximise their personal wealth), on the one hand; and on the other hand, the growth of a new 'precariat' on zero-hours or spurious self-employment contracts, who often take several jobs to make ends meet and are particularly vulnerable to economic distress (with all its well-known social consequences).

The pattern of UK employment now has three distinctive features, which it is possible to try to align, suggestively and speculatively, with patterns of education:

- There certainly is indeed a growing 'precariat' – 'lousy jobs' in the terms of the Maarten and Manning article title. But not all 'precarious' jobs are necessarily low-paid or low-status. For example, in the cultural and creative industries, self-employment is common, as it is among the expanding ranks of 'consultants', although some of these consultants, of course, are making the best of a bad job, having lost, or never acquired, corporate or bureaucratic security. It would also be misleading to suggest that members of the 'precariat' can easily be aligned with those who have lost out in the educational race. Many are comparatively well educated or are even graduates, who are disadvantaged for personal reasons or because they suffer from forms of institutional racism or other forms of discrimination (in particular, their minority ethnic status).
- There is also just as clearly a super-rich category. But even among those with 'good' (if not 'lovely') jobs, there has been a marked polarisation between the top 20 per cent whose incomes have rapidly increased and the majority of those in 'good jobs' who have seen their incomes grow at a more modest rate. Partly, this is a reflection of new economic sectors, particularly financial services. Partly, it reflects the cumulative effect of low income-tax regimes and the ease with which taxes on inherited wealth and unearned income can be evaded. Once again, there is little evidence of a strong correlation between the super-rich and the well-educated. The most highly educated, clustered in the traditional and scientific and technical professions, typically enjoy generous but not excessive salaries. Rather, explanations for the 'success' of the super-rich have to be looked for in terms of flows of inherited wealth, family and peer networks, or attendance at elite schools and universities.
- The middle range of income holders is perhaps the most interesting. It also offers the best fit with advances in higher education. Employment data suggests that, while this middle group has enjoyed only a modest increase in incomes as a result of the development of the economy, they have benefited from a large-scale inflation in job titles. As a result, many apparently high-status jobs now only attract middle-range salaries. Once again, several explanations are available. Prominent among these explanations are the comparative (although not absolute) decline in moderately paid (but secure) public sector jobs at the expense of more keenly priced private sector jobs; and the depressing effect on wages of the decline in the influence (and membership) of trade unions. A third explanation may be that the mass production of graduates has begun to outrun the capacity of even a dynamic economy to generate sufficient suitably highly skilled jobs – generating, as a result, graduate under-employment. A fourth explanation is that the skills levels required for middle-range jobs have increased to match the development of more sophisticated roles they now represent – in other words, job titles had

been modified to reflect these higher skills levels. A final explanation is that a widespread strategy has been adopted by employers to 'buy off' better-educated and more aspirational workers by offering them high-status job titles rather than offering them higher salaries. All these interpretations suggest a close, but complex, relationship between new divisions of labour in the UK economy and the educational revolution, in particular the development of mass higher education. This middle group is particularly interesting because it embraces the bulk of graduates from the mass higher education system.

Graduate employment – and a graduate economy?

Is it possible to talk of an emerging 'graduate economy'? Here, there are two competing, and even contradictory, narratives. The first is unambiguously positive, emphasising the ways in which the mass production of skilled graduates has contributed to economic success. This is still, just about, the dominant narrative. Although the size and shape of mass higher education systems are overwhelmingly determined by student demand, in other words social 'push', the case for investment in universities and colleges is often made in terms of meeting the need for a skilled workforce – in other words, economic 'pull'. The second narrative, touched on briefly in the previous section and now catching up fast in terms of political support, is more sceptical, emphasising instead ideas of graduate 'under-employment' (or 'over-education'). It is often expressed in terms of the desirability of curbing, or even reversing, the growth of higher education, and a diversion of resources into technical and further education.

Of course, the choice between the two narratives is not simply a matter to be resolved by careful economic analysis but also involves political and ideological choices. For example, calls to curb higher education expansion are also clearly motivated by social and academic elitism. But the emphasis in this chapter is on the former, the economic benefits of the UK's mass higher education. Crudely, do we have a mass system because we need one out of economic necessity, or because we can afford one and it is a desirable social good? Far too simple a question, of course, because economic success requires certain social conditions to be met (not least in terms of generating demand for goods and services). There is also significant evidence to support the view that more equal societies also tend to have more developed economies and greater national wealth. There is, of course, a counterargument that, as with mass higher education systems, it is only rich countries that can afford redistributive tax regimes and generous social spending.

But perhaps it is a question still worth considering because of these clashing narratives. It is also a timely and relevant one because of the debate about what constitutes a 'graduate job'. In formal terms, 'graduate jobs' are defined with reference to standard occupational classifications, which in turn are largely determined by job titles. But, as was also discussed in the previous section, there has been a tendency to inflate job titles, which partly reflects genuine increases in skills content but may also be a form of status compensation for restrictions on pay. Either way, job titles do not map easily onto skills levels. They also reflect the comparative social and cultural status of jobs. One of the major impacts of the COVID-19 pandemic has been to emphasise the UK's dependence on what have traditionally been regarded as medium- or even low-skill jobs. This opens up the possibility, although far from certainty, that there may be some radical reordering of the status of jobs.

However, whatever the narrative, there has clearly been a substantial growth in the proportion of jobs in the UK, and other advanced economies, that require applicants to be graduates. In 1997, 15 per cent of jobs fell into this category, and by 2017, the proportion had almost doubled to 29 per cent. What is interesting is that, although in the first of these decades (1997–2006) almost all of the 5 per cent increase in the proportion of jobs requiring graduates could be explained by up-skilling (in other words, the changing nature and content of these jobs), in the second decade (2006–17) up-skilling explained only a quarter of the 8 per cent increase (Henseke et al, 2020). One, short-term and expedient, explanation for this contrast is that employers took the opportunity of the greater competition for jobs following the 2008 crisis to upgrade the new workers they recruited. Another, longer-term and more speculative, explanation is that this change reflected more fundamental changes in the nature of the labour market.

Attempts to measure the skills 'density' of various jobs depend not only on an 'objective' analysis of the skills they require but also on the – inevitably subjective – perceptions of workers themselves about the skills they need and use. It is worth noting in this context that an overwhelming majority of graduates believe they are using the skills they learned during their courses, although this could logically lead to the unhelpful conclusion that a graduate job is just a job done by a graduate. A further complication is that salaries, although they indicate the market price of different forms of work, cannot simply be used as proxies for skills levels either, despite the temptation to define 'graduate jobs' in reductionist terms of higher salary levels, especially when there is a need, as there is in England where students are charged high fees, to demonstrate they have received 'value for money'. More than a third (37 per cent) of graduates in jobs that are labelled 'high skilled' according to SOC (standard occupational classification) categories are earning less than £24,000 a year 15 months after graduation, according to the most recent data.

The minority of graduates who take 'non-graduate' jobs do so for a wide variety of reasons – for example, to earn money or to gain experience – not simply because their qualifications have limited uses in the labour market. Interestingly, even if graduates end up in 'non-graduate' jobs, they are still paid more on average than non-graduates. Why is their labour priced more highly than that of people in apparently identical jobs? The most plausible conclusion that employers are paying for the intangible qualities associated with 'graduate-ness'. In other words, non-graduate jobs may be done 'better' by graduates, either because they are easier to train (because of the greater cognitive skills they have acquired) or because they are more productive.

The definition of a 'graduate job' is not only fuzzy but volatile. As a result, the accompanying concept of graduate 'under-employment' is equally problematical. But, even if this definition and concept are accepted as givens, the available evidence still suggests that, despite the large increases in the number of graduates, the proportion of 'under-employment' among graduates has not significantly increased. To the extent it has varied at all, it appears that the actual skills gained by graduates play a comparatively minor role compared with overall changes in the structure of UK employment (and associated rewards). After all, no reasonable person would attribute the stagnation of wages over the past decade predominantly to stagnant skills levels rather than to the state of the economy.

Going to university, of course, has always conferred on graduates non-financial benefits which they value highly, for example in terms of individual empowerment, social and cultural emancipation, and access to attractive lifestyles. These non-financial benefits may be particularly important if the underdevelopment of the UK economy in key areas, compared for example with some other European countries, and its skewed characteristics have made it more difficult to generate a sufficient number of 'highly skilled' jobs. After all, there is evidence that the links between jobs and social identity and status have loosened. As has already been argued, participation in higher education has become not only a route to highly skilled employment but also a component of this non-economic (in the sense of job titles) identity and status. As the 21st century progresses, this loosening between paid employment and individual identity and social status is likely to gather pace, not just in the UK but in all advanced economies. Some strategies have been attempted and failed, notably depressing wage levels to remain competitive with lower wage cost economies. Others have yet to be seriously attempted, for example a reduction in working hours. All these considerations leave the conventional debate – about securing a better fit between graduate skills and employment needs (which is actually pretty good) or adjusting priorities in tertiary education to reduce graduate 'under-employment' – appearing increasingly irrelevant.

Conclusion

The social landscape in the early decades of the 21st century, unsurprisingly, is post-industrial. In other words, it is no longer structured in terms of the particular class alignments that flourished in the age of industry from approximately the 1880s to the 1970s (although some historians would prefer to start that period in the early 1800s). In retrospect those nine decades were an exceptional time, characterised in particular by an organised labour and trade union movement representing the interests of a proletarian working class (and by attenuated Marxist ideas about capitalism and its exploitation of labour through the appropriation of the surplus value). In short, class consciousness was highly developed. The pre-industrial social landscape was even more stratified and unequal – but structured in much looser terms in which there was less clarity about the place of workers in the process of a horizontally imagined process of production, and more attention was given to other characteristics such as those in vertically organised, guild-like trades.

In terms of these looser structures, the contemporary post-industrial social landscape may appear to have much in common with the pre-industrial social landscape that prevailed before the high tide of heavy industry. The particularly acute proletarian class consciousness typical of the intervening period has declined. But this does not mean that real differences in the conditions of life and opportunities for social advancement have become more equal, rather the reverse. The UK is a much more unequal society in 2020 than it was in 1970 by almost every available measure. However, these differences are now more fluid and heterogeneous, and no longer so easily described (or experienced) in terms of social class. Other old-and-new affiliations have emerged. For example, the rise of nationalism and the decline of 'labour', especially in Scotland, cannot be explained solely as a reaction against the manifest incompetence of the archaic UK state and its political and administrative structures. Rather, it may suggest that categories such as 'British' (as opposed to Scottish, Welsh, English or Irish) may also have peaked in the age of industry – and, of course, 'empire', however uncomfortable it may be to associate 'labour' and 'empire' in this way. As a result, it is not at all surprising that social class, in this historical sense, is no longer such a powerful indicator. But to suggest that the UK is moving in the direction of becoming a classless society, in terms of more equal life chances, is a leap far too far.

This social landscape is reproduced in the economic landscape. The churn in occupational categories cannot disguise the persistent trend towards greater inequality of incomes, less extreme in the UK than the US but more extreme than in other mainstream European countries. This suggests that greater income inequality is not simply a structural feature of advanced economies, the result of factors such as growing competition from low-wage economies in an integrated global economy or the deskilling caused by the widespread adoption of more intelligent information technology systems. Rather, it reflects political choices grounded in ideology. Growing income inequality, in terms of wages, salaries and other benefits, seems to reflect a loosening of moral restraints. What was once unacceptable is now accepted, legitimised by dominant new neoliberal market ideologies. The increasing inequality of wealth of all kinds reflects a decline in taxation levels (especially between generations), as well as structural changes such as capital appreciation (especially of real property) and the end of the destruction of capital in the first half of the 20th century. The result is a polarisation of wealth.

The clear implication is that, although mass participation in higher education may have played a role in creating new forms of 'graduate' identity, it has played a subordinate role in any move away from describing identity in the language of social class. The advance of mass higher education has been a social leveller in many respects. But in other respects, it is a social divider. Most obviously, it has created divisions between graduates and the rest, the employment and reward consequences of which are clear in labour market statistics (and wider social and cultural behaviours). As a result of institutional stratification within mass systems, sharper divisions have also emerged between different types of higher education experience (crudely put, between elite universities and the rest).

In economic terms, universities play a key role, but again often at the margins (for example, as producers and, crucially in terms of regional development, retainers-in-place of skilled graduates, or as centres of material and cultural consumption). In terms of culture, the experience of higher education clearly plays an important role in shaping the habits and preferences of its graduates, although on a highly differentiated basis. In many ways graduates are trendsetters, early adopters of new technologies. The presence of universities also helps to shape urban environments, often literally so as they increasingly intrude into the urban landscape, and also to foster cosmopolitan cultures. But once again, in the context of overarching trends towards new communicative cultures and virtual identities, universities are far from being the only, or even the decisive, players.

However, this attempt to sketch the outlines of contemporary society, culture and economy in the UK and to position mass higher education within them in more nuanced (and less triumphalist?) terms does not absolve universities of their wider social responsibilities. If anything, it intensifies those obligations. This book began with an assertion that there is now something resembling a 'general crisis' of mass higher education. Its final chapters will set out ways in which it can respond to, and even resolve, that crisis.

8

COVID-19 emergency and market experiment

Introduction

The argument in this book is that mass higher education, for all its multiple and irreversible achievements, is experiencing a general crisis. This crisis can be attributed in part to contradictions that may be inherent in the project itself.

The most important of these contradictions is between the promise of wider opportunities (and outcomes) for all and the emergence of a new graduate class, no longer perhaps framed so oppressively in terms of gender, race or even social class, but nevertheless still a middle class from which key sections of the community are excluded. The graduate class itself is also strongly segmented as the result of the emergence of a more explicit hierarchy within, calibrated by types of institution. This hierarchy continues to reflect social and cultural advantage as much as intellectual merit. Both this new class and the hierarchy within it seem to mock the possibilities of a democratic higher education.

A second contradiction is between the belief that the expansion of higher education would be a major driver of a new skills- and knowledge-based economy and its apparent reality – the production of a mass graduate population. That mass population is sometimes seen as over-educated, or at any rate inappropriately or miseducated, and many graduates struggle to find satisfying jobs and careers. Once again, the graduate workforce is increasingly segmented between those in elite – or, if not elite, highly remunerated – occupations; those in the expert and technical professions; and those who, despite their high level of education, are under- or precariously employed and may sometimes enjoy limited career satisfaction. Such a segmentation has the potential for increasing social discontent: the able but under-employed or under-appreciated have always been a restless force in history. In any case, it hardly accords with the optimistic vision of a knowledge society.

A third contradiction is between the ideal of universities as self-governing communities of students and scholars, and the contemporary reality of universities as corporate organisations. The communitarian values of the former are mocked by the competitive imperatives of the latter. The *habitus* of the university has also changed profoundly. Mass expansion has often been blamed. But, as has been argued in earlier chapters, it is not necessarily the only culprit; organisational shifts towards more corporate forms across wider society are also important. A fourth is the tension between the increasing emphasis in many countries – but notably in England within the UK and wider Europe – on individual goods at the expense of public benefits and placing these individual goods at the heart of the conception of the contemporary university, on the one hand, and, on the other, the equally or more powerful growth of global consciences, exemplified by social movements on human rights and the environment. At the heart of these new movements, paradoxically, are often to be found the expanding populations of graduates produced by mass access.

A key part of the argument in this book is that these contradictions do not stand alone. This crisis of mass higher education is only one of several crises afflicting modern society more broadly – for example, the widening inequalities of income (and social conditions); the weakening of democratic legitimacy in an age of fake news and dark money; the rise of populist or, better, nativist revolts against the optimism, progressivism and cosmopolitanism of modernity; the explosion of aggressive (and politically charged) culture wars linked to fears of radicalisation and sometimes of immigration (and 'otherness' more generally); the growing concentration of corporate and financial power in an age of globalised capitalism; a corresponding increase in global distress and inequality; and the urgency of environmental degradation and species destruction fuelled by global warming (the dystopia of the dawning Anthropocene age).

As a result, anxieties about whether mass expansion has led to a more open society, and greater democracy, or to the consolidation of a new class – or, worse, a legitimation of hierarchy as an organising principle of society – have increased. These anxieties also cannot be divorced from the wider, confused and confusing, conversations about social mobility (in place of social equity and equality), which is naively assumed to be overwhelmingly upward, and political rhetoric about 'levelling up'. Equally, parallel anxieties about the ambiguous impacts of mass expansion on the labour market, careers and economic life-chances cannot be separated from the radical changes in occupational structures. Some of these changes can be attributed to near-inevitable economic and technological changes – for example, the decline of heavy manufacturing and extractive industries or, indeed, the impact of mass access to advanced education. But some are attributable to ideological choices – for example, the enforced shrinking of core public services provided by the state and parallel growth of a para-state of privatised and outsourced services.

Viewed through the lens of these multiple crises, the challenges facing mass higher education can appear almost overwhelming. Many of the standard responses are not so much wrong as underwhelming. They do not rise to the challenge of the times. Instead, they are constrained within the narrow limits of what counts as higher education policy, which is sometimes treated as a near-autonomous domain of public policy. Within these narrow limits, typical policy choices offered are between abolishing tuition fees or increasing them (while tinkering with student support and loan repayment systems); between increasing institutional differentiation (into the 'best' and , presumably, the 'rest') or seeking to establish wider tertiary education systems; between more intrusive 'steering' by politicians and bureaucrats or opening up the higher education 'market' to new forms of academic enterprise (which, in practice, often seems to require precautionary regulation difficult to distinguish from state steering); between encouraging even more management by metrics or creating more democratic forms of university governance.

Such policy choices, of course, are not trivial. They raise complex technical issues about their feasibility (and unintended consequences), which are the main diet of higher education policy. But these choices should also involve asking more fundamental, even moral, questions. Some of these questions are very old, such as those about the core purposes of a university; some are new questions about the place and responsibilities of higher education in an age beset by these multiple crises. Asking these questions takes many higher education policy makers, and the new class of institutional leaders and managers, out of their (technocratic) comfort zones. As a result, these more fundamental questions tend to be avoided or to receive less attention.

None of this relatively narrow, even technocratic, focus is new. Debates about expansion in the second half of the 20th century were also often framed in terms of detailed, and almost always inaccurate, projections of future demand rather than in wider terms of extending the higher education franchise in a democratic society. Debates about how the system should be organised were largely structured in terms of rivalry between central and local government or, later, membership of university 'clubs', rather than wider considerations of optimal system design. In the past, these rather narrow, and essentially technocratic, terms of engagement for discussions about policy choices may have mattered less. There were few fundamental doubts about the overall benefits of university expansion, and today's crises of democracy, modernity, inequality and the environment had yet fully to emerge. Under current conditions, this silence about the wider implications of these choices about the future direction of higher education, and how they relate to the wider crisis-beset environment, is a more serious weakness.

This chapter, the first of the two concluding chapters, will focus on two issues familiar to higher education leaders, policy makers, researchers and commentators: the implications of the public health emergency posed by the COVID-19 pandemic on the future direction of higher education; and the attempted development of a strongly market-oriented system of higher education in England, an experiment of more than local significance because it speaks to the wider question of whether there are limits to the application of market principles to the organisation of higher education. The final chapter will move on from discussing these episodes in *histoire événementielle*, as opposed to the *longue durée* (to adopt Braudelian language), to consider instead a set of reforms that might go some way towards resolving the general crisis facing mass higher education. But even here it is important to recognise that higher education is not an island but, in the words of John Donne, 'part of the main'. Any reforms that help mass higher education overcome its current contradictions – a radical 'leap forward' – can only be effective within the context of wider social and economic reform and cultural renewal.

The impact of COVID-19

The sudden appearance of COVID-19 in China at the end of 2019 and beginning of 2020, and its rapid spread around the globe in the first half of 2020, has been described as a 'black elephant' event, which could have been, and was, widely predicted but was largely ignored. This is a good description. Epidemics and pandemics have been coterminous with civilisation itself, and the emergence of organised urban societies with sufficiently concentrated populations to allow disease to spread. Human history has been punctuated by plague – in the 6th century in the reign of the Eastern Roman Emperor Justinian, through the Black Death in the 14th century, to the 'Spanish' flu of 1918–19. Many had major social and economic impacts. The role played by the mobility of peoples in the spread of exterminating diseases is also well understood. The most extreme example is still the near-extinction of the indigenous Indian population in the Americas in the 16th century as a result of exposure to routine diseases to which Eurasian populations had become partly immune following long-term exposure. But, in the second half of the 20th century, infectious diseases appeared to have been conquered.

The eruption of COVID-19 was preceded by earlier tremors which should have alerted the world to the complacency of that view. In the 1970s and 1980s HIV/AIDS demonstrated the terrible effects of a virus that jumped across the boundaries of species, exposing humans to the reservoir of disease among other animals. In the present century, precursors of COVID-19 such as SARS and MERS were further earlier warnings from which the wrong lessons – the feasibility of rapid containment – were learnt. Four factors, none of which is new but all of which have been intensified, have powered the COVID-19 pandemic.

The first is the increasing encroachment of human beings on the natural world, including on other animal species. Deforestation, intensive cultivation, the burning of fossil fuels, industrialisation of animal husbandry, global supply chains – all have created the conditions for the emergence and rapid spread of pandemic disease as surely as of global warning and species extinction. The consequences of humanity's heavy and oppressive footprint are apparent in the COVID-19 public health emergency.

The second is the accelerating pace of globalisation. There were direct flights from Wuhan, the Chinese city at the epicentre of the pandemic, to major cities across the world. Chinese tourists spread the virus to Italy. From there it was rapidly transferred to northern Europe by holiday makers returning from the ski slopes. Similar near-instantaneous vectors emerged around the world. Business travel, mass tourism and the increasing flows of international students are all aspects of this accelerating globalisation. It is revealing that the first cases of COVID-19 in the UK were of a foreign student and his visiting family. Later mutations spread rapidly across the world. In mitigation, other forms of globalisation were massively stimulated by the public health emergency, notably international efforts to develop and produce vaccines, and communication tools such as Zoom.

The third factor has been the fragility of international institutions, and the erosion of habits of global solidarity, both of which have been attributed to the popularity of neoliberal ideas now toxically layered with nativist populism. This fragility of global governance has been reflected in a fragility of national governance in some countries, which not coincidentally perhaps have been among those hardest hit by the pandemic. It has yet to be seen whether the world can rediscover its moral poise and resist the spread of vaccine nationalism.

The fourth factor is the vulnerability created by the growing interdependence of social and economic systems. Everything depends on everything else in the context of global supply chains, just-in-time delivery, multiple outsourcing – and, it might be added, instantly shared scientific data. Efficiency has often been calibrated in terms of cost rather than of resilience. The increasing dependence on technology in social life and the noise created by the media have perhaps intensified these vulnerabilities of interconnectedness.

The impact of the COVID-19 public health emergency on higher education was immediate (Commissioner for Fair Access, 2020). Across the world, most universities largely closed during the first wave, remaining open only for stranded students in campus residences and a few others, and some core services. Student learning moved online, as did the elaborate administrative and deliberative bureaucracy that is an inescapable feature of modern university life. The longer-term effects of these measures were not considered in any detail, on the initial assumption that any effects would be essentially temporary. This assumption was strengthened when the first wave appeared to recede in the summer of 2020. Universities opened their doors again, with only limited public health hygiene measures in place.

The inevitable result of large-scale student migration at the start of the new academic year, even on a much reduced scale, and of the repopulation of campuses was, inevitably in retrospect, a rise in infection rates which coincided with a second, and more virulent, wave of the pandemic. This second wave, in the last three months of 2020 continuing into the spring of 2021, closed campuses again. The hope of some kind of return to normality then increased with the growth in the number of vaccinations in the spring of 2021 (Hillman, 2020b). But, at the same time, it has become more difficult to ignore the longer-term consequences of an emergency the intensity of which more than compensated for its hoped-for brevity.

One of these longer-term consequences is the potential for setting back the access agenda, which has always been at the heart of the mass higher education project (in spirit, if not always in effect). A second is the reversibility of – or the desirability of reversing – the enforced shift to blended learning for students, within which online provision has played the dominant role. A third is the need to consider the consequences for the wider student experience which, in the UK and many other countries, emphasises the campus experience, often in a residential mode, the academic *habitus*. This is particularly true in the case of elite universities. A fourth longer-term consequence is the impact of COVID-19, in terms not only of public health restrictions but also of potential changes in habits and behaviour, on internationalisation, which has become such a prominent feature of higher education systems over the past generation.

Access

The COVID-19 public health emergency has the potential to derail the democratisation of higher education at multiple levels: initial access to higher education; the experience of being a student; and graduate outcomes, particularly in terms of employment. The overall impact of COVID-19 has been that, to adapt the famous words of St Matthew's Gospel, 'from those with the least the most has been taken away'.

Catch-up, bridging and access programmes offered by universities, designed not only to remedy deficits in attainment but also to overcome cultural barriers, necessarily rely on personal engagement. As a result, they have struggled to be as effective in an online environment, although it has been argued that online programmes extend their reach. But the impact has been felt not only by the immediate cohort of 2020 applicants. The future supply of applicants from more socially deprived communities, or who are otherwise disadvantaged, has been compromised by school closures. School attendance has always acted an equaliser, despite unequal patterns of funding particularly between independent and state schools. Restrictions on attendance are likely to widen the attainment gap, so often cited by more selective universities as a defence of their socially skewed student populations. Schools' reliance on online learning has highlighted the alarming digital divide between rich and poor, between those with expensive MacBooks and others with cheap mobile phones. This digital divide, and the cancellation of school examinations which frame the upper-secondary school curriculum, have inevitably eroded motivation and aspiration.

Within higher education itself, the same digital poverty has put disadvantaged students at further disadvantage. This poverty is reflected not only in the availability of appropriate IT equipment and connectivity, which can to some extent be remedied. It is also reflected in the availability of the space and ambience that encourages students to study, a more intractable issue. As with schools, campus attendance is a social equaliser. The collapse in part-time jobs, often in hospitality, has placed poorer students at a further disadvantage. Finally, a depressed graduate labour market, even temporarily, will exacerbate existing inequalities between graduates coming from a privileged hinterland and those who lack the same degree of personal connections and confidence.

The immediate evidence suggests that the proportion of higher education entrants from more disadvantaged social groups did not suffer in the immediate aftermath of the pandemic. However, the damage to access may simply be delayed. While it is possible to develop mitigating action for potential applicants in a short-term emergency, it may be more difficult to compensate for the widening of the attainment gap and erosion of aspiration in the middle (or even early) years of education. The potential setbacks to widening participation and promoting fairer access to higher education, and especially elite universities, highlight not only the need for decisive action to prevent longer-term scarring of opportunities but also the key role access plays in helping to resolve mass higher education's general crisis. Urgent and sustained restorative action is needed.

Learning

In recent years most universities have incrementally increased the amount of learning material available to students online, although nearly always to supplement rather than substitute for traditional modes of teaching. But the near-total closure of university campuses enforced a sudden and whole-system displacement of face-to-face teaching by online learning. Institutions were largely successful in adapting courses to largely online delivery as an emergency measure during the first wave of the pandemic. Limited exceptions were made for some practice-based courses that require hands-on experience. What is remarkable, to paraphrase Samuel Johnson, is not that it was always done well but that it was done at all. Just as not all students had the same capacity to access online courses, not all online courses were of a similar pedagogical and technical standard. Sometimes conventional lectures and seminars were simply video-recorded and supplemented by chatrooms and other interactive tools. The question now is whether this far-reaching system-wide experiment should be consolidated or (partially) reversed.

With the reopening of campuses in the late summer of 2020, and again in the spring of 2021, some face-to-face teaching was restored. Uncertainty about the future trajectory of COVID-19, and the continuing need for public health restrictions, makes it difficult to predict how far and fast this return to 'business as usual' in learning and teaching will proceed. But it is clearly important to evaluate the experiment in shifting radically to online delivery of higher education. Preliminary research into students' attitudes suggests that, while they recognise some benefits such as their improved digital skills and better time management, they see few other positive benefits – particularly when other constraints on the wider student experience are taken into account (Hewitt, 2020). Despite this, universities may be attracted by possible efficiency gains, although previous experience suggests that, done well, online delivery is not a cheap option. The impact of online delivery on this scale on learning styles remains largely unexplored. The webinar clearly has different dynamics from the seminar. Using social media is not the same experience as attending class. But these differences are elusive and, again, largely unexplored, except in micro-studies.

On the larger canvas, it is unclear how important the communitarian practices of in-person and on-campus teaching are to the essence of a university education, even in an age of mass higher education. What rites and rituals are being performed – and can they be performed online? Certainly, there remains a strong conviction among academic staff that at its best a university education must retain some element of direct personal engagement between students and their teachers, and crucially with other students, that is difficult to reproduce online. The conviction is even stronger that such engagement is particularly important for students from more diverse backgrounds with more limited academic and social capital for whom the rites of academic life are especially important (Montacute and Holt-White, 2021).

However, the experience of the radical shift to online and blended learning in the COVID-19 emergency may have produced a step-change in attitudes to the delivery of higher education – revolutionary substitution in place of evolutionary enhancement. It may also have reinforced the more radical view that in a digital age in which shopping, entertainment and most interactions with bureaucracy are rapidly moving online, a parallel shift in higher education is inevitable. According to this view, for many students the future lies with more self-curated forms of education such as massive open online courses (MOOCs) and micro-credentials alongside whole-course assessments (Bishop, 2021). COVID-19 has sharpened these debates.

Habitus and community

This leads to the third possible longer-term consequence of the COVID-19 emergency – its impact on the evolution of the university as a *habitus* for students, and also for teachers and researchers. The growth of mass higher education since the 1960s has greatly increased the spatial and visual presence of the university. In the 1960s and 1970s designer campuses were planned, often on greenfield sites. Within cities, 'signature' buildings were constructed to front more coherent university precincts. Later still, in response to the emerging view that students were now consumers, institutions further developed their academic, and social, estate to make it more student friendly. But the COVID-19 emergency left campuses and precincts almost deserted. Even when universities reopened, continuing public health restrictions have made it difficult to restore the 'buzz' of campus life.

The analogy with hollowed-out high streets and smarter offices is almost inescapable. Just as many predict that high streets will need to be reinvented, as boutique consumer spaces, or that offices will become occasional venues for hot-desking and team meetings, it seems possible that equally radical changes will need to be made in how campuses are used. To some extent, these changes were under way before COVID-19. Fewer lecture theatres were being built, and more brightly designed social spaces for students created. Monumental libraries with imposing book stacks were being replaced by learning resource centres designed to access more digital content. But these changes were essentially adjustments to how university campuses were configured. They were designed to update how these dedicated spaces – which were the embodiment of academic communities, whether among students or researchers – are used. Far from abolishing the need for such spaces, the intention was to make them more attractive and more vibrant.

The experience of the pandemic, with the enforced and temporarily near-complete closure of many campuses, may accelerate and radicalise some of these trends. If more student learning moves online, arguably the need for traditional lecture halls and seminar rooms will decline still further. However, on-campus spaces to access online learning will still be needed. For many students, the main attraction of online delivery is that it can be accessed at convenient times, not that it is available 'at a distance'. A lot of access, therefore, is still very local, and campus based. In any case, the need for more learning space, part-study and part-social, will correspondingly increase.

The COVID-19 shock seems unlikely to deconstruct the physical university in a more fundamental sense, even to the (limited?) extent that it may have that effect on the high street or the office. Instead, enforced closures may have produced a powerful nostalgia for renewed face-to-face connections. Creative entrepreneurs have long recognised that they need to meet in coffee shops as well as on screens, which is why they cluster in certain districts in cities. This is even more true in higher education. The co-location of universities, research establishments and some forms of enterprise is not mere convenience. The residential model of a university also remains immensely influential, especially in the elite sector. The university's presence is not simply instrumental – a more or less convenient collection of buildings – but also normative – an expression of the ideal of a learning community, only part of which can be transferred onto the virtual plane. The impact of COVID-19 changes none of that.

Internationalisation

The fourth longer-term consequence of COVID-19 is for the internationalisation of higher education. There have always been international flows of students and scholars, from the medieval university through the colonial connections during the age of empire to the diasporas of refugees in the 20th century. But in the past half century the scale of internationalisation has transformed the character of many universities. Before the COVID-19 pandemic there were confident predictions that the numbers of internationally mobile students would increase two or even threefold by the middle of the present century.

The imperatives of internationalisation have also grown more urgent. The North American and Western European higher education and research systems have become increasingly dependent on an inflow of students from other parts of the world, especially at doctoral and postdoctoral level, to make good the shortfall in domestic production – in short, brain gain. In the UK the recruitment of high fee-paying international students has also provided an essential funding stream. In most countries the intensity of internationalisation has been seen as evidence of prestige and excellence, because the proportion of international students and staff is a key metric in league tables of so-called 'top universities'.

None of these imperatives has diminished in force. But restrictions on travel have sharply reduced flows of international students and staff in the short run. The relative success of different countries in coping with COVID-19 has probably also influenced their national images, and their attractiveness as academic destinations. Most of the major importing countries have struggled, but none more so than the US and the UK, which has been further burdened by negative perceptions of its decision to leave the European Union. The endorsed shift to largely online learning has also adversely affected international students, many of whom, in addition to the course and credentials, seek a wider experience of acculturation in their host countries.

Most universities probably anticipate, once the pandemic has been tamed, a return to business-as-usual, with only a few course corrections, notably greater emphasis on sustainability. They also anticipate that the upward trajectory of internationalisation will be restored. National strategies are now being refurbished which continue to embody these optimistic assumptions (Department for Education, 2021). Of course, incremental change had already been expected, and accepted. Gradual shifts in flows of international students were already anticipated. In particular, as higher education systems in East Asia developed it was widely anticipated they would cease to 'export' students to North America and Europe on the same scale. The greater use of online courses was also already expected, allowing more mixed-mode delivery for international students. Virtual mobility and internationalisation-at-home were familiar concepts.

However, two features that predated COVID-19 but have been highlighted by the pandemic may create greater difficulties for the smooth path of internationalisation. The first is the way in which the pandemic has exposed inequalities in higher education in a harsher light than ever before. The profile of international students is skewed even more heavily than that of home students to the most privileged social groups. The rapid increase in international students in the past two decades has been powered by the rising aspirations of the expanding middle classes in countries often marked by extremes of wealth and poverty. Aid and development programmes, and accompanying scholarship programmes, have contributed comparatively little to the recent growth in the number of international students. International partnerships have also been dominated by exchanges between elite universities. Limited attempts have been made in the recent past to allow considerations of equity to influence this internationalisation drive. Post-Covid, and in a world of increasing global inequality and stress, will such an agnostic position on access and equity be possible to sustain?

The second feature is the rapid growth of what might be termed an ecological conscience across the world, most strongly in the most developed countries and among those of their citizens with the highest levels of education. The COVID-19 pandemic itself is an example of the consequences of the exploitative relationship between human beings and the rest of the natural, and animal, world. Internationalisation, as currently practised, also has a heavy environmental footprint, which the sharp reduction of global circulation in response to the pandemic has highlighted. Once again, is that practice any longer sustainable? Greater emphasis on sustainability action plans to reduce the heavy CO_2 footprint of international student and staff exchanges hardly seem adequate to address the concerns expressed in this emerging 'global conscience'.

A market experiment

The second major theme of this chapter is the experiment in applying market principles to the organisation of English higher education, often stigmatised as marketisation. This experiment was begun a decade ago and has already been discussed in greater detail in Chapter 3. But two further aspects of these reforms will be considered here. The first is the most recent developments since 2018, which arguably have seen a retreat from marketisation. The second is that these reforms constitute probably the most radical experiment in applying market principles to the operation of a public system of higher education anywhere in the world. Therefore, they have more than local significance.

Retreat from the market

As has already been said, there are many excellent analyses, mainly critiques, of the reforms in English higher education since 2010, which have already been referred to in earlier chapters (Brown and Carasso, 2013; Callender and Scott, 2013; McGettigan, 2013; Collini, 2012, 2017). The framers of these reforms have also responded to their critics, provoking a lively debate (Willetts, 2017). This book has not been designed principally as another intervention in that debate. Instead, the intention is to highlight the main consequences of these reforms, both intentional and unintended, in the spirit of the book's focus not on the *histoire événementielle* but the *longue durée*.

England's market experiment did not come out of nowhere. Before the Second World War universities in the UK still enjoyed significant non-state funding, mainly from student fees, (limited) philanthropic donations, and support and sponsorship from (mainly local) industry and business, although a system of state grants had been instituted just before the First World War and regularised with the establishment of the University Grants Committee in 1919. Increasing financial support to students to pay fees and living expenses had also been made available, but mainly in the form of local authority scholarships for those who had high marks in school examinations and would not otherwise be able to go to university. Over the course of the two decades after 1945 all this changed. By the mid-1960s the predominant source of funding for universities came from the state, which had also taken a leading role in establishing new universities. For a while fees continued notionally to be charged but they were now fully reimbursed from public funds. At the same time a universal system of grants for living expenses to which all students were eligible had been established, although the parents of students from richer families were still expected to make a contribution.

This prehistory is important because it can too easily be assumed that until the current market reforms a predominantly state-funded system of public higher education was the historical norm in the UK, as in most other European countries (although they too have their own intriguing prehistories). It is more accurate to see almost wholly publicly funded higher education as a development of the second half of the 20th century and, as such, an important element in the post-war welfare state. When that welfare state began to unravel from the 1980s onwards, the public funding of higher education also came under threat. But not immediately – Margaret Thatcher's government made no serious effort to deny the principle of state funding, although it did attempt sharply to reduce the funding available. The erosion of the principle of public funding through state grants came a decade later in the 1990s when student grants for living expenses were progressively replaced by repayable loans and the groundwork was laid for charging fees again.

As has been discussed in Chapter 2, the formal decision to reintroduce tuition fees was taken not by a Conservative government but by the incoming Labour government in 1997. Fees were charged, first at the modest annual level of £1,000 but later increased to £3,000. Initially these decisions were pragmatic rather than principled. The income from fees was in addition to direct state funding, in effect a top-up. The new fees, paid upfront by the state and repaid after graduation, were largely a device to leverage extra public expenditure without coming into direct competition with other public services, notably the NHS, which had greater political and public support.

According to one reading, therefore, the market-oriented reforms pursued since 2010 were a return to pre-welfare state patterns of higher education funding and even enjoyed, in a limited and highly provisional way, bipartisan political support. Over the next decade, these reforms moved through three phases. The first, beginning in 2010, saw the tripling of tuition fees from a standard contribution of £3,000 to a maximum fee of £9,000 (subsequently upgraded in line with inflation), the so-called extended fee cap. This increase represented a clear move beyond Labour's essentially pragmatic use of fees to leverage extra public funding towards the deliberate design of a more explicitly market-oriented funding regime in which students were put, in the title of the 2011 White Paper, 'at the heart of the system' (Department of Business, Innovation and Skills, 2011). Students were now required to make a much larger contribution to the cost of their higher education. But in return they were to be recognised as 'customers', with their choices and preferences shaping future provision. That was the deal.

However, as discussed in Chapter 3, two design faults rapidly emerged. First, it had been expected that universities would charge variable fees depending on the cost of providing particular courses and also on their own standing within the 'market' (or, more accurately, hierarchy of institutions). Second, it had also been expected that higher education would be opened up to 'alternative providers', essentially private institutions, most of which were for-profit, which would challenge the existing public institutions. The first never happened and the second only to a limited extent and belatedly.

In the second phase of the reforms neither design fault was directly addressed. Instead, there was an attempt to revive the momentum towards a market, mainly by removing the overall cap on student numbers that had existed since the 1990s to limit the state's total funding commitment. The effect was not so much to kickstart a new expansion in the total number of students in England, but to redistribute students within the system from less selective universities, which were, by definition, more open to new kinds of students (and incidentally were more vocationally oriented), to more selective universities. The removal of the student numbers cap was also expensive, because more students meant more initial outlay of public money to fund the loans to which all students were entitled.

This background is important to understand the most recent changes in higher education policy since 2018, which mark a retreat from the market established in 2010–11 and modified by the Higher Education and Research Act 2017. Four changes have taken place.

First, the income level at which graduates began to pay back their student loans was increased. As a result, the Research Accounting and Budgeting (RAB) charge was also increased, raising the long-term burden on public expenditure. Receipts declined while outgoings increased, as a result of the removal of the student numbers cap and consequent increase in the student population.

Second, the Office for National Statistics changed the way loans paid to students by the Student Loans Company (SLC) should be accounted for in the national accounts. Instead of the total amount being 'off the books', and therefore not counting as public expenditure (or adding to the government's official borrowing requirement), all outgoing loans should count as public expenditure, on the reasonable grounds that they were provided by the state, minus actual repayments by graduates. The effect was that the UK Government's deficit sharply increased. Any supposed savings produced by a reduction in direct state funding of universities were exposed as what has been termed a 'fiscal illusion' (Roff, 2021).

Third, the then prime minister, Theresa May, dismayed by the Labour Party's appeal to young people in university constituencies, established the Augar Committee to review student fees and funding. The clear steer given to the committee was that it should reconsider the existing tuition fee cap, which had led to all students in public institutions being charged the maximum £9,250 that was allowed. The Augar Committee duly obliged, recommending a reduction to £7,500, but with the possibility that some universities might be able to charge more (Augar Report, 2019). This recommendation satisfied two objectives: to reduce the standard fee, while opening the door to the development of variable fees, as the framers of the original 2010–11 reforms had hoped. Although the government, now under Mrs May's successor Boris Johnson, did not immediately accept the Augar recommendation for a cut in the standard fee, the possibility of charging still higher fees – to reflect, as some universities argued, the true cost of teaching – was effectively foreclosed.

Taken together, these first two changes cast serious doubt on the long-term affordability of the system of student – and, by extension, institutional – funding established in 2010–11. If the Augar recommendations are accepted, there is likely to be a further dilution of the market principles on which the 2010–11 reforms were based.

However, in the short run, the immediate impact of the COVID-19 emergency imposed an effective standstill on the development of higher education. The UK government dithered over its response to Augar, and essentially ignored the inescapable consequences of the higher graduate repayment threshold and the redesignation of student loans in the national accounts. As 2020 ended and 2021 began, ministers showed very little interest in attempting to rescue or refine the market experiment begun a decade earlier.

Instead, they embarked upon a very different, and interventionist, policy agenda – the fourth big change. The Office for Students (OfS) came under sustained pressure to act as much more *dirigiste* regulator. Sometimes this was for noble purposes, such as promoting widening participation and fair access. But increasingly it was for openly political and ideological purposes. The centrepiece of the government's agenda was to combat supposed threats to academic freedom by left-wing activists to 'woke' or 'cancel' culture which, it was alleged, had not been vigorously resisted by university managers. This was to be achieved by new legislation and toughened instructions to the OfS. Another measure was a top-down adjustment to the newly relabelled 'strategic funding grant', successor to the block grant once made to universities in long-gone 'arm's length' days. These adjustments were presented as tough action against undesirable subjects such as media studies – undesirable, that is, to politicians, not to students. Other measures included the downgrading of the National Student Survey and of the Teaching Excellence Framework, and their effective replacement by metrics such as 'Start to Success', which covers continuation rates and graduate earnings; and action to combat so-called 'grade inflation' in degree classifications, the increase in the number of 'firsts' and 'two-one' degrees. This metric was quickly complemented by another similar metric, Proceed (Projected Completion and Employment data). These acronyms reek of a narrow instrumentalism.

All these measures had two common features. The first was a downgrading of student choices. The government increasingly acted as if it knew better than students what was good for them. The second was an openly political and ideological policy agenda, implemented through familiar forms of system 'steering' directly by the state or its subordinate agents. In the threadbare disguise of regulation to protect student customers, top-down state control of higher education has not only been restored but imposed with a degree of intrusiveness once unimaginable. Their common effect was to step back from the intention to establish a market-led system of higher education, which in effect has been largely abandoned. Whatever view is taken of the direction of higher education policy in England, supportive or critical, it is now difficult to label it marketisation. Centralisation or politicisation are much more accurate labels.

The English experiment

The English experiment between 2010 and 2018 was the most sustained and fully developed attempt to apply market principles to the organisation of a public system of higher education. As a result, its effective abandonment since 2018 raises an important question. Should this abandonment be regarded simply as a local failure of no wider significance for the viability of marketisation as a general strategy for the development of higher education, or does it demonstrate that privatisation is fatally flawed?

It is tempting, and even comforting, to regard the faltering of England's market experiment as simply a local failure. The experiment had two design flaws, over and above the specific failures to introduce variable fees and open the doors to alternative providers. Both flaws are rooted in conflicts of interests. The first applies to the OfS, which is both a regulator and also a provider of funding, now avowedly in the form of funding strategic initiatives. It is impossible for a body to be both outside the market as a regulator and at the same time an active player in that market. The second applies to the state, which is both a banker, providing loan financing to students, and a policy setter, which directly impacts on the risk of non- or under-payment of the loans it has made. Put simply, as banker, the state has a responsibility to minimise the RAB charge – in effect to reduce bad debts – and an incentive to save public expenditure. But, as policy setter, it is likely to take decisions that run counter to that responsibility – for example, by encouraging students to study subjects in the wider national interest which may not command high salaries (and, therefore, reduce their ability to repay their loans in full). Even if these conflicts of interest had been recognised, they would have been difficult to resolve. Two separate state agencies, one to regulate the market and the other to set policy, would not be credibly independent of each other. Even if commercial lenders were prepared to take over the student loan book from the state, they would not be prepared to accept a transfer of risk, so bad debts would remain the ultimate responsibility of the state.

At a broader level, England's higher education market experiment has been contaminated by the natural inclination of Whitehall to centralise decision making, discussed in earlier chapters. This centralising instinct is now reinforced by the rise of ideological polarisation accompanying Brexit, which has encouraged a (right-wing) radicalisation of many UK government policies. The failure, therefore, is simply another example of collateral damage caused by the over-centralisation of decision making, and a rotten electoral system that manufactures majorities in the House of Commons out of minorities and undermines moderate politics. Both are diseases that are eating away the UK state. But there are no wider lessons to be learnt in terms of the generic development of higher education policies. In another country with a greater taste for devolution and for non-confrontational politics, marketisation could still work.

On the other hand, the faltering of the English experiment may suggest that any attempt to create a functioning higher education market is likely to encounter serious contradictions – for two reasons. The first is the applicability of market principles to higher education. A university education is a highly complex (and usually once-in-a-lifetime) experience. It is not a consumer good or service that can be 'purchased' several times over, activating genuine market choices. Even in terms of the private benefits it brings to individuals, which of course are largely positional benefits, the experience is savoured over a lifetime. It is not cashed in immediately or soon after graduation.

The second reason is it is almost impossible to take the politics out of higher education – both in limited terms of regulation to ensure the market operates fairly, and in wider terms of recognising that there are essential public, or collective, goods that cannot be produced simply by the operation of a market in which the preferences of individuals, and their expectations of private benefits, are the sole determining factors. In practice, these two rather different reasons for political intervention tend to get confused.

First, it is difficult to define where market regulation ends, and political intervention begins. Inevitably, the rules of regulation are written to reflect the preferences of those who set them: those with political and bureaucratic power. This is particularly the case when, as in England, the state provides loans to pay tuition fees and only partially reclaims them. In theory these loans could be provided by banks, although probably on the basis that the state continues to bear all the risk by underwriting any losses through default – which would transform these bank loans into *de facto* public expenditure. As a result, the role of the state in higher education, far from shrinking, has simply been changed and even been aggrandised. The on-the-ground differences between state regulation and state 'steering' can be difficult to define. Their common effect is to constrain the freedom of action of universities. But, arguably, a more fundamental reason for this erosion of institutional autonomy is to be found in the development of mass higher education systems.

Second, political interventions inevitably extend beyond the protection of a well-regulated market. Even if only private benefits to individuals are considered, it is clearly unacceptable in a democratic society for access to higher education to be rationed by the ability to pay, on grounds of both social equity and economic efficiency. But higher education also has important community, national and international roles, even if these collective benefits are difficult to measure. Universities exist not just now but in history. Once again, some form of active political intervention is required to safeguard these collective benefits. But any form of intervention, except the most passive simply to ensure fair competition and the smooth working of the markets, undermines the rationale of having a market in the first place.

There is a final and fundamental argument against the marketisation of higher education, even in less polarised environments than in England. To attempt to organise a public higher education largely according to market principles – as opposed to enhancing student choice, which as the English example has shown, is a very different matter – is also to make an ideological statement about the purposes of higher education. It asserts that its primary purposes are to maximise benefits for individuals – benefits moreover that are denominated in terms of earning power – and also to add to economic wealth by contributing to greater productivity and faster growth. In other words, these purposes are framed within an essentially free-market neoliberal world view. This frame of reference leaves out some of the traditional purposes of higher education, to help build nations in the 19th century and to educate citizens in a democracy in the 20th century, as well as its core educative function to promote liberal learning and critical understanding. This neoliberal frame also leaves out some new purposes: to address the challenges of inequality (locally, nationally and globally) and of urgent threats to humanity and the planet – of which the COVID-19 pandemic and the global environmental crisis are the most obvious examples.

9

What is to be done?

Introduction

This book has taken the long view – deliberately. It has focused on Braudel's *longue durée*, with a backward gaze to 1960 and detours into wider social and economic change. The issues of the moment, namely the longer-term impact of COVID-19 and the stuttering progress of England's market experiment in higher education – *histoire événementielle*, in Braudel's terms – were discussed in Chapter 8. But it is still too early to reach settled conclusions about either. In any case, the emphasis on the long view is fundamental to the argument in this book, that the crisis now facing higher education, in England, the wider UK and many other advanced countries, is only one of a number of intersecting crises in contemporary society, culture and the economy. It cannot be examined, let alone resolved, on its own.

This final chapter discusses four main themes, focusing on the ways in which this crisis might be resolved:

- further expansion and a decisive shift towards a universal system of tertiary education;
- fair access to reduce current inequity in terms of participation, progression through higher education, achievement levels and graduate success;
- a better balance between 'steering' and regulation, within a broader framework of democratic accountability and the abandonment of surveillance metrics at the system level, combined with the root-and-branch reform of institutional governance and management; and, perhaps most important,
- the reassertion of the public character of the university and its crucial, and critical, role in maintaining an open society.

Expansion

First on the 'What is to be done?' list of reforms must be a large-scale expansion of higher education, a step-change beyond a mass to a universal system. But old, and bad, habits die hard. In 2020 in the UK, ministers in the recently re-elected Conservative government publicly stated their belief that the 50 per cent participation target associated with the former Labour prime minister Tony Blair should be abandoned, overlooking the awkward fact that it has already been achieved. Just like the 'more means worse' opponents of the Robbins expansion more than half a century ago, they appeared to believe that too many 18-year-olds were going into higher education. Higher education should be reserved for the intellectually able (who possessed the social and cultural capital, whether acquired or inherited, to benefit from it), while most school leavers should go instead into technical education or apprenticeships. That belief is interesting not because there is any serious prospect of higher education growth being thrown into reverse but as evidence of how deeply unchallenged notions of 'the brightest and the best' and 'excellence' have remained rooted in both the academic and political spaces in the UK despite decades of successful expansion. It also highlights the persistence of an anachronistic taxonomy of different sectors of post-secondary education, long ago abandoned in the US, where 'college' or 'higher education' has swallowed up these hierarchical and discriminatory sub-categories.

Expansion is not going to be reversed. According to surveys of social attitudes, the overwhelming proportion of parents in the UK now expect their children to go on to higher education. Parental ambitions are mirrored in the aspirations of their children. The social pressure for more higher education, therefore, will be irresistible. One survey found that even in the most socially deprived communities 97 per cent of would-be parents – in effect, all – anticipated a future in higher education for their children (Centre for Longitudinal Studies, 2010). These high levels of ambition are not in themselves particularly surprising after two generations or more of expansion. They are actually higher than in the US, perhaps because there has been less time (and therefore opportunity) for the experience of mass higher education to sour, which has happened to some extent in the US mainly because of inflationary fee levels (a lesson there perhaps for policy makers in England?).

Instead, it is key elements in the social (and academic) elites in the UK who appear to have the greatest doubts about the value of further increasing student places in higher education. They, not the public, worry that mass expansion has been at least a partial 'failure'. They also seem determined to maintain a high degree of differentiation between institutions because only a suitably trained-up minority can benefit from a traditional university education. To the extent there is a crisis of confidence about mass higher education, it seems to be among these elites not among the general population.

Rather than contemplating a retreat from the 50 per cent participation 'target', now more than two decades old, the UK should plan to push up the participation rate to 70 or even 80 per cent of young people. This reflects what parents expect with regard to their own children and what young people aspire to. Nor is it especially ambitious. There are already many examples of high-participation higher education systems enrolling substantially more than 50 per cent of young people. Renewed growth to more than three quarters of school leavers (and a corresponding uplift in opportunities for adults) might appear radical. Rather, it would be a game of catch-up. Participation on that scale would only match the rates already achieved in many other countries, notably in some East Asian countries such South Korea.

Building a tertiary system

Even if – still a big 'if' – the case for expansion is accepted, the question then arises of how such growth should be distributed. There has been extensive, although rather sterile, discussion about the correct balance between universities and other institutions, such as local colleges and new providers, and within the university sector between traditional universities – that is those which are most research intensive– and other universities – which focus more on teaching and also recruit students from more varied social backgrounds. There has also been a parallel discussion about the correct balance between academic and vocational subjects and also between degrees and other courses such as Higher National Diplomas (HNDs) and Certificates (HNCs), often disparagingly labelled 'sub-degree' or 'non-degree' (a label that reveals which is regarded as the academic gold standard). None of these discussions has been especially productive, mainly because they tend to rely on binary either/or choices with limited purchase in the real world.

For example, the distinction between research-intensive and teaching universities is predicated on a narrow and perhaps outdated view of subject-bound and curiosity-driven research at a time when there is widespread agreement about the development of more open forms of knowledge production (Gibbons et al, 1994). Even within traditional modes of research there is a strong trend towards placing greater emphasis on issues and problems and less on the development of disciplinary knowledge. But, if it is accepted that 'research' has become a more extensive and diffuse category, any categorical distinction between research-intensive universities, where esteem is measured in terms of highly cited publications in traditional journals or scholarly books, the production of PhDs and high volumes of research income, on the one hand, and, on the other, different types of university engaged in more open forms of knowledge work, for example applied or activist research, also becomes much less clear.

The near-impossibility of devising a satisfactory distinction between 'academic' and 'vocational' (or, better, professional) subjects has been broadly accepted for many years. Yet it continues to be part of the essential vocabulary of higher education policy-speak. The more cynical, of course, have always seen this demarcation (correctly?) as a code, a proxy to distinguish between more and less 'noble' forms of higher education, according to their student profiles. The pronounced bias against 'vocational' higher education, a perennial cause of complaint about the supposedly ingrained contempt for entrepreneurialism in English culture, can readily be explained by the transparency of that code. Who wants to be in second place? The divide between degrees and sub- or non-degree courses such as HNDs has been made wider, and less porous, by the failure to develop effective articulation pathways through higher education so familiar in the US (although not in the rest of Europe).

Much of the difficulty – the disjunction between policy debates and the real world – is due to the survival of outdated and divisive categories: higher and further education, with adult education as an afterthought; within higher education, bizarrely and anachronistically, pre-1992 and post-1992 universities; academic and professional education; degrees and non-degree courses … A much broader and more inclusive language of tertiary education needs to be developed at both conceptual and operational levels (outside of the pages of OECD, UNESCO and World Bank statistics where it currently exists). The concept of lifelong learning, so often lauded as an idealistic policy goal, has struggled to establish itself in more concrete policy terms. There has only been limited movement towards broader and more inclusive categories of post-secondary education. Within the UK, the Welsh Government proposes to establish a tertiary education committee following the recommendations of the Hazelkorn Review (2016). The Scottish Government launched a 'Learner Journey 15–24' initiative that attempted to embrace the multiple pathways into different forms of education, training and work, although its impact has so far been limited (Scottish Government, 2018). In England sadly, and let it be hoped temporarily, there has so far been a doubling-down on traditional demarcations.

A tertiary future is perhaps as inevitable in a post-mass, or universal, system as the increasing coordination of universities and other forms of higher education was in the second half of the 20th century when mass higher education systems were developed. In many universities, in the UK and around the world, new roles, once regarded as peripheral (or the responsibility of other institutions and organisations), are moving ever close to the core of their mission. In effect, through this process of mission creep, they are becoming markedly more comprehensive. The need now is to develop system structures that are equally comprehensive. Instead of being deliberately engineered, competition between institutions should be curbed. Collaboration, local partnerships, regional consortia between different universities, and between universities and colleges (and, more broadly, other educational and cultural organisations) should be encouraged through formal coordination, joint funding and other methods.

Important changes would flow from the shift towards much higher levels of participation, and perhaps a lower proportion of residential on-campus students, and towards a system structure based on networks of comprehensive institutions. For example, community identity would become more important than corporate branding; the recent emphasis on reviving the idea of the 'civic university' is an early indication of this important shift. The Kerslake Report on the civic university will be discussed further later in this chapter (Kerslake Report, 2019). Surveillance systems such as the REF and TEF, the primary use of which is to 'empower' students as consumers in an academic marketplace by ranking institutions, would need to be radically revised (if they were retained at all). Current definitions of student satisfaction heavily influenced by a traditional, often residential, campus experience and face-to-face teaching would also need to change, along with how 'performance' is defined and measured.

The development of a high-participation tertiary education system would inevitably, and perhaps radically, modify the social situation of universities and colleges. It would no longer be possible to argue, as has sometimes been strongly argued in the case of mass higher education, that expansion has overwhelmingly benefited the middle class (even if that middle class has itself been stretched and become more open in terms of gender and, less certainly, race and social origins). Although rates of participation would no doubt continue to vary, that variation would be within a narrower range of near-universal participation. The language of 'elites' and 'the left behind' would become less persuasive. The impact of the development of a high-participation tertiary education system on patterns of employment would also be far-reaching. On the one hand, there would be a general elevation of overall levels of knowledge and skills, which few people doubt will be essential in the 21st-century workforce. On the other hand, the often invidious and arbitrary distinction between 'graduate' and 'non-graduate' jobs would largely disappear.

Fair access

Of course, 70 or 80 per cent participation and the development of comprehensive systems of tertiary education are not the whole solution to mass higher education's 'general crisis'. Not enough would change if existing inequalities were to be simply reproduced, even if in a less rigidly structured way, within a larger system. Not only has the standing – and divisiveness – of elite universities (and the prestige of traditional disciplines) not been diminished but arguably it has been increased by the development of mass higher education systems. The same could happen again without vigorous counteraction. This is why, second on the list of 'What is to be done?' reforms must be greatly intensified efforts to achieve fair(er) access – and also fair success, in terms of progression and outcomes, covering both academic qualifications and degree classifications and employment opportunities. There is a – very – long way to go. A similar pattern of inequity in university admissions can be observed in many countries despite having different types of higher education system, different dominant political ideologies, different social structures and different cultures. Young people from the most socially advantaged groups are between three and four times more likely to participate in higher education, especially university education, than those from the most socially deprived groups. This participation gap reflects deep-rooted inequality. Moreover, students from less socially advantaged groups, and from minority groups, tend in most countries to be concentrated in newer institutions lacking the historical advantages, and cultural capital, of elite universities.

Widening participation by under-represented groups, and fair(er) access to higher education, are declared goals in many higher education systems. Indeed, it is difficult to find one in which these goals are not being pursued to some degree, although the degree of active commitment, of course, varies widely. The need to widen participation, therefore, is common ground. There is a general concern to make entry to higher education more equitable. However, there is much less agreement about the policies best designed to achieve these goals. A variety of strategies have been adopted in various countries.

Free tuition

The most important strategy is to make tuition in universities and colleges free and to fund higher education from general taxation. The underlying principle is that the ability to pay should play no part in determining who has access to higher education (any more than access to healthcare). Free tuition is still the standard pattern across large parts of Europe and Latin America, at any rate in public institutions. In Germany, for example, where some of the *Länder* governed by right-wing parties had briefly charged fees, free tuition was restored following a legal judgment that charging fees for university education was contrary to the constitutional right of access to education. In the UK, tuition is free (to Scottish students) in higher education in Scotland, while in England (and, to a lesser extent, Wales and Northern Ireland) students are required to pay fees. In the past many US state systems of higher education offered free tuition to in-state students or only charged low fees. Fees have increased significantly in recent years for reasons outlined in Chapter 3. In contrast, fees are common in higher education in most Asian countries, and also in large parts of Africa.

Focused support

The standard argument against free tuition is that, because the majority of students in almost every country continue to come from more socially advantaged groups, it amounts to a subsidy of the middle class. At the very least, free tuition is a blunt instrument that fails to target students in the greatest need. A second strategy, therefore, is designed not to make tuition free to all students but to develop various forms of financial support: state-provided loans to pay tuition fees; fee waivers or reductions; scholarships and bursaries (sometimes for high-achieving students as well as those in financial need); grants or loans to pay for living expenses and similar interventions. Inevitably, this is the strategy adopted by private institutions. Typically, it is only generously endowed, not-for-profit private universities established as charitable foundations that are able to come anywhere close to needs-blind admissions. Most for-profit institutions, 'alternative providers' as they are labelled in England, usually have neither the means nor the desire to forgo substantial amounts of fee income in order to provide fair access, even if in practice they recruit more marginal students in academic terms.

State-provided or state-backed loans to pay for tuition suffer from many of the disadvantages of free tuition. If they are universally available, and repayment terms are generous (high repayment thresholds, or write-offs after a fixed term), they too represent an indiscriminate subsidy – to the same middle class. In addition, the desire to keep graduate debt within sustainable limits tends to push up default rates, leading to continuing high levels of public expenditure. Other forms of financial support come in all sizes and shapes – both national loan schemes and institutional scholarships and bursaries.

Targets – and their enforcement

The third main strategy to promote widening participation and fair access is to require universities themselves to take direct action to increase the proportion of their students from more deprived social or racial and cultural groups, or of women students in subjects and courses with an (unjustified) preponderance of men. Direct action takes three main forms. The first is through outreach work with schools and deprived communities to seek to raise levels of aspiration (and achievement). The second is to develop more flexible admissions systems in which past social and economic disadvantage is taken into account and formal entry requirements correspondingly reduced (so-called 'contextual admissions'). The third is to set quotas for students from more deprived backgrounds. There has been extensive experience of positive discrimination/affirmative action in the US to increase participation by Black students from the 1960s onwards. Equivalent efforts to do the same for students suffering social and economic deprivation in the UK and the rest of Europe have sometimes been pejoratively labelled 'social engineering' and, as a result, have struggled until recently to secure the same degree of political and public support.

Within the UK there are two contrasting approaches. In England the Office for Students (OfS) requires institutions to have approved access and participation plans with clear targets as a condition of registration and also if they wish to charge more than the minimum regulated fee. When the OfS was established, it incorporated the formerly independent Office for Fair Access (OFFA), which had a similar approval process. The OFFA regime was open to two main criticisms. The first was that institutions were free to set their own targets on access and participation (and some were not exactly challenging …). The second was that no university ever failed to get its plan approved. Like all 'nuclear options', the prospect of a major university being refused permission to charge higher fees (which in practice would have amounted to a multi-million pound 'fine') was difficult to contemplate. Early indications are that the OfS will take a tougher line, partly because it has a more extensive range of regulatory powers and a more explicit mandate to protect the interests of students.

In Scotland a more direct, and interventionist, approach has been adopted. The Commission on Widening Access recommended in 2016 that a national target should be set, echoing the earlier commitment by Nicola Sturgeon, Scotland's First Minister, that by 2030, 20 per cent of entrants to higher education should come from the 20 per cent most deprived communities. If achieved, this would lead to the total elimination of the historical imbalance in participation in favour of the socially advantaged – although across the system as a whole, not in each individual institution, an important caveat. Interim national targets were set to be achieved in 2021 and 2026, with minimum targets for individual institutions. The Scottish Government enthusiastically accepted this recommendation, requiring the Scottish Funding Council to monitor progress by institutions through its outcome agreements and appointing a Commissioner for Fair Access to make annual reports. So far, progress has been rapid, with the 2021 target being met two years early and only a handful of universities lagging behind the 10 per cent target for individual institutions. In England institutions set their own access and participation targets, although within the framework of an overall national goal. In Scotland there is a top-down national target. However, it is worth noting that the Scottish Government, and the Scottish Funding Council, lack the legal powers enjoyed by OfS in England. Instead, they rely on the moral force represented by a strong consensus in favour of fair access. There may be a danger of exaggerating the difference of approach.

Quotas

More radical strategies to secure fair access have also been suggested – including the setting of quotas for entrants from different social and school backgrounds for universities to meet, an extension of the approach taken in Scotland. Such an approach is usually dismissed without serious debate as 'social engineering'. But it is worth remembering that in the 1960s and 1970s affirmative action policies in the US were based on a similar principle, in effect reparation for past discrimination. In order to be eligible for federal government research funding, US universities had to demonstrate the seriousness, and effectiveness, of their action plans to redress historical imbalances not only in terms of student recruitment but also of staff employment.

However, quotas based on socio-economic status would be more difficult to implement. Ethnicity appears simple, almost a Black/White distinction, although definitions of Black and other minority ethnic groups in the UK is not always straightforward, and all quasi-racialist categories present difficulties. But social disadvantage is much finer grain. It has many dimensions – parental occupations (or unemployment), type of school attended, incidence of family breakdown, care experience, home location, physical or mental disability and so on. To calibrate all these, plus of course gender, ethnicity and age, into a workable system of quotas would be almost impossible. What would be possible, although very controversial, would be to limit the proportion of entrants from private schools (in particular, in the most selective universities) to the proportion of sixth-form students in private schools in the general secondary school population. As a significant motive for parents sending their children to private schools is to increase their chances of being admitted to a 'top' university, such a limited positive discrimination could be justified on the grounds that family wealth should pay no (direct) part in determining access to higher education.

Remedying 'deficits' or transforming institutions?

Beneath these different strategies to secure fair access, pursued with different levels of urgency and commitment, lie radically different interpretations about how fair access – or, indeed, fairness generally – should be defined. One interpretation, more common perhaps in the context of widening participation to the most selective research universities, is sometimes characterised as 'getting poor kids into posh universities'. It focuses on the idea of educational deficit. The aim is to help socially disadvantaged applicants meet the (high) academic standards required to benefit from an elite university education. In other words, the value, style and content of such an education are accepted as uncontested givens; the deficit is on the part of applicants who do not come from the elite social groups which still provide a disproportionate number of students in what are now labelled 'top universities'.

According to this first interpretation not so much has changed in the access game, except in scale, since the middle of the 20th century when 'scholarship boys' (and a very few girls) – comparatively small numbers of high-achieving entrants from lower-income families – were admitted to what was still an elite university system. The underlying model was, and remains, co-option into existing social and political elites. This interpretation, of course, has a strong resonance with mass higher education's wider and more general crisis. How can fair access, in this limited register, be regarded as an essentially progressive project if one of its main effects, if not intentions, is to refresh these traditional elites, and give legitimacy to the elitism that is at the heart of the inequality that disfigures many (or most) contemporary societies? Essential as it is to require elite universities, with their all their historical prestige and dominance of many key graduate labour markets, to have much wider and more balanced student intakes, the primary focus of a tertiary education system must be on the 80 per cent as much as, or maybe more than, the top 20 per cent of institutions (and entrants); on the rest, not the (self-affirming) 'best'. Perhaps because of its near-universal reach, not just across all social classes but across generations too, the concept of lifelong learning might enjoy a second life.

The second interpretation of fair access focuses instead on the need for higher education itself to change, rather than on potential students from currently under-represented groups being required to and helped to adapt. The balance of proof therefore is reversed. In other words, any potential deficit is on the part of universities, not the less traditional applicants. For example, the use of 'contextual admissions' should be seen not just as a series of limited and technical adjustments of entry standards to remedy or compensate for shortcomings in applicants' previous education experience. Instead, they should provide an opportunity to ask radical questions about the extent to which current entry requirements may be inherently biased in favour of particular forms of academic knowledge which are bound up in traditional elite acculturation.

There is clearly a connection between this second, and more radical, interpretation and current debates about the university curriculum. These debates include highly politicised controversies about the extent to which the curriculum in some of the humanities and social sciences is gendered or racialised, and the counter view that free speech and academic freedom are being constrained by so-called 'cancel' culture. But they also include more reasoned debates about, for example, the poor fit between the ambitions of many medical students, who often aspire to work in high-profile and high-prestige hospital specialties, and the needs of most health services, which are in primary care and general practice. These wider controversies and debates, of course, require re-examination not just of entry requirements and of curriculum content but also of exit standards still expressed in terms of, always archaic and often inaccurate, degree classifications and of the skills and qualities graduates bring to the labour market. In short, they concern the aims of a university education. These debates about the curriculum may raise important questions about the place of the mass university in a democratic society – islands of academic and scientific excellence; bastions of critical enquiry in an open (and civil) society; beacons of civic and community life; corporations in the knowledge industry; people's universities …

Fair access, especially in the context of greatly expanded tertiary education systems, needs to be seen as a key element in the debates about these wider reforms. But this requires a step-change in current practice. The advance to much higher levels of participation of between 70 and 80 per cent demands an intensification of efforts to widen participation and secure fair access at all levels of higher education, not a reduction of these efforts on the grounds that more, or even most, people will be able to participate as a result of the establishment of a wider tertiary education system. Equity, therefore, of access to all levels within these tertiary education systems.

In contrast, a collateral effect of the development of mass systems in the 20th century was to protect elite selection by providing wider opportunities. The primary achievement of mass higher education was to produce much wider participation, in aggregate. Within the elite university systems that preceded mass higher education the disproportionately large number of students from the most socially advantaged groups was a significant embarrassment. But that imbalance appeared to reduce, or at any rate to become less blatant, with the expansion of student numbers and establishment of new universities, and new kinds of higher education institution. Participation was certainly greatly increased, but did access become fairer?

Under the heading of 'fair access' in the 'What is to done?' list must be a sustained effort to equalise the social profile of students across all kinds of institution, including (and especially) major research-focused universities, not just to meet challenging aggregate national targets for fairer access. A 70–80 per cent participation rate must be accompanied by at least a halving of the current access gap. To achieve that wholehearted acceptance of the need for fair access, a radical interrogation of academic standards (both on entry and at exit), of the aims and contents of the university curriculum, of graduate skills and qualities, of the respective claims of academic and 'popular' knowledge, even of the social position of the university, will be required.

Systems, governance and management

The governance of UK higher education has major flaws:

- At the system level there is an unstable balance between the steering and coordination of a 'public' (in the broadest sense) system, on the one hand, and, on the other, the regulation of a quasi-private system (again in the broadest terms). In England that balance has tilted dangerously but unrealistically towards the latter. As a result, most policy instruments, funding regimes and measurement tools like the REF and the TEF operate in a kind of void, with more unplanned consequences and inappropriate uses than clear and consistent aims.
- Arrangements for institutional governance are essentially oligarchic and as a result unaccountable, except perhaps in terms of compliance with the rickety system-level superstructure. Moreover, the membership of governing bodies is still disproportionately White, middle-class and middle-aged (or older). The representation of stakeholders – students, staff, communities – is minimal and marginal.
- A belief in the right-to-manage has largely triumphed over the idea of an academic community, in most institutions completely so and in a fortunate few more conditionally, although the direction of travel is plain. As a result, a new class of managers (senior and intermediate, academic and professional) has developed, shunting aside older arrangements, whether of academic hierarchy or collegiality, and displacing traditional 'civil service' forms of public administration.

The reasons for these characteristics and trends have been discussed in earlier chapters. The question here is how to remedy their most negative features.

A key issue is that it is difficult to discern the underlying principles according to which governance, at every level, is currently organised. What is being governed (and managed) and why? Who should have a voice? Is higher education regarded as a coherent national system (or, now in most respects, four national systems across the UK), subject to some degree of political (that is democratic) scrutiny and control? Whether at arm's length or close-up *dirigiste* is a second-order question. Or is it seen essentially as a collection of separate and independent organisations that simply require limited regulation to ensure that there is fair play and that they do not operate contrary to the public interest? Once again, whether these organisations are conceived of as autonomous academic institutions of the traditional type or as quasi-commercial organisations competing in some kind of market is a second-order question although, of course, it is a key issue to be resolved before deciding the best arrangements for the formal governance and management of universities. The lack of clear answers to these questions, or even an informed debate about them, is the first striking feature of the governance of UK higher education.

The second, and closely linked, feature is its democratic deficit. At a system level the governance of UK higher education is littered with quangos. In the case of the OfS, the Scottish Funding Council and the Higher Education Council for Wales, and UK Research and Innovation (UKRI) (and the research councils), their members are appointed by the respective governments. The chairs of these bodies, in particular, are seen as strategic political appointments. The degree of partisan politicisation varies – disturbingly high in the case of the OfS, as the recent appointment of a new chair has highlighted; moderate in the case of the Scottish and Welsh councils; less pronounced still in the case of UKRI and especially the research councils. The members of other agencies, such as UCAS, HESA, the QAA and Advance HE, are typically appointed by their corporate stakeholders, including bodies such as Universities UK. Significantly, Advance HE, which (as the Higher Education Academy and earlier still the Institute of Learning and Teaching) was initially a body controlled by individual members, a professional body, is now a corporate organisation.

At an institutional level, members of university governing bodies effectively appoint themselves, although most make (valiant and/or token) efforts to have more diverse memberships. Admittedly, the small number of staff representatives, where they exist, are elected. Student members are appointed by governing body on the, effectively non-negotiable, recommendation of their student unions. The recently imposed requirement that the chairs of Scottish university courts should be elected was typically regarded with bizarre incredulity (Von Prondzynski, 2012). Within the management structure, election for fixed periods of office has been almost completely replaced by appointment to executive positions. None of these practices is without justification or merit. But the cumulative effect is to deny that the democratic principle has any serious role to play in the governance of higher education.

There is a price to pay for both features. The silence on first principles has made it difficult to mobilise public support. Is UK education a system or a market? Is it an autonomous domain, a part of civil society distinct from state and market; or a public service; or a key element in the knowledge services industry? Although there is widespread support for the extension of opportunities for higher education, in terms both of broad public opinion and the aspirations of individuals and families, that support has sometimes been difficult to translate into more general public esteem – and political bargaining power. There are several reasons for this, which have been discussed earlier in this book. These include the belief that mass higher education is still a middle-class game; the suspicion that the high fees charged in England backed by state loans, although a very real burden from the perspective of students, have been an accounting scam that has enabled universities to avoid the worst effects of austerity; even the sense of elite entitlement, or vestigial *de haut en bas* tone, which sometimes seeps into university leaders' contributions to public debates. But an important reason is the lack of clarity about where higher education sits within the political economy. No longer regarded as a public service, like the NHS, it is not really part of the private market either. Instead, universities seem to be located in an ill-defined (and unpopular?) para-state hinterland. Inevitably the messaging is muddied.

The price paid by the absence (denial?) of democracy in terms of mobilising public support is also clear. Cities, which were the prime movers in the original creation of many universities, and communities, which enthusiastically sponsored the establishment of new ones, are now allowed no meaningful role in their governance. Recent efforts to create more effective regional government frameworks by creating metro mayors, in Greater Manchester, the West Midlands and elsewhere, have not extended to even the most limited control over higher (or further) education despite their importance in urban and regional life. As a result, local and regional engagement with higher education is seen largely through the lens of universities and colleges as job providers, economic multipliers, development agents (particularly with regard to advanced technology), part of the social and cultural scene. They are not part of local democracy (Scott, 2014a). In contrast, the provinces in Canada, states in Australia and *lander* in Germany are key players in higher education.

The bulk of staff are similarly excluded from a direct role in governance. Most senates spend much of their time on process rather than strategy. Senior academics have increasingly been limited to playing a blocking role, unless they hold management positions. More junior staff are firmly regarded as employees first, and colleagues only as a rhetorical afterthought. The result has been the growth of often adversarial employer-and-employee relations. Complaints about excessive vice-chancellors' salaries are countered by rival complaints about 'unnecessary' strike action – hardly the context for creative dialogue. No university, with the possible but elitist and archaic exception of Oxford and Cambridge colleges, operates as a mutual or cooperative like John Lewis, despite the obvious fit with collegial values.

Students are treated as customers rather than as citizens of academic communities. As a result, they are very welcome to fill in satisfaction surveys – the TEF as TripAdvisor – as the increased emphasis on improving the 'student experience' demonstrates. But wider student engagement is stigmatised as 'political' activism. Even that limited student consumer voice is likely to be muted if the UK (English) Government goes ahead with its plans to review – that is to downgrade or even abolish – the annual National Student Survey (NSS). The curious charge is made, by supposed market enthusiasts, that the NSS has encouraged universities to pander to students and, as a result, needs to be replaced by a wretched algorithm focused on 'graduate job' employment rates.

System(s)

What is to be done with the governance of higher, or tertiary, education? The need for a system must be firmly accepted. The primary task must be to focus on producing optimal provision on the basis of an appropriate balance of types of institution, subjects, levels, delivery models – and geographical access. Establishing a regulatory framework is a secondary – and subordinate – task, not an alternative goal. It is an illusion to imagine that an optimal system can ever be produced by some miracle of self-organisation on the part of autonomous institutions, still less of quasi-commercial corporations, for two reasons.

The first reason is that, when higher education was dominated by a small number of like-minded universities, it might have been able to produce a kind of 'collegial gravity' or informal coherence which might have made self-organisation feasible, although only by ignoring other types of post-school education. The development of mass higher education, greatly expanded and much more heterogeneous, made reliance on this kind of loose self-organisation impossible more than half a century ago. The shift towards a universal tertiary education has made the establishment of a formal system even more imperative.

The second reason is that in recent years universities, especially in England, have been encouraged to compete rather than collaborate with each other. This clearly undermines any notion of informal systemic self-organisation. The belief that by contriving a 'market' an optimal provision of tertiary education will ever be produced is naively ideological. It also denies there is any legitimate public interest, or role for democracy, in the provision of tertiary education, although in practice in any political system there are always more acceptable market outcomes (students choosing STEM courses) than others (students choosing courses with apparently poor records of graduate employment).

It is not within the scope of this book to propose a detailed scheme of how a system of tertiary education should be organised. But certain principles are important. One is that the scale and complexity of tertiary education across a country the size of England is such that a single monolithic national agency can never work. Instead, building on the success of the separate Scottish and Welsh systems, some regional substructures are essential. At one time the Higher Education Funding Council for England developed a number of regional scenarios for the English regions, recognising that planning and coordination at a national level was ineffective. Much tertiary education provision will inevitably be local in character, just as much higher education has always been. The disadvantages of trying to coordinate local delivery from Whitehall–Westminster are obvious, and have been on cruel display during the COVID-19 pandemic. A multi-layered approach to system governance is the only way forward.

A second principle is that there must be safeguards to insulate the governance of higher/tertiary education from excessive politicisation, especially in the present age of angry ideology and increasing polarisation of political views. But this insulation must not compromise sensible democratic scrutiny. As has been discussed in an earlier chapter, the invasion of SPADS and partisan think thanks with a vested interest in ideological confrontation has exposed the weaknesses of the UK's highly centralised constitution, which in the past was disguised by the anonymous gentility of the Civil Service. This is another reason why the involvement of local and regional politicians, who generally are less caught up in this extreme politicisation, in a plural system of governance should be encouraged.

A number of approaches can be taken to developing safeguards: a clear and categorical (and respected) demarcation of powers between ministers (and their Whitehall departments) and any national agencies enshrined in new legislation; direct election of some members of agencies to combat political patronage; greater representation of staff and students … None of these is a magic bullet and, it will be argued, some already exist, such as the formal separation of powers in the Higher Education and Research Act 2017 (although it has been honoured more in the breach than in the observance). It is a tough call. The need for safeguards cannot be allowed to degenerate into a denial of democracy. Higher/tertiary education must be politically accountable although not just to the overheated Whitehall–Westminster core but to regional and local communities, and to civil society at large.

Institutional governance and management

The current oligarchic pattern of university governance must be abandoned. Governing bodies need to be more democratic in their composition and more transparent in their operation. This is not intended as a criticism of the efforts of individual governing bodies to recruit members from a more representative cross-section of society and to consult and communicate more widely. However, such efforts can make little difference unless the model of governance itself is radically changed.

This too will not be easy. As has been discussed in Chapter 4, the trend in higher education governance in recent decades has been in the opposite direction – towards smaller, more closed and (supposedly) more expert governing bodies. That trend must be reversed, to re-emphasise representation. The main unrepresented group of stakeholders at present is local and regional communities. Where local communities are represented, this takes the limited form of the appointment of local business and professional leaders. Also, many universities, especially perhaps those with stronger national and international profiles, deliberately seek board members with national and international profiles. A bolder approach is needed. Regional mayors and local authorities, both in their generic role as agencies of local government and in the context of their specific responsibilities for school education, should have non-token representation. Many governing bodies, sometimes despite their best efforts, also have a legitimacy problem in the eyes of many academic and other staff within their institutions. That can only be remedied by a substantial increase in the elected element on governing bodies. In addition, there should be a substantial increase in student representation. It is vital that the sense of 'ownership' of universities is more widely spread.

The deliberate reduction in the size, and representativeness, of university governing bodies has inevitably reduced transparency. This lack of transparency cannot be compensated for by the (often tardy) publication of sanitised minutes of meetings. Many governing bodies compound this lack of transparency by even excluding their staff and student members from key parts of their meetings or membership of important subcommittees on spurious grounds of supposedly commercial confidentiality, or conflicts of interest. Why should meetings not be open to all staff and students, with very limited and specified exceptions? Of course, their dynamic would change – but in positive as well as negative ways. Although a shocking idea in the UK, most state-wide boards in the US have to operate under so-called 'sunshine laws', and in other European countries university councils are treated as public bodies accessible to the public (and the press). No doubt it would be an uncomfortable experience but interest in and engagement with universities would greatly increase. They would get closer to the people – a key gain in an unsettled age of populism, growing inequality and increasing social divisions, media manipulation and 'fake news'.

The current balance between governance and management, so often repeated as a kind of mantra, also needs to be reset. There has been a tendency for some governing bodies to take on more openly strategic, even quasi-executive, roles. Indeed, they have been encouraged to do so directly by being reminded of their responsibility for oversight of academic quality (impossible) and standards (difficult). Muscle-flexing rhetoric about sharpening 'brands' and 're-engineering' management processes has had a similar effect. There has been a much stronger countertendency for senior managers to over-influence the processes of governance which are designed to hold them to account, mainly through their stranglehold on the key information available to governing bodies (and effective silencing of rival voices from within institutions). Sometimes there have been close and collusive relationships between chairs and chief executives, which is desirable within limits but also encourages management 'capture' and can disempower other members of governing bodies. Either way, the result is a confusion of roles. Maybe governing bodies should be redesigned as supervisory boards on the model of German industry, or with their own support staff like most US university trustees and regents. Informal task-oriented senior management groups should be reorganised as formally constituted management boards with a clear and specified role in governance. Of course, charters, articles of government and other formal quasi-legal documents specify and demarcate these roles. But contemporary practice has moved on, and often far away.

Within institutions it is essential to achieve a better balance between academic governance (and the student voice) and executive management. The current balance is badly out of kilter as senior managers have consolidated their power with intermediate academic managers accountable solely to them in a strict line-management hierarchy and buttressed by a growing number of subordinate professional managers. But there is little point in simply complaining about the iniquities of a poorly defined 'managerialism', or even trying to reassert the power of senates as blocking agents. Inevitably universities, colleges and other tertiary education institutions are complex academic bureaucracies which must be expertly managed. But that does not mean that centralised command-and-control regimes are equally inevitable.

The issue to be addressed is the regime of control. The current regime is expressed in the language of 'delivery' and 'accountability'. It is embodied and enforced through metrics, dashboards, algorithms, rankings and surveillance tools like the TEF and the REF. This 'delivery' regime is further intensified in England by a funding system dependent on high fees, and a redesignation of students as customers. The problem with such a regime of control is that the data on which it relies is partial, in the sense that it has been designed with specific political agendas in mind (and so is not neutral or objective), and that it is inherently inaccurate (as just one example, there is no reason to suppose that degree classifications are more than 80 per cent accurate, the level achieved by A-levels in schools). The problem is also that a data-driven regime of control changes behaviour in unpredictable and unanticipated, as well as intended ways. For example, the REF has fundamentally changed behaviour – at every level from individual researchers to institutional managers and policy makers – and not always (not often?) for the better. At its worst, this control regime descends into a cult of measurement in which peer review or the opinions expressed by students through the NSS end up being regarded with suspicion and as inferior to 'data', however flawed, so doubling down on its defects.

Once again, it must be emphasised that mass higher education, and even more so universal tertiary education systems, and the comprehensive and heterogenous institutions that make them up, need to be managed properly. In the case of universities in particular, an alternative control regime is needed that allows room for safe spaces, spaces for undirected reflection, room to draw intellectual breath (for students as well as academic staff). Perhaps full-on nostalgia for 'a state-funded institution whose low-pressure otherworldliness allowed for imagination and experimentation, diversity and discovery' is no longer realistic (Gaskill, 2020). 'Otherworldliness' is clearly going too far, although there is perhaps more to be said for 'low-pressure'. An arm's-length state is a gentler master than an ideologically contrived market under close political, and openly partisan, supervision. But any control regime, any management culture, that is inimical to imagination and experimentation, diversity and discovery has lost its way.

The delicate task is to achieve the best balance between the need for universities to be professionally managed, both strategically and operationally, and the need to maintain, or restore, a sense of collegial ownership among academics (and other staff) and students, and a wider sense of community ownership too. Within institutions, principles of devolution (not delegation) and subsidiarity should be more widely applied. Accountability should be downwards as well as upwards. The roles of deans and heads of department, and other academic post-holders, are diminished and disempowered if they are regarded as simply executive; their key role is as academic leaders and role-models. A change in organisational culture is long overdue, although in a contrary sense to that in which that phrase has come to be used.

The place of higher education in contemporary society

The final section of this chapter focuses on how the place and purpose of higher education (or higher education-plus in a wider tertiary education system) can be re-imagined in order to address the disappointments, misunderstandings and perverse labels attached to mass higher education – its general crisis. There is a long, and honourable, tradition of writing about the purposes of higher education, beginning with John Henry Newman, and still vigorous today in both rhetorical and analytical terms (Collini, 2012, 2017; Barnett, 2017). But Newman's experience is salutary. Even in the 1850s his efforts to distil the essence of a university education failed because (the few) contemporary universities, not to mention the other institutions that would eventually be incorporated into 20th-century mass higher education systems, were already too various to be characterised in a simple or even coherent way. One hundred and seventy years later, any attempt to capture the essence of a tertiary education system in which the majority of people participate at some stage in their lives is even more fraught. My instinct is that it is not always worth the considerable scholarly effort. It can only be at such a high level of abstraction and generalisation to which there are likely to be so many exceptions to any rule, and which is very unlikely to help higher education address the current challenges it faces.

Equally pop-up *schemas* are also unhelpful, however intellectually fascinating they may be, because they also inevitably oversimplify (when they do not misread or distort) an almost infinitely complex reality. A recent example is David Goodhart's distinction between the domains of 'head', 'hand' and 'heart', his attempt to align them with different types and modes of education, and his conclusion that too great a value has been placed on 'head', in the form of academically accredited cognitive skills, and, more controversially, therefore that the expansion of higher education should be reversed (Goodhart, 2020). Newman would certainly have retorted that the development of 'heart', although he would have preferred to call it 'character', should be a central preoccupation in a true university. Others will point out that there is an awful lot of 'hand' in modern universities. But, interesting as such debates can be, I also believe they are not worthwhile. Instead of seeking some 'theory of everything' about contemporary higher education, or the 'clever' ideas of fashionista intellectuals (usually on the right), perhaps we would settle for a more down-to-earth 'story' that universities can tell about themselves and tell the world.

A key strand in that 'story' is how higher education relates to … let's avoid for a moment that loaded word 'state' … but to the commonwealth or more mundanely the community. At one level this is uncontested territory. Even the most enthusiastic neoliberal supporters of a higher education market emphasise the role of universities – and colleges – as 'anchor' institutions within, if not their communities, at any rate their local and regional economies. There has also been a marked trend to emphasise the 'civic' responsibilities of the university, notably in the Kerslake Report (2019). These responsibilities have also been highlighted in the revised code of governance published by the Committee of University Chairs (CUC, 2020). But, as has already been pointed out, there is still an equally marked reluctance to grant locally elected representatives any significant say in the governance of higher (and further) education. Instead, the blander and non-committal idea of 'engagement' with communities is preferred.

Paradoxically, although the 21st-century state has not been slow to assert its growing control over higher education, whether through direct edicts or indirect regulation, there has been a reluctance to countenance a return to the predominantly state funding of higher education that powered mass expansion in the 20th century. The reasons for this are partly pragmatic – reducing (apparently, if not in reality) the funding requirement of universities and colleges at a time when other demands are increased against a background of a perceived crisis of affordability in public finances; and partly ideological – the right-wing desire to create yet another market on the ruins of the public sector. Many of the detailed debates for and against free tuition and fees have focused on elaborate calculations of how much the middle classes benefit from free tuition, and the attractions of a fee-based system with targeted financial support for the 'deserving poor'. These debates are important. But there has been little discussion of the bigger issue of the messages that free tuition and fees send out, both to society and to individuals. Free tuition is the firmest possible affirmation of the public character of higher education, a message surely that urgently needs reinforcing at a time of increasing inequality and divisions, populism and supposed 'culture wars'. It is also an affirmation that a higher education is not simply a kind-of-commodity, or ticket to a job, but that it also incurs an obligation, and responsibilities, to a wider community – more 'us' than 'me'.

A second, closely linked, strand in the story is the key role played by universities in particular within an open society, and civil society poised between the direct domain of the state and the encroaching domain of the market. Here it is sometime difficult to escape from under the weight of clichés, many of which are compromised in reality – 'talking truth to power', blue-skies research and disinterested scholarship, critical enquiry, a university education as a transformative experience for the individual. In practice, talking truth to power is rarely popular. The choice is often between oppositional rhetoric or obeisance to power with no measured mean. Research is constrained by politically mandated themes and priorities and disciplined by targets. A higher education is also a private good which is leveraged in the labour market (rates-of-return). Sometimes the mass expansion of higher education is blamed for this erosion of these historic freedoms, ignoring the much wider erosion of civil society itself. But it is not inevitable that a much more open system of tertiary education, higher education-plus, must also be a more subordinated system. The contrary can apply – a system that is more open demographically can, and must, be more open intellectually too. In any case, a key strand in the story must be that higher education is 'free', not simply in terms of access but also spirit, and that it is vitally connected with the advance of liberty and democracy.

A third strand of the story is that the purposes of the university – or indeed any tertiary education – should be considered in a down-to-earth and practical sense that does not require grand Newmanesque statements. The development of mass higher education in the 20th century, and even more so the hoped-for development of a universal tertiary system in the 21st century, has been accompanied by a shift towards more explicitly vocational and professional courses. An emphasis on problem solving and generic skills has been apparent in – almost – all subjects, even the avowedly academic. Of course, as has been argued earlier, a clean and clear divide between vocational and academic education has always been impossible. Oxford PPE has become, not without intention, a kind-of-apprenticeship for much of the UK's political class, while there must always be room for self-discovery and reflection in, let us say, recreational management or computer games courses. But no sensible person can deny that the development of skills, whether expressed in terms of building human capital in the economy or improving rates-of-return for individual graduates, is a major purposes of 21st-century higher education.

However, to jump from there to the conclusion that the main purpose of higher education should be meeting economic needs is going much too far. Its primary purpose remains educative (Ashwin, 2020). Just as the Robbins Report back in the 1960s asserted (supposedly quoting Confucius) that no one aimed for higher education 'without some thought of pay', few people in the 2020s aim for higher education solely for pay. Aspirations, ambitions, identity, dreams – all are bound up in a complex web of motives for pursuing higher education, expressed at the family as well as the individual level. The experience of mass higher education has been that, while its impact on the economy has sometimes seemed unclear and contested (graduates in 'non-graduate' jobs, the opening up of a graduate–non-graduate gap with damaging consequences, and so on), its impact on society has been far-reaching and uncontested. For better or worse, we live in a graduate society in which there have been far-reaching cultural shifts. The advance of 'populism' has been attributed to the effects of, and reactions to, these shifts. A more plausible explanation is that that advance has been much more in response to increasing inequality linked to disruptive economic change, and to the opportunities that social media offer to spread extremist (and once marginal) views. But the very fact that mass higher education, and the graduate society it has produced, has been one of the drivers of 'populism' is a – back-handed – acknowledgement of the profound significance of its social dimension.

These are only three strands within the story of how contemporary higher education can better relate, and explain itself, to a society that has perhaps fallen a little out of love with the consequences of mass expansion. No doubt there are others. Any story inevitably must be complex and will not always be convincing. But there is no alternative to a messy story. No fully explanatory theory-of-everything can be satisfactory, or even possible, in the face of the scale of the challenges that higher education faces, its general crisis.

Coda

The argument in this book is that higher education faces a general crisis that goes beyond the perennial challenges of financial sustainability, adjusting to new learning paradigms and new patterns of knowledge production, evolving new models of organisation and so on, and even beyond more immediate and urgent challenges such as the COVID-19 pandemic and global warming. The roots of that crisis are to be found in the doubts that have accumulated about the development of mass higher education over the past 60 years, its balance sheet of gains and losses. Has expansion merely consolidated existing social hierarchies, lightly modified them, or has it challenged and eroded them? Has it created a middle-class meritocracy, still largely shaped by family fortune? In the economy, has the large-scale production of graduates powered growth and productivity by boosting skills, or has it created new divisions between the academically and professionally credentialised and those resentfully left behind? In the cultural sphere, has it created 'citizens of nowhere', cosmopolitan metro-elites, and patronisingly eroded more traditional forms of identity, community and meaning?

Once, these questions could be answered with confidence. Mass higher education was a work in progress, with an overwhelmingly positive balance sheet. Today, the doubts have accumulated, within higher education itself and in wider society (at any rate, as expressed through public and political discourses; the choices and aspirations of individuals continue to tell a different story). Not everyone will accept that this shift in mood has taken place, denying the seriousness or even reality of this general crisis. With entire justification, they will offer as counterevidence an accumulation of 'good news' about universities and colleges. But it sometimes feels like whistling nervously in the dark.

There are three possible responses to this general crisis. The first, closely linked to the belief that such a crisis does not exist or is essentially trivial, is to muddle through. Forget the big picture, which will take care of itself, any clouds will disperse, and focus instead on detailed reforms. In an important sense, such a response is correct and necessary. In the short run, what else is to be done, especially by policy makers and institutional leaders but also by rank-and-file academics? The second response is to roll back mass expansion, to argue that retrenchment to a more traditional university core is necessary in order to preserve higher education's quality and essential purpose. That purpose is to produce elites, not the straggly semi-elites produced by today's mass system, but more focused and disciplined ones. Perhaps more effort needs to be made to uncouple these elites from their anchorage in social privilege. But, even if these efforts are only partly successful, the integrity of higher education, and especially elite universities, must be maintained. So be it.

The third response, advanced in this book, is take a radical leap forward. The momentum from mass to universal provision must be maintained. The historic link between higher education and elites, however attenuated, must be finally broken. Instead, tertiary education should be available to – almost – all in a democracy worthy of that name. Fair access must challenge restricted and rationed access within a hierarchy of institutions, some noble, others less so. The system should be depoliticised, with regard to centralist Whitehall–Westminster control (which is increasingly tainted by toxic ideology), and then re-politicised, by reaching out to local communities and new social movements. Current regimes of control and surveillance must be replaced by new forms of popular accountability, not least with regard to students and staff. Not only should the curriculum be student-centred, and in a normative not simply a procedural sense, but it must be people-centred, in humanistic and democratic terms, to reflect the pluralism of modern society. In short, higher education must be re-centred as a progressive project.

Not all will agree. But, for better or worse, that is the programme that has been advanced in this book.

References

Data sources

HESA (2021a) *Higher Education Student Statistics: 2019–20. Statistical Bulletin SB 258*, Cheltenham: HESA, https://www.hesa.ac.uk/news/27-01-2021/sb258-higher-education-student-statistics

HESA (2021b) *Widening Participation: UK Performance Indicators 2019–20*, Cheltenham: HESA, https://www.hesa.ac.uk/data-and-analysis/performance-indicators/widening-participation

HESA (2021c) *Higher Education Staff Statistics: 2019/20. Statistical Bulletin SB 259*, Cheltenham: HESA, https://www.hesa.ac.uk/news/19-01-2021/sb259-higher-education-staff-statistics

HESA (2020a) *What is the Income of Higher Education Providers?*, Cheltenham: HESA, https://www.hesa.ac.uk/data-and-analysis/finances/income

HESA (2020b) *What is the Expenditure of Higher Education Providers?*, Cheltenham: HESA, https://www.hesa.ac.uk/data-and-analysis/finances/expenditure

OECD (Organisation for Economic Co-operation and Development) (2019) *Education at a Glance 2019: OECD Indicators*, Paris: OECD Publishing, https://doi.org/10.1787/f8d7880d-en

OECD (2020) 'Education at a glance: Educational finance indicators, *OECD Education Statistics* (database), https://doi.org/10.1787/c4e1b551-en

ONS (Office for National Statistics) (2015) *2011 Census analysis: Ethnicity and religion of the non-UK born population in England and Wales*, https://www.ons.gov.uk/peoplepopulationandcommunity/culturalidentity/ethnicity/articles/2011censusanalysisethnicityandreligionofthenonukbornpopulationinenglandandwales/2015-06-18

ONS (2019) *Overview of UK population: August 2019*, https://www.ons.gov.uk/peoplepopulationandcommunity/populationandmigration/populationestimates/articles/overviewoftheukpopulation/august2019

ONS (2020a) *Sexual Orientation: UK 2018*, https://www.ons.gov.uk/peoplepopulationandcommunity/culturalidentity/sexuality/bulletins/sexualidentityuk/2018

ONS (2020b) *Gross Domestic Product (at market prices)*, https://www.ons.gov.uk/economy/grossdomesticproductgdp/timeseries/ybha/qna

ONS (2020c) *Gross Domestic Product (quarter-by-quarter growth)*, https://www.ons.gov.uk/economy/grossdomesticproductgdp/timeseries/ihyq/qna

ONS (2020d) *SOC 2020*, https://www.ons.gov.uk/methodology/classificationsandstandards/standardoccupationalclassificationsoc/soc2020

Reports

Augar Report (2019) *Review of Post-18 Education and Funding: Advisory Panel Report*, https://assets.publishing.service.gov.uk/government/uploads/system/uploads/attachment_data/file/805127/Review_of_post_18_education_and_funding.pdf

Browne Report (2010) *Independent Review of Higher Education Funding and Student Finance Securing a Sustainable Future for Higher Education*, London, https://assets.publishing.service.gov.uk/government/uploads/system/uploads/attachment_data/file/422565/bis-10-1208-securing-sustainable-higher-education-browne-report.pdf

Commissioner for Fair Access (2020) *The Impact of COVID-19 on Fair Access to Higher Education: Interim Report*, Edinburgh: Scottish Government, https://www.gov.scot/publications/impact-COVID-19-fair-access-higher-education/

CUC (Committee of University Chairs) (2020) *The Higher Education Code of Governance,* September 2020, https://www.universitychairs.ac.uk/wp-content/uploads/2020/09/CUC-HE-Code-of-Governance-publication-final.pdf

Dearing Report (1997) *National Committee of Inquiry into Higher Education: Higher Education in the Learning Society*, London: HMSO.

Department for Education (1991) *Higher Education: A New Framework*, London: HMSO, www.educationengland.org.uk/documents/pdfs/1991-wp-higher-ed.pdf

Department for Education (2021) *International Education Strategy: 2021 Update. Supporting Recovery, Driving Growth*, London: Department for Education, https://www.gov.uk/government/publications/international-education-strategy-2021-update/international-education-strategy-2021-update-supporting-recovery-driving-growth

Department for Education/National Statistics (2018) *Participation Rates in Higher Education 2006/07–2016/17*, https://assets.publishing.service.gov.uk/government/uploads/system/uploads/attachment_data/file/744087/Main_text_participation_rates_in_higher_education_2006_to_2017_.pdf

Department for Business, Innovation and Skills (2011) *Higher Education: Students at the Heart of the System*, London: HMSO.

Department for Business, Innovation and Skills (2015) *Fulfilling our Potential: Teaching Excellence, Social Mobility and Student Choice*, London: HMSO.

Department of Education and Science (1966) *A Plan for Polytechnics and Other Colleges*, London: HMSO, http://filestore.nationalarchives.gov.uk/pdfs/small/cab-129-125-c-70.pdf

Department of Education and Science (1972) *Education: A Framework for Expansion*, London: HMSO, http://www.educationengland.org.uk/documents/wp1972/framework-for-expansion.html

Department of Education and Science (1985) *The Development of Higher Education into the 1990s* [Green Paper], London: HMSO.
Hazelkorn Review (2016) *Towards 2030: A Framework for Building a World-Class Post-Compulsory Education System in Wales* [a report to the Higher Education Funding Council for Wales by Professor Ellen Hazelkorn], https://gov.wales/sites/default/files/publications/2018-02/towards-2030-a-framework-for-building-a-world-class-post-compulsory-education-system-for-wales.pdf
Jarratt Report (1985) *Report of the Steering Group for Efficiency Studies in Universities*, Committee of Vice-Chancellors and Principals, March, http://www.educationengland.org.uk/documents/jarratt1985/index.html
Kerslake Report (2019) *Truly Civic: Strengthening the Connection between Universities and their Places*, Final Report of the UPP Foundation Civic University Commission, London: UPP Foundation, https://upp-foundation.org/wp-content/uploads/2019/02/Civic-University-Commission-Final-Report.pdf
Pearce Report (2021) *Independent Review of the Teaching Excellence and Student Outcomes Framework: Report to the Secretary of State for Education (TEF), August 2019*, https://assets.publishing.service.gov.uk/government/uploads/system/uploads/attachment_data/file/952754/TEF_Independent_review_report.pdf
Public Accounts Committee [House of Commons] (1967) *Parliament and the Control of University Expenditure*, London: HMSO.
Robbins Report [Committee on Higher Education] (1963) *Higher Education: A report by the committee appointed by the Prime Minister under the chairmanship of Lord Robbins 1961–63*, London: HMSO.
Scottish Government (2018) *15–24 Learner Journey Review: Report*, https://www.gov.scot/publications/15-24-learner-journey-review-9781788518741/
Scottish Government (2019) *University Applications, Offers and Acceptances: Trends*, https://www.gov.scot/publications/university-applications-offers-acceptances-scottish-universities-trends/
Scottish Tertiary Education Advisory Committee (1985) *Future Strategy for Higher Education in Scotland*, London: HMSO.
Von Prondzynski Report (2012) *Report of the Review of Higher Education Governance in Scotland*, Edinburgh: Scottish Government, https://www2.gov.scot/Resource/0038/00386780.pdf

Books, articles and blogs

Amis, K. (1960) 'Lone voices', *Encounter*, 82, July.
Ashwin, P. (2020) *Transforming University Education: A Manifesto*, London: Bloomsbury Academic.

References

Barnett, R. (2017) *The Ecological University: A Feasible Utopia*, London: Routledge.

Bauman, Z. (1999) *Liquid Modernity*, Cambridge: Polity Press.

Bell, D. (1973) *The Coming of Post-Industrial Society: A Venture in Social Forecasting*, New York: Basic Books.

Bell, D. (1976) *The Cultural Contradictions of Capitalism*, London: Heinemann.

Berdahl, R. (1959) *British Universities and the State*, Berkeley, CA: University of California Press.

Bird, R. (1994) 'Reflections on the British Government and higher education in the 1980s', *Higher Education Quarterly*, vol 48, no 2, pp 73–85.

Bishop, M. (2021) 'Micro-credentials and credit transfer: giving credit where credit is due', Oxford: Higher Education Policy Institute (blog, 5 February).

Bocock, J., Baston, B., Scott, P. and Smith, D. (2003) 'American influences on British higher education: science, technology and the problem of university expansion', *Minerva* vol XLI, no 4, pp 327–46.

Bray, C. (2014) *1965: The Year Modern Britain Was Born*, London: Simon & Schuster.

Brown, P. and Lauder, H. (2012) 'The great transformation in the global labour market', *Soundings: A Journal of Politics and Culture*, vol 51, pp 41–53.

Brown, R. and Carasso, H. (2013) *Everything for Sale? The Marketisation of UK Higher Education*, Abingdon: Routledge (Society for Research into Higher Education).

Bukodi, E. and Goldthorpe, J. (2009) *Class Origins, Education and Occupational Attainment: Cross-cohort Changes among Men in Britain*, London: Centre for Longitudinal Studies Institute of Education, University of London (December 2009), https://cls.ucl.ac.uk/wp-content/uploads/2017/07/CLS_WP_2009_3-1.pdf

Calderon, A. (2018) *Massification of Higher Education Revisited*, Melbourne: Royal Melbourne Institute of Technology.

Callender, C. and Scott, P. (eds) (2013) *Browne and Beyond: Modernizing English Higher Education*, London: Institute of Education Press.

Cantwell, B., Marginson, S. and Smolentseva, A. (2018) *High-Participation Systems of Higher Education*, Oxford: Oxford University Press.

Carswell, J. (1986) *Government and Universities in Britain: Progress and Performance 1960–1980*, Cambridge: Cambridge University Press.

Castells, M. (2000, revised edition) *The Rise of the Network Society: The Information Age – Economy, Society and Culture Volume I*, Chichester: Wiley-Blackwell.

Castells, M. (2009, with a new preface) *The Power of Identity: The Information Age – Economy, Society and Culture Volume II*, Chichester: Wiley-Blackwell.

Centre for Longitudinal Studies (2010) 'News: Millennium mothers want university education for their children', London: Centre for Longitudinal Studies, Institute of Education, University of London, 15 October, https://cls.ucl.ac.uk/millennium-mothers-want-university-education-for-their-children/

Christensen, T. and Laegreid, P. (eds) (2006) *Autonomy and Regulation: Coping with Agencies in the Modern State*, Cheltenham: Edward Elgar.

Collini, S. (2012) *What are Universities For?*, Harmondsworth: Penguin.

Collini, S. (2017) *Speaking of Universities*, London: Verso.

Daiches, D. (1964) *The Idea of a New University*, London: Andre Deutsch.

Davie, G. (1961/2013) *The Democratic Intellect: Scotland and her Universities in the Nineteenth Century*, Edinburgh: Edinburgh University Press.

Davie, G. (1986) *Crisis of the Democratic Intellect: The Problem of Generalization and Specialization in Twentieth Century Scotland*, Edinburgh: Polygon Books.

Deem, R., Hilyard, S. and Reed, R. (2007) *Knowledge, Higher Education, and the New Managerialism*, Oxford: Oxford University Press.

Dorling, D. (2018a) *Peak Inequality: Britain's Ticking Time Bomb*, Bristol: Policy Press.

Dorling, D. (2018b) *Do We Need Economic Inequality?*, Cambridge: Polity Press.

Etzkowitz, H. and Leydesdorff, L. (eds) (1997) *Universities and the Global Knowledge Economy: A Triple Helix of University-Industry-Government Relations*, London: Pinter.

Gaskill, M. (2020) 'Diary: On Quitting Academia', *London Review of Books*, vol 42, no 18 (September).

Gibbons, M., Limoges, C., Nowotny, H., Schwartzman, S., Scott, P. and Trow, M. (1994) *The New Production of Knowledge: The Dynamics of Science and Research in Contemporary Societies*, London: Sage.

Goodhart, D. (2020) *Head Hand Heart*, London: Allen Lane.

Halsey, A.H. (1992) *Decline of Donnish Dominion*, Oxford: Clarendon Press.

Harvey, D. (2005) *A Brief History of Neoliberalism*, Oxford: Oxford University Press.

Hennessy, P. (2006) *Never Again: Britain 1945–51*, Harmondsworth: Penguin.

Hennessy, P. (2007) *Having It So Good: Britain in the Fifties*, Harmondsworth: Penguin.

Hennessy, P. (2019) *Winds of Change: Britain in the Early 1960s*, Harmondsworth, Penguin.

Henseke, G., Feslstead, A., Gallie, D. and Green, F. (2020) 'Unpacking the rising degree requirements in the British labour market' (see https://www.researchcghe.org/perch/resources/goloslides.pdf).

HEPI (Higher Education Policy Institute) (2016) Woolwich Polytechnic speech by Anthony Crosland, 27 April 1966, https://www.hepi.ac.uk/wp-content/uploads/2016/08/Scan-158.pdf

Hewitt, R. (2020) *Students' Views on the Impact of Coronavirus on their University Experience 2020–21*, Policy Note 27, Oxford: Higher Education Policy Unit.

Hillman, N. (2016) 'The Coalition's higher education reforms in England', *Oxford Review of Education*, vol 42, no 3, pp 330–45.

Hillman, N. (2020a) 'Universities and Brexit: past, present and future, The UK in a changing Europe', Kings College London, 11 July, https://ukandeu.ac.uk/universities-and-brexit-past-present-and-future#

Hillman, N. (2020b) 'The future of higher education after COVID', Oxford: Higher Education Policy Unit (blog – 16 October) https://www.hepi.ac.uk/2020/10/16/the-future-of-higher-education-after-covid/

HMSO (1956) *Technical Education*, London: HMSO.

HMSO (1969) *In Place of Strife: A Policy for Industrial Relations*, London: HMSO.

Holmwood, P. (ed) (2011) *A Manifesto for the Public University*, London: Bloomsbury Academic.

Kerr, C. (1963) *The Uses of the University*, Cambridge, MA: Harvard University Press.

Kingston, P. (2000) *The Classless Society*, Stanford CA: Stanford University Press.

Kirp, D. (2019) *The College Dropout Scandal*, New York: Oxford University Press.

Koch, J. (2019) *The Impoverishment of the American College Student*, Washington DC: Brookings Institution Press.

Kynaston, D. (2008) *Austerity Britain 1945–51*, London: Bloomsbury.

Kynaston, D. (2010) *Family Britain 1951–57*, London: Bloomsbury.

Kynaston, D. (2013) *Modernity Britain: Opening the Box*, London: Bloomsbury.

Larkin, P. (1983) *Required Writing: Miscellaneous Pieces 1955–1982*, London: Faber.

Little, A.N. (1961) 'Will more means worse? An enquiry into the effects of university expansion', *British Journal of Sociology*, vol 12, no 4, pp 351–62.

Maarten, G. and Manning, A. (2007) 'Lousy and lovely jobs: The rising polarisation of jobs in Britain', *Review of Economics and Statistics*, vol 89, no 1, pp 118–33.

Machin, S. and Vignoles, A. (eds) (2018) *What's the Good of Education? The Economics of Education in the United Kingdom*, Princeton NJ: Princeton University Press.

Mandler, P. (2020) *The Crisis of the Meritocracy: Britain's Transition to Mass Education since the Second World War*, Oxford: Oxford University Press.

Marginson, S. (2016) 'The worldwide trend to high participation higher education: Dynamics of social stratification in inclusive system', *Higher Education*, vol 72, pp 413–34.

McGettigan, A. (2013) *The Great University Gamble: Money, Markets and the Future of Higher Education*, London: Pluto Press.

McMillan Cotton, T. (2018) *Lower Ed: The Troubling Rise of For-Profit Colleges in the New Economy*, New York: The New Press.

Montacute, R. and Holt-White, E. (2021) *COVID-19: The University Experience*, Sutton Trust Research Brief, https://www.suttontrust.com/wp-content/uploads/2021/02/COVID-19-and-the-University-Experience.pdf

Moodie, G. and Eustace, R. (1974) *Power and Authority in British Universities*, London: Allen and Unwin.

Nybom, T. (2003) 'The Humboldt legacy: reflections on the past, present and future of the European University', *Higher Education Policy*, vol 16, pp 141–59.

Perkin, H. (1989) *The Rise of Professional Society: England since 1880*, London: Routledge.

Perkin, H. (1991) 'Dream, myth and reality: new universities in England 1960–1990', *Higher Education Quarterly*, vol 45, no 4, pp 294–310.

Piketty, T. (2014) *Capital in the Twenty-First Century*, Cambridge, MA/London: Belknap Press of the Harvard University Press.

Piketty, T. (2015) *The Economics of Inequality*, Cambridge, MA: Harvard University Press.

Piketty, T. (2020) *Capital and Ideology*, Cambridge, MA: Harvard University Press.

Power, M. (1997) *The Audit Society: Rituals of Verification*, Oxford: Oxford University Press.

Pratt, J. (1992) *The Polytechnic Experiment 1965–1992*, Buckingham: Open University Press

Robinson, E. (1966) *The New Polytechnics: The People's Universities*, London: Cornmarket [Penguin Education Special, 1968].

Roff, A. (2021) *Student Finance in England from 2012 to 2020: From Fiscal Illusion to Graduate Contribution*, Oxford: Higher Education Policy Institute (Debate Paper 25), https://www.hepi.ac.uk/wp-content/uploads/2021/01/Student-Finance-in-England-from-2012-to-2020-From-fiscal-illusion-to-graduate-contribution.pdf

Rustin, M. and Poynter, G. (eds) (2020) *Building a Radical University: A History of the University of East London*, Chadwell Heath: Lawrence and Wishart.

Ryan, D. (1998) 'The Thatcher Government's attack on higher education in historical perspective', *New Left Review*, vol 1, no 227, January–February.

Sandel, M. (2020) *The Tyranny of Merit: What's Become of the Public Good?*, London: Allen Lane.

Scott, P. (1977) '14 years later the Robbins faith remains unshaken', *Times Higher Education Supplement*, 4 November.

Scott, P. (1989) 'Higher education', in D. Kavanagh and A. Seldon (eds) *The Thatcher Effect*, Oxford: Oxford University Press.

Scott, P. (1994) 'Education policy', in D. Kavanagh and A. Seldon (eds) *The Major Years*, London: Macmillan.

Scott, P. (2014a) 'The reform of English Higher Education: Universities in global, national and regional contexts', *Cambridge Journal of Regions, Economy and Policy*, vol 7, no 2, pp 217–31.

Scott, P. (2014b) 'Robbins, the binary policy and mass higher education', *Higher Education Quarterly*, vol 68, no 2, pp 147–63.

Scott, P. (2021) 'Unpacking the social dimension of universities', in M. Klemencíc and S. Gaber (eds) *From Actors to Reforms in European Higher Education*, Dordrecht: Springer.

Sharp, P. (1987) *The Creation of the Local Authority Sector of Higher Education*, London: Falmer Press.

Shattock, M. (2012a) *Making Policy in British Higher Education 1945–2011*, Maidenhead: McGraw-Hill/Open University Press.

Shattock, M. (2012b) 'Parallel worlds, the California Master Plan and the development of British higher education', in R. Rothblatt (ed) *Clark Kerr's World of Higher Education Reaches the 21st Century*, Dordrecht: Springer.

Shattock, M. and Horvath, A. (2020) *The Governance of British Higher Education: The Impact of Governmental, Financial and Market Pressures*, London: Bloomsbury Academic.

Slaughter, S. and Leslie, L. (1997) *Academic Capitalism: Politics, Policies and the Entrepreneurial University*, Baltimore: Johns Hopkins University Press.

Slaughter, S. and Rhoades, G. (2004) *Academic Capitalism and the New Economy*, Baltimore: Johns Hopkins University Press.

Sloman, A. (1963) *A University in the Making*, London: BBC.

Svallfors, S. and Taylor-Gooby, P. (eds) (1999) *The End of the Welfare State*, London: Routledge.

Thomas, K. (2011) 'Universities Under Attack', *London Review of Books*, vol 33, no 24, 15 December.

Trow, M. (1973) *Problems in the Transition from Elite to Mass Higher Education*, Berkeley, CA: Carnegie Commission on Higher Education.

Trow, M. (2010) *Twentieth-Century Higher Education: Elite to Mass to Universal* (ed M. Burrage), Baltimore, MD: Johns Hopkins Press.

Truscot, B. (1951) *Redbrick University*, Harmondsworth: Penguin.

Turner, A. (2013) *A Classless Society: Britain in the 1990s*, London: Aurum Press.

Watson, D. and Bowden, R. (1999) 'Why did they do it? The Conservatives and mass higher education', *Journal of Education Policy*, vol 14, no 3, pp 243–56.

Willetts, D. (2017) *A University Education*, Oxford: Oxford University Press.

Wolf, A. (2002) *Does Education Matter? Myths about Education and Economic Growth*, London: Penguin.
Young, M. (1994) *The Rise of Meritocracy*, London: Transaction Publishers (first published 1958; London: Thames & Hudson).
Zaloom, C. (2019) *Indebted: How Families Make College Work at Any Cost*, Princeton, NJ: Princeton University Press.

Index

A

academic boards 68, 94, 95
'academic capitalism' 72
academic culture, shared 104
academic landscape, changing 103–4, 108
academic staff 71, 90–1, 107
   female 91
   in management roles 15, 68, 70, 95, 96, 185
   from overseas 91, 115
   role in governance 181, 186
'academic' vs. 'vocational' subjects 170–1, 188
access to higher education 4, 12–14
   COVID-19 pandemic and impact on 155–6
   fair 172–8
   focused financial support 174
   and free tuition 173
   quotas 174–5, 176
   and remedying 'deficits' 176–7
   targets for participation, and their enforcement 174–5
   and transforming of institutions 177–8
achievements and transformations of mass higher education 5–11
   disenchantment with 7–11
   reasons for doubts regarding 12–18
'active' learning 105
Advance HE 76, 101, 180
adversarial politics 22, 24, 27–8, 29
'alternative providers' 52, 60, 66–7, 84, 162, 165
   size 87
   students enrolled with 82, 83
   tuition fees 174
   validating of degrees 85
Amis, Kingsley 17, 40
art colleges 38, 39, 42, 64
assessment regimes 16, 17, 75, 76, 78, 100, 101–2, 106
Augar Committee 163–4

austerity policies 25, 33, 51, 181
Australia 54, 113, 181
autonomy of universities 10–11, 62, 65
   legal 65, 91
   nostalgia for 90
   'steering' and limits on 40, 45, 166

B

banking crisis 2008 25, 33, 47
Bell, Daniel 3, 129
binary system of higher education 84
   ending 8, 23, 47–8, 65
   establishment 41–2
   in Europe 57, 77
Black and other minority ethnic (BAME) groups
   academic staff 91
   access to higher education 176
   participation in higher education 5, 13, 74, 83, 133
   and recruitment to governing bodies 93
Black Lives Matter (BLM) 137–8
Blair, Tony 22, 23, 32, 40, 47
Bologna Process 54, 57, 78, 120, 121
Brexit 18, 26–7, 54, 109, 140
   and binary view of UK politics 136
   educational attainment divide in vote for 10
   ideological polarisation 166
Brown, Gordon 25
Browne Report 23, 50
budget for higher education 70, 80
business and administration studies 103

C

Calderon, Angel 110
California Master Plan 55, 118
Cameron, David 24, 25, 26
Campaign for the Public University 15–16
campuses, design of university 158–9

Canada 111, 113, 181
cap on student numbers 51, 52, 163
Cathedrals Group 86
census 1961 35
Cental and Eastern Europe 56, 57, 120, 121
centralisation of political decision making 27, 29, 165–6
   and hollowing out of local government 23, 25, 27, 29
   over- 29, 35
charities 92, 102
chartered universities 69, 84, 85, 91–2, 94–5
chief executive officers (CEOs) 69–70
Chile 116
China 58, 78, 114, 123
   exporting of students 58, 83, 113
   importing of students 113, 114
   tertiary education graduate numbers 110
'civic' responsibilities of universities 187
civic universities 38, 86, 87, 172
Clarke, Kenneth 47
classless society 5, 48, 128–9, 130–1, 135, 148
Coalition government, Conservative-led 25–6, 27, 33, 66
   higher education 'market' 50–2, 162
codes of practice 71
colleges of advanced technology (CATs) 38, 41, 63, 64
colleges of education 38, 45, 61, 63, 64
Committee of University Chairs (CUC) 71, 85–6, 93–4, 187
Committee of Vice-Chancellors and Principals (CVCP) 37, 72, 76
communication technologies, revolution in 129, 138, 139
'Confucian' model of education 58, 123, 124–5
Conservative governments from 2015 onwards 26–7, 130–1
   opposition to expansion of higher education 168–9
   retreat from higher education 'market' 52–3, 161–5

Conservative governments under Major 22, 23, 32, 47
Conservative governments under Thatcher 21–3, 27, 30, 34, 162
   1981 funding 33, 44
   development of mass higher education 43–5, 46–7
   liberalisation of financial services 31
contemporary higher education 80–108
   academic profession 90–1
   development of mass higher education 46–9
   funding, 'steering' and regulation 97–103
   governance and management of institutions 91–7
   income and expenditure 88–90
   institutions 83–8
   persistence of elite attributes 80–1
   research 106–8
   size and shape 81–91
   students 81–3
   teaching 103–6
corporate organisations, universities as 14–16, 17, 45, 72, 150–1
cosmopolitanism 14, 126, 129, 137, 138
Council for the Defence of British Universities (CDBU) 15
councils, governing 39, 68, 69, 91, 92, 93
courts, university 91, 94, 180
COVID-19 pandemic 26, 29
   access to higher education 155–6
   economic shock 141
   face-to-face connections 157, 158–9
   factors powering 153–4
   habitus and community 158–9
   impact on graduate employment 113–14
   impact on higher education 11, 18, 153–60
   internationalisation and 18, 114, 159–60
   learning and 156–7
   and possible reordering of status of jobs 146
   and 'steering' by OfS 97–8
credit, availability of 140

crisis of mass higher education 4–5
  contradictions and challenges 150–3
  reforms to address 168–89
    building a tertiary system 170–2
    expansion 168–70
    fair access 172–8
    place of higher education in society 186–9
    systems, governance and management 179–86
  three possible responses to 190–1
Crosland, Anthony 41–3, 46
cultural capital 12, 134, 135, 169, 173
cultural change 19–20, 33–5, 35–6
  mass higher education and 6–7, 14, 138–9, 149
culture 136–9
  'graduate' 13, 138
  new intellectual 73–7, 103–4
  shared academic 104
  wars 10, 26–7, 56, 119, 136, 151
curriculum
  attempts to 'de-colonise' 17
  current debates around 177–8
  new intellectual cultures and new 73–4
  polytechnics and new approaches to delivery of 16, 17, 42
  universal principles in organisation of 105–6
  see also subjects
customers, students as 99, 162, 181–2

D

deans 68, 70, 95, 186
Dearing Report 49
debt levels 140
degree-awarding powers 75–6, 85
de-industrialisation 31, 139
demographics, UK 127–8
development of mass higher education 37–58
  advances and setbacks 43–6
  beyond UK 53–8, 77–9
  coordinating and funding higher education 63–7
  Crosland and 41–3

higher education in 1960 37–9
higher education 'market' 50–3
institutional governance and management 68–73
Robbins Report 2, 28, 34, 37, 40–1, 42–3, 49, 110, 188
second wave 46–9
'steering' and regulation 59–63
devolution 24, 48, 66
digital divide 156
'dispersed' higher education, delivery of 43

E

East Asia 58, 110, 114, 116, 123–5
  'Confucian' model of education 58, 123, 124–5
  US influences in 117
economy 139–47, 148–9, 189
  COVID-19 pandemic and impact on 113–14
  division between graduates and non-graduates 135, 147, 149, 189
  evolution 29–33, 139
  graduate employment and a graduate 145–7, 149
  income inequality 35, 130, 139, 143, 148–9
  labour market 143–5
  role of higher education and science 141–3
Education: A Framework for Expansion 43
Education Reform Act 1987 45, 64
educational and cultural themes in mass higher education 16–18
educational attainment and social attitudes 134–5
elite university system 3, 67, 71, 138
  access to 12–13, 172–3, 176–7, 178
  flourishing of science and intellectual life 6
  golden age 2–3
  mass higher education seen as a threat to 3–4, 8, 72, 190
  and production of elites 138, 190
  recruitment of international students 55
  residential model 155, 159

elite university system (continued)
  retaining 'feel' of 80–1
  size 81, 87
elites
  Brexit divide between 'people' and 10, 136
  concerns over mass higher education 169
  elite university system and production of 138, 190
  insiders and 10–11
  international student 112
  mass education and refreshing of traditional 177
  old and new 13
employment
  aligning education patterns with segmentation of 143–5, 150
  COVID-19 pandemic and impact on 113–14
  divide between graduate and non-graduate 135, 147, 149, 189
  graduate 113, 135, 145–7, 149
  'graduate under-employment' 144, 145, 147, 150
  loosening of link between social status and 128, 130, 147
  restriction of opportunities for non-graduate 14
  see also labour market
engineering, subject of 104
environmental issues 141, 160
Erasmus Programme 54
ethnicity 133
  of academic staff 91
  of governing bodies 93
  quotas and 176
Europe 57, 120–3, 125
  adoption of managerial practices 78
  Bologna Process 54, 57, 78, 120, 121
  Central and Eastern 56, 57, 120, 121
  comparisons with US 122
  international students and 54–5, 83, 113
  main challenge to higher education project 122–3
  modernisation process 121–2

  'quality culture' 78, 121
  research programmes 54, 121
  student numbers 56, 80
  systems of higher education 11, 77
  UK academic staff from 91
European Higher Education Area (EHEA) 54, 55, 121, 122
European Research Area (ERA) 54, 55, 121
European Union (EU)
  Conservative Party divisions over 23, 26
  referendum 10, 26
executive management 69, 92, 95–7, 185–6
expenditure on higher education, income and 88–90
  budgets 70, 80
experts 28–9, 62, 139

F

faith-based institutions 117
female
  academic staff 91
  identity 5, 132
  members of governing bodies 93
  participation in higher education 5, 73, 83
financial services sector 31, 35, 140, 142, 144
France 56, 57, 113, 121, 141
free tuition 173, 188
funding of higher education 59, 161–2
  in competition with other public sectors 49
  coordinating and 63–7
  crisis in US 119–20
  cuts under Thatcher to 33, 44
  focused financial support for students 174
  fragmentation into three national systems 48, 61, 65–7
  with free tuition 173, 188
  higher education expansion and challenges of 43
  and 'market' for higher education 50–3, 162–4

nationalisation of 64–5, 67
under New Labour 47, 49, 162
OfS responsibilities 60, 97
reluctance to countenance a return to state 187–8
research funding 53, 66, 88–9, 98
in Scotland 48, 61, 63, 65, 98, 99–100
'steering', regulation and 97–103
systematisation of 63–4, 67
tree stump in forest metaphor 38–9
in Wales 48, 61, 98, 99–100
see also student loans; tuition fees
further education colleges 38, 64, 84, 85

G

gender
　roles, revolution in 5
　and social identity 129, 132
General Certificates of Secondary Education (GCSEs) 46–7
Germany 56, 57, 113, 121, 141, 173, 181
global higher education data 110–11
globalisation 112, 129, 137, 140, 154
glossary vi–x
golden age of higher education 2–3
Goodhart, David 187
Gove, Michael 26
governance of higher education 179–86
　in 1960s 38–9
　in 2020s 91–7
　academic boards 68, 94, 95
　democratic deficit 180, 181
　executive management 69, 92, 95–7, 185–6
　governing bodies 91–4, 180, 183–5
　insulation from excessive politicisation 183
　lack of clear underlying principles 179–80, 180–1
　management and institutional 68–73, 91–7, 183–6
　new systems 182–3
　regimes of control 185–6
　senates 69, 93, 94–5, 181
　staff excluded from role in 181

transformation of system 45, 59–63
governing bodies 91–4, 180, 183–5
graduate class 13, 150
'graduate' culture 13, 138
graduate employment 113, 135, 149
　COVID-19 pandemic and impact on 113–14
　divide between non-graduate and 135, 147, 149, 189
　and a graduate economy 145–7, 149
　growth in 146
　in 'non-graduate' jobs 147
　segmenting of 150
'graduate society' 134, 135, 189
'graduate under-employment' 144, 145, 147, 150
graduates, numbers of tertiary education 110–11
gross domestic product (GDP) 88, 139
Guild HE 85, 86

H

Halsey, A.H. 68
Harvard University 117, 118, 119
heads of departments 68, 70, 95, 186
healthcare disciplines 5, 64, 70, 82, 103
Heath, Edward 22, 31
hierarchy of types of institution 150, 151, 170–1
　'mission groups' representing 86–7
Higher Education and Research Act 2017 99, 163, 183
higher education corporations (HECs) 84, 85, 92, 94, 95
Higher Education Funding Council for England (HEFCE) 47, 50, 52, 60, 61, 65, 66, 97
Higher Education Funding Council for Wales (HEFCW) 65, 98, 100
Higher Education Statistics Agency (HESA) 81, 88, 89, 90, 93, 101, 103, 180
history, subject of 103–4
Holmwood, P. 16
Hong Kong 110, 113, 114, 124
hybridity 125, 126, 137–8

I

immigration 128, 133
Imperial College, London 89
In Place of Strife 30–1
income
    and expenditure 88–90
    inequality 35, 130, 139, 143, 148–9
India 110, 113, 116
industrial decline 29–30, 31, 139
    and changing understandings of 'social class' 131
industrial relations 30–1, 96
inequality
    of access for international students 160
    income 35, 130, 139, 143, 148–9
    participation in higher education and compounding of existing 134
    and polarisation of labour market 143, 149
    rising 9–10, 130–1
institutional governance and management 68–73, 179, 180–1
    in 2020s 91–7
    beyond UK 78
    future of 183–6
    ideological drivers for transformation in 72–3
    structural reasons for transformation of 70–2
institutions 83–8
    hierarchy of 150, 151, 170–1
    themes in an expanded higher education system 14–16
    three organisational types 83–4
    US classifications of 118
intellectual culture, changing landscape of 73–7, 103–4
intermediate public agencies 99–100, 101
international students 46, 55, 83, 111–15
    difficulties in counting 111–12
    fees from 55, 88, 90
    patterns of importers and exporters of 15, 114–15
internationalisation 111–15
    COVID-19 pandemic and impact on 18, 159–60
internet 138
Iraq war 24–5

J

Japan 58, 110, 111, 123–4
Jarratt Report 44, 72
job titles, inflation of 144–5
Johnson, Boris 26, 163
Joseph, Keith 44, 47

K

Kerslake Report 172, 187
'knowledge society' 30, 129–30
Kuhn, Thomas 74

L

Labour governments 1997 to 2010 *see* New Labour
Labour governments of 1960s and 1970s 20, 22, 23
labour market 143–5
    mass education and reshaping of 5–6, 13–14
    polarisation of 143, 149
    push and pull factors 142
    see also employment
languages 133
Larkin, Philip 3, 34
Latin America 110, 116, 173
law, subject of 104
league tables, global 58, 87, 107, 115, 117, 159
learning
    in COVID-19 pandemic 156–7
    and teaching 104–6
    technologies, new 16, 77, 105, 139
    see also online learning
legal
    autonomy of UK higher education institutions 91
    and regulatory requirements 71
    status of universities 84–5
Liberal Democrats 25, 26, 50
lifelong learning 171, 177
local education authorities 38, 39, 42, 45, 61, 64
local government, hollowing out of 23, 25, 27, 29

Index

M

Major, John 22, 23, 32, 47
Malaysia 113, 114, 124
'managed universities' 14–16, 17
management, institutional governance and 68–73, 179, 180–1
   in 2020s 91–7
   beyond UK 78
   future of 183–6
   ideological drivers for transformation in 72–3
   structural reasons for transformation of 70–2
Mandler, Peter 13
'market' for higher education 50–3, 160–7
   discourse of 'best' and 'worst' universities 51–2
   neoliberal framing 167
   reasons for failed English experiment 165–7
   retreat from market 161–5
marketisation 139
mass higher education 3–4
   achievements and transformations 5–11
   disenchantment with 7–11
   expansion in less mature education systems 111
   global data 110–11
   historical development 37–58
   opposition to 10, 40, 168–9, 190
   reasons for doubts regarding 12–18
   size and shape today 81–91
   as a threat to elite universities 3–4, 8, 72, 190
mass higher education, crisis of 4–5
   contradictions and challenges 150–3
   reforms to address 168–89
      building a tertiary system 170–2
      expansion 168–70
      fair access 172–8
      place of higher education in society 186–9
      systems, governance and management 179–86
   three possible responses to 190–1

massive open online courses (MOOCs) 77, 157
'maximum aggregate student numbers' (MASNs) 60
May, Theresa 26, 137, 163
medicine 5, 64, 70, 82, 102, 103
meritocracy 13, 130
middle class
   expansion 128–9
   free tuition and loans as a subsidy to 174, 188
   mass higher education and 4, 13, 83, 150, 172
Middle East 116
Million Plus 86
minority ethnic groups *see* Black and other minority ethnic (BAME) groups
'mission groups' 86–7
modernisation
   in East Asia 123–4
   in Europe 121–2
   and links with modernity 114, 125
   New Labour and 23, 24, 27, 32, 47
multiculturalism 35, 127–8
multi-disciplinary courses 105

N

National Advisory Body (NAB) 45, 61, 64, 65
National Student Survey (NSS) 164, 181–2, 185
nationalisation 27, 67
   of higher education funding 64–5, 67
   of public policy 62–3
nationalism 26–7, 131–2
neoliberal
   framing of higher education 167
   values, shift to 62, 72, 149, 154
Netherlands 109, 121
New Labour 23–5, 72
   funding of higher education 47, 49, 162
   modernisation and 23, 24, 27, 32, 47
New Left student activists 74
New Public Management (NPM) 72, 96

'new' universities of 1960s and 1970s 16, 39
  development 34, 41, 46, 68
  'market' reforms and 51
  and similarities with new US campuses 116–17
Newman, John Henry 186, 187
1994 Group 86
non-graduates
  employment 14, 135, 147, 149, 189
  social divisions between graduates and 12
  and support for Brexit 10
non-university sector
  in 1970s and 1980s 45
  in 2020 84
  art colleges 38, 39, 42, 64
  colleges of advanced technology (CATs) 38, 41, 63, 64
  colleges of education 38, 45, 61, 63, 64
  funding 61, 63, 64
  further education colleges 38, 64, 84, 85
  Guild HE representation of 85
  institutional governance 61, 68–9
  local education authorities' responsibilities for 38, 39, 42, 45, 61, 64
  oversight of courses and degrees in 75–6, 85
  in Scotland and Wales 48
  see also polytechnics
North East London Polytechnic 42
Northern Ireland 67, 86, 98, 173
novelty of mass higher education 7
numbers of students *see* student numbers

O

occupation and social class 128, 130, 147
Office for National Statistics (ONS) 52, 127, 130, 132, 133, 139, 140, 163
Office for Students (OfS) 18, 52, 53, 59, 92, 99
  approval of access and participation plans 175
  COVID-19 pandemic and 'steering' by 97–8
  design flaw 165
  funding responsibilities 60, 97
  political appointments to 180
  as regulator 43, 60–1, 99, 164
one-size-fits-all system 42–3, 88
online learning 77, 105, 158
  in COVID-19 pandemic 155, 156–7, 159
  digital divide 156
Open University 4, 6, 64
opponents of mass higher education 7–9, 10, 40, 168–9, 190
Organisation for Economic Co-operation and Development (OECD) 110, 111
organisational culture
  transformation of 68–73
  in US 78

P

'para-state' 22, 32
participation in higher education 12
  Black and minority ethnic groups 5, 13, 74, 83, 133
  female 5, 73, 83
  global 110–11
  targets and their enforcement 174–5
  see also access to higher education; numbers of students
part-time students 51, 81, 82
Pearce Report 77
Piketty, Thomas 143
political change from 1960s to Brexit 20–7
  themes and trends 27–9
political consensus, decline of 22, 27–8
polytechnics
  amalgamation of non-university institutions 42, 45, 63, 64
  awarding of degrees 76
  development and expansion of 45–6
  ending of binary division between universities and 8, 23, 47–8, 65
  establishment 42

Index

funding 64, 65
governance 45, 61, 68–9
local authority control 27, 45, 61, 64, 69
'nationalising' of 45
new approaches to delivering curriculum 16, 17, 42
as 'post-1992' universities 65
Polytechnics and Colleges Funding Council (PCFC) 45, 47, 61, 64, 65
population, UK 127–8
'populism' 62, 137, 154, 189
'post-1992' universities 8, 154
distinctions between 'pre-1992' and 84–5
governance 69–70, 92
legal autonomy 65
mission groups 86
postgraduate students 6, 74, 82, 83
post-industrial social landscape 129, 142, 148
practice-based learning 105
principals 68, 85
privatisation 22, 23, 32
professional bodies 75, 85, 102
professional qualifications, awarding of 75, 85
professionalism 6, 28–9
professors 68, 70, 90–1, 94
pro-vice-chancellors (PVCs) 68, 70, 95
public administration, erosion of competence in 29
public spending cuts 25, 33, 44
public-private partnerships 32

Q

Quality Assurance Agency (QAA) 76, 85, 101–2, 180
quality industry 76, 78
quotas 174–5, 176

R

ranking regimes 76–7, 101, 172
global 58, 87, 107, 115, 117, 159
red-brick universities 38, 42

reform of higher education
building a tertiary system 170–2
expansion 168–70
fair access 172–8
systems, governance and management 179–86
regulation and 'steering' 59–63, 97–103, 164–5, 166, 168, 179
religion 133
representative bodies 102
research 16–17, 75, 170
centres of excellence in East Asia 114
complex environment in 2020s 106–8
European programmes 54–5, 121
funding 53, 66, 88–9, 98
institutes in Europe 121
quasi-industrialisation of 74–5
volume of activity 106–7
Research England 53, 59, 66, 97–8, 100
Research Excellence Framework (REF) 17, 60, 67, 75, 76, 100, 172, 179, 185
Resource Allocation Budgeting (RAB) charge 51, 52, 163
Robbins Report 2, 28, 34, 37, 40–1, 42–3, 49, 110, 188
Royal College of Art 42, 64
Russell Group 86, 87
Russia 111, 113, 122

S

salaries 143, 144, 149
graduate jobs and 144, 146
job title inflation and 144–5
vice-chancellors' 70, 96
Sandel, Michael 13
scholarly and learned societies 102
science
'brain drain' and workforce in 115
growth in research 6, 74–5
mass higher education and influence on 6
role in economy of higher education and 141–3
students studying 82

Scotland
    central institutions 48, 63, 64, 66
    courts, university 91, 94, 180
    devolution 24, 48, 66
    divergence from England on policy and structure 66, 67
    funding of higher education 48, 61, 63, 65, 98, 99–100
    higher education in 1960s 38
    Learner Journey 15–24 171
    participation in higher education 12, 82
    regaining control of Scottish universities 48, 65–6
    research funding 53, 66, 98
    'story' of universities 17
    targets to widen access 175
    tuition fees 53
Scottish Funding Council (SFC) 66, 98, 100
Scottish Higher Education Funding Council (SHEFC) 65, 66
secondary education 21, 27, 28, 35
    expansion of Academies 25–6
    private schools 176
    public exam reform 46–7
sector agencies 101
senates 69, 93, 94–5, 181
service industries 31, 128
    financial services sector 31, 35, 140, 142, 144
sexual identities 132
Shattock, Michael 37, 44, 54, 92
Singapore 114, 124
size and shape of higher education 81–91
social and cultural change 19–20, 33–5, 35–6
social capital 12, 134, 157, 169
social class 128–9
    classless society and decline of 5, 48, 128–9, 130–1, 135, 148
    and correlation with education level 13
    working class 12, 128, 131
    see also middle class
social composition of student population 83

social identities 128–9, 132
social mobility 130–1, 151
social reformism, post-war 9–10
social revolution of higher education 5–11
    disenchantment with 7–11
    reasons for doubts regarding 12–18
society, contemporary 129–35, 148
    decline of social class 5, 48, 128–9, 130–1, 135, 148
    educational attainment 134–5
    fundamental changes 127–9
    gender, ethnicity, language and religion 131–4
    place of higher education in 186–9
sociological themes of mass education 12–14
South Asia 116
South Korea 111, 113, 114, 124
Soviet Union 110
'Start to Success' 164
statutory universities 69
'steering'
    creeping process of state 40, 44–5, 47–9
    and regulation 59–63, 97–103, 164–5, 166, 168, 179
'story' of universities 17–18, 187–9
student loans 51, 88
    changes in accounting for 52, 163
    conflict of interest for state 165
    disadvantages 174
    non-recovery of 52, 89–90
    raising of repayment threshold 163
    shift from maintenance grants to 49
Student Loans Company (SLC) 51, 88, 163
student numbers 80, 81–2
    cap on 51, 52, 163
    in Europe 56, 80
    global 110–11
    international students 83, 111–12
    MASNs and control of 60
    postgraduate 74, 82
    projections 43–4
    in United States 56, 117

students
    characteristics of 81–3
    as customers 99, 162, 181–2
    see also international students
subjects
    'academic' vs. 'vocational' 170–1, 188
    action against 'undesirable' 164
    in a constant state of flux 103–4
    healthcare 5, 64, 70, 82, 103
    most popular 82–3, 103
success of mass higher education 5–11
    disenchantment with 7–11
    reasons for doubts regarding 12–18
Sweden 57, 121
systems of higher education 63–7
    architecture of 97–103
        intermediate public agencies 99–100
        other agencies 101–2
        sector and interest groups 102–3
        UK and devolved administrations 98–9
    organisation of institutions 83–8
    reform of higher education 182–3
    regional substructures 182–3
    unstable balance in 179
    world 55–8
    see also binary system of higher education; unified system of higher education; universal systems of higher education

T

Taiwan 114, 124
targets for participation, and their enforcement 174–5
tax 33, 149
    avoidance and evasion 143, 144
teaching 103–6
    academic landscape 103–4
    control and regulation of 75–7
    learning and 104–6
Teaching Excellence and Student Outcomes Framework (TEF) 16, 76–7, 100, 164, 172, 179
Teaching Quality Assessment (TQA) 76, 101
technical colleges 38, 39, 41, 42
technology, investment in 20, 30
Thatcher, Margaret 21–3, 27, 28, 30, 31, 33, 34, 43, 44
themes and transformations 59–79
    beyond UK 77–9
    coordinating and funding higher education 63–7
    institutional governance and management 68–73
    new agendas 73–7
    'steering' and regulation 59–63
themes and trends, long-term 27–33
    advance of adversarial politics 27–8
    centralisation of political decision making 27
    erosion of competence in public administration 29
    experts 28–9
Thomas, Keith 15
trade unions 22–3, 30–1, 102, 140, 144
transparency 106, 183–4
Treasury 30, 38, 63, 98
Trow, Martin 3, 80, 81
tuition fees
    abolition of 173, 188
    'alternative providers' and 174
    Augar Committee recommendations 163–4
    design faults 50–1, 162–3
    focused financial support 174
    income from 88
    increase under Coalition government 25, 50, 162
    New Labour's reintroduction of 49, 162
    in US 117, 119
    in Wales and Scotland 53
Turing scholarships 54–5

U

UK Research and Innovation (UKRI) 53, 66, 98, 99–100, 180
UNESCO 110

unified system of higher education 84
 ending of binary system and creation of 8, 23, 47–8, 65
 hierarchies within 150, 170–1
 legal differentiations 84–5
 sectoral bodies and mission groups 85–7
 size differentiations 87–8
United States (US) 11, 54, 58, 109, 116–20, 125
 assessment and measurement of performance 78
 birth of mass higher education in 9, 116
 categorising institutions 118
 comparisons with Europe 122
 dominance of higher education system 55–7
 fragmented system of higher education 77, 117
 funding crisis 119–20
 governing bodies 92
 international students 113
 organisational culture 78
 student numbers 56, 117
 tertiary education graduates 111
universal systems of higher education 12, 80, 81
 building 170–2
 expansion to 168–70
 and fair access 178
Universities Funding Council (UFC) 45, 47, 48, 60, 61, 64, 65
Universities UK (UUK) 85, 86
University Alliance 86
University and College Admissions Service (UCAS) 101, 180
University and College Employers Agency (UCEA) 101
University College London 80, 89
University Grants Committee (UGC) 37, 41, 43, 44, 59, 63
 abolition of 45
 administering of funding cuts 44
 distribution of funding to universities 38–9, 63
 letters of guidance 60, 97

University of Cambridge 38, 39, 87, 89, 92
University of Edinburgh 89
University of Manchester 87, 89
University of Oxford 38, 39, 44, 46, 87
 governance 92
 income 89
 PPE 39, 188
University of Strathclyde 63

V

vice-chancellors 68, 69–70, 85, 92, 95–6
 salaries of 70, 96
vocational subjects 82–3, 103, 105
 vs. 'academic' subjects 170–1, 188

W

Wales
 devolution 66
 funding of higher education 48, 61, 98, 99–100
 Hazelkorn Review 171
 higher education strategy 99
 intermediate public agencies 100
 research funding 53, 66
 tuition fees 53
wealth, polarisation of 143, 149
 see also income inequality
Western universities, erosion of dominance of 115
Williams, Shirley 44
Wilson, Harold 20, 27, 30
working class 12, 128, 131
World Bank 110
'world class' universities 8, 115, 117, 124
world higher education systems 55–8, 115–25
 global data 110–11
'wrong side of history', universities on 9–10

Y

Young, Michael 13

www.ingramcontent.com/pod-product-compliance
Lightning Source LLC
Chambersburg PA
CBHW071157070526
44584CB00019B/2830